What a find! A gem of a book about a rough diamond of genius/ provocateur/creative philosopher and, ultimately, a true conquistador of humanistic challenges. The deeply engaging writings of Dr. Mike Arons leap off the page and wrestle playfully with your more obedient thoughts, resulting in a chaotic symphony of profound realizations about the very essence of life. Tracking the inner linings of humanistic ideas with his bright lantern, shedding light where none have ever trodden before, Mike reveals an entire universe of new concepts, hardly stopping to take a breath before venturing off to the next idea, always brilliant, insightful, and ultimately satisfying the soul of the reader. Hop into the depths of this magic realm. You'll never be the same.

David Ryback, PhD, co-author (with Carl Rogers) of
One Alternative to Nuclear Planetary Suicide

This finely edited book is a treasure for anyone interested in humanistic psychology. Mike Arons was a towering figure as the founder of the humanistic psychology program at West Georgia and as a compelling and erudite presenter at conferences around the world. This book brings together some of his most significant writings, covering topics ranging from his extraordinary life journey to the value of creativity. Each chapter demonstrates the depth of his philosophical understanding as well as his passion for developing a psychology that provided a holistic view of persons and society. The editors have done an exceptional job of introducing Mike Arons as a person and a scholar, providing the context for his work, and constructing a comprehensive index.

Steen Halling, PhD, Professor Emeritus of Psychology, Seattle
University; author of *Intimacy, Transcendence, and Psychology*

Reading the various chapters in *The New-Old: Recollections, Reflections, and Reconnoiterings of Mike Arons* is like taking a stroll with Mike as he tells the story of his own developmental journey, while at the same time continually inviting you to do the same. Though most of these papers I am reading for the first time, the tone is familiar. Mike was a teacher—my teacher—and these papers reflect the power of his pedagogy. For those who knew Mike or who had the opportunity to study with him, he became the doors to the recognition he alludes to in the first sentence of this collection. As we walk with Mike through this story, our own start to resonate as well.

David Polizzi, PhD, MA, LCAC, Professor, School of Criminology
and Security Studies, Indiana State University; editor of the
Journal of Theoretical and Philosophical Criminology

From the founding of West Georgia's renowned psychology program to courses on hermeneutics and creativity, students and colleagues of Mike

Arons know intimately his pedagogical genius. The collected essays in this volume equally testify to Mike's brilliance as a philosophical and psychological thinker. This book is a necessary and fitting tribute to a pioneer of humanistic psychology in America.

Peter J. Columbus, PhD, co-editor of *Alan Watts in the Academy* and *Alan Watts: Here and Now*

This work goes well beyond an important tribute to a path breaker in existential, humanistic, and transpersonal psychologies; at this time of unprecedented challenge, these chapters put consciousness, creativity, and culture at center stage. Mike's writings harness a whirlwind of energy and perspective—historical, personal, philosophical, psychological, and more—into a generous, incisive, and humane argument, one that stimulates and invites, like the conversations with Mike always seemed to do. There is vital creative force in this, an evolutionary current that he tapped, lived, and transmitted. This wonderfully curated collection is fresh, important, and touching.

Tobin Hart, PhD, Professor, Department of Psychology, University of West Georgia

This book is a festschrift for one of the great unsung forebears of humanistic psychology; it is also a history of the field itself. Page after page teems with gems by and about Mike Arons, but the book also brims with insights into the humanistic movement as a whole and Mike's critical part in nourishing it. As a former student and close colleague of Mike's, I was deeply moved by the many memories the book evoked—from Mike's trailblazing ideas about teaching to his reflections on creativity to his rich metaphors for the flow and complexity of life. Mike was persistently grappling and perpetually venturing wherever his soul and spirit beckoned, and for this we are grateful. For, as Andrew Bland suggests in the closing chapter, Mike anticipated—and in many ways helped to shape—the present configuration of our field, and that gift, that hope, is our future.

Kirk Schneider, PhD, author of *The Spirituality of Awe, The Polarized Mind,* and *Existential–Humanistic Therapy*; co-editor of the *Wiley World Handbook of Existential Therapy*

Mike Arons was alive, present, open and fearless, abundantly creative, while deeply connected to those he encountered, their complexities, and ongoing positive potential. And—alas!—to the challenges of our often beleaguered world. A student of Maslow, he was founder of two humanistic programs, including at the U of West Georgia. His students adored him. Complex, subtle, scholarly, master of paradox, and integrator of diverse traditions and systems, he also stood as beacon of truth and champion of inquiry through the immediacy of lived personal experience and the wisdom of dialogue. Not to mention the boons of fun, humor, caring, the gifts of human creativity, and even a cartoon or two. This book has it all. It shows Mike's humanity and range, his prescient intuition and insight, his unique intention to draw others into a dynamic process of growth toward our higher possibilities and profound interconnection.

Ruth Richards, MD, PhD, author of *Everyday Creativity and the Healthy Mind* (Silver Nautilus Award); editor of *Everyday Creativity and New Views of Human Nature*

Mike Arons was a Western Zen Master who told stories that helped repair this world of duality and complexity by pointing to a shared center where the soul of things exists. He held the world open for those more sensitive souls to enter and belong. Mike was an educator in the truest sense of the word—and helped bring out those subtle and latent potentials in those he touched within his extended global community. To truly connect with another, you must have a keen sense of where they reside in their understanding—and it is from this exact place of intimacy that he was so impeccable in walking with others into the reality of the Unknown, thereby making the process of education a true initiation and expression of a sublime and rare Art.

Howard S. Whitehouse, PhD

Mike Arons was a force of nature, a man who was truly larger than life. He traversed continents, created academic programs, and taught untold numbers of students. Some people are happy that he touched their lives; others are grateful that he changed their lives. When the history of humanistic psychology is written, every thread will have passed through the eye of Mike Arons' needle.

Stanley Krippner, PhD, co-author of *Personal Mythology*

Mike Arons artfully wove together existential, phenomenological, hermeneutic, humanistic, and transpersonal approaches to psychology to disclose a powerfully transformative vision of the potentialities of full human living. It is a vision of the person being intuitively and creatively in tune with the upsurging of improvisational possibilities—opportunities that we can engage when we are free to be available to whatever comes to us. Not only was he able to articulate this vision so well, he also lived it with inspiring authenticity. In so doing, he incited literally thousands of students, as well as many colleagues, friends, and other fellow travelers to become our truest selves, for which we are forever grateful.

Chris Aanstoos, PhD, Professor Emeritus, Department of Psychology, University of West Georgia

I came to West Georgia in 1983 to study psychology with Mike Arons. I was his student, friend, and unindicted co-conspirator for the next twenty-five years. He shared himself, his life, and his ways of being with me, always with unwavering encouragement to find *my* own way. Just before he died, when he saw the tears in my eyes, he squeezed my hand, smiled, and said, "Life doesn't owe me *anything*." When I met Sandrine, she was a child, perhaps naïve to the uniqueness of her family. Andrew honed his bright and curious intellect and heart in our program. Together, they have conveyed authentically and beautifully this reflection of his life and enduring contribution to human understanding, for which we owe much.

Larry Schor, PhD, Professor, Department of Psychology, University of West Georgia

I first met Mike Arons in 1971 at the second international conference on Humanistic Psychology, which was held at the University of Wurzburg, Wurzburg, Germany. That fortuitous meeting led to a deep personal and professional relationship that lasted until his death in 2018. This current volume by Bland and Arons, in an uncanny way, creates an almost virtual reality of who Mike Arons was as a person, psychologist, educator, and cultural influencer. It clearly is a major contribution to our understanding of the development and trajectory of humanistic psychology post Maslow. It also gives us a unique glimpse into the life of Mike Arons, who, once he discovered his path in life, never veered but went forth with the full force of nature behind him.

Donadrian L. Rice, PhD, Professor and Chair Emeritus, Department of Psychology, University of West Georgia

The New-Old:
Recollections, Reflections, and
Reconnoiterings of Mike Arons

Edited by
Andrew M. Bland & Sandrine M. Arons

University
PROFESSORS PRESS

Colorado Springs, CO
www.universityprofessorspress.com

Table of Contents

Acknowledgments

The editors wish to thank:

Dr. Louis Hoffman and the staff at University Professors Press for providing a forum to make this book possible.

Dr. Kand McQueen and the numerous librarians who assisted with locating and obtaining hard-to-find materials—including Krista Higham, Ramie Millar, and Loree Strickler at the McNairy Library at Millersville University and Arianna Iliff at the Drs. Nicholas and Dorothy Cummings Center for the History of Psychology, University of Akron.

Adele Hutchinson (Permissions Manager at the American Psychological Association) and Mary Ann Price (Rights Coordinator at SAGE Publishing) for generously granting permission to republish Mike's papers without a fee. For granting permission to republish, the editors also thank Drs. Nathaniel Granger (Chapter 4), Ruth Richards (Chapter 7), Stanley Krippner (Chapter 8), and Tracy Cross and Anne Richards (Chapters 9 and 11). More information about copyright and permissions is included as a footnote at the beginning of each chapter.

Carlos Morla (Andrew Bland's graduate assistant at Millersville University, 2018–2019) for assisting with typesetting.

Mary Hogan Barber (Andrew Bland's wife) for her patience, support, and careful proofreading.

Wanis Kabbaj (Sandrine Arons' husband) for his support through Sandrine's emotional journey through old papers, photos, and memories.

Christiane Arons for providing specific details about Mike's past and, most important, for giving Mike the space to always be himself.

Preface

by Sandrine M. Arons

When Andrew and I first discussed putting this book together, I offered to write a preface with the hope of sharing a more personal view of my father so that others could understand the man behind his writings. Now that the time has come, I'm finding it more difficult than I imagined for various reasons. It means going back in time with him. It means revisiting memories, letters, photographs, recorded conversations, e-mails, and chats. It means remembering him fully alive, and then it means remembering him in his last days. It is a journey of pain but also of great peacefulness and gratitude and beauty. Our 37-year journey together was not an academic one, although we did some research together and he was my teacher in so many ways. Our journey was a bond so strong that we sometimes communicated telepathically. Our connection was on the plane of the emotional and the spiritual. Though we often didn't need words to speak, we both loved words and language so much that over the years we wrote countless letters and e-mails to each other in order to share our experiences at particular junctures in our journey.

If there is one thing I was certain of, it was that my father loved loving me and he loved being a dad. And I also understood that it was the years of him becoming a person, finding his place in a world with no template for him, that guided him to carve his own mold and become the wonderful father that he was. Perhaps when others read his writings, they will read concepts and theories from an academic mindset; they will read the genesis of his ideas about creativity, humanistic psychology, and education and how these interconnect, how naturally he danced with them all and invited them all to dance in unison. But when I read his papers, I also read his childhood, his struggles, his search for legitimacy, and his commitment to remain authentic. I read his unbound desire to help others tap into their personal truths. I read the writings of a man who wanted others to

Daughter and father, circa 1978.
(Photographer unknown. Contributed by Sandrine Arons.)

experience what it feels like to find their innate gifts and to seize that peak experience as a jumping-off point for their life journey. I read about a boy who broke the codes, who shattered expectations, who seized his wave and rode it fully to the end of his life. I read the words of a man who wanted everyone to recognize and catch their wave. In *The Growing Chasm Between Mission and Job* (Chapter 9 in this book), he spoke of this in terms of "the confidence of empowerment." He wrote about the feeling of being on the right path as an empowering one. For him, that path was the path of an educator. As he explained,

This includes but is not encompassed by teaching. It is teaching out through and beyond these particulars which gives a fullest sense of life and meaning.... A call or vocation is a big intuition. It is seeing something way ahead of yourself that, if you follow the path, comes to be validated along the way.

This explanation struck me because this was the lesson my father reiterated to me throughout my life. He felt personally responsible for teaching me how to fly. But for him flying did not mean success in school or in work, it meant being your most authentic self even when it was the most difficult.

When I was 23 and traversing a moment of self-doubt and uncertainty about my future, my father handwrote me a 14-page letter detailing the struggles he was having at work with some of his colleagues and their desired changes in the psychology department that he had chaired for 25 years. To be honest, I never truly understood the full context and scope of this departmental shake-up, but I saw my father torn apart and doubting himself and suddenly doubting his own calling. He used his personal struggle to speak to mine. As two people in very different stages of our lives, we had something in common. But his problem seemed much worse. I had yet to build my life, I had yet to catch my wave, and I was searching the far horizon for a sign. He, by contrast, had built a home, and a storm came to tear it down. He was in full crisis mode, re-examining his life. Had he used the wrong tools, the wrong materials, the wrong sketch or design? Had he misunderstood something, had he misread his own vision? This was 1994, and it was our summer of shared questioning. We spent a month together traveling through France without my mother, which was quite unusual. Both of us in full self-doubt and both needing the other's loving reflection and empathy.

Some may read self-doubt as a negative, but I was raised to believe that the harm would be to ignore the doubt and push it aside. The thing to do would always be to dive straight in full throttle, to face the doubt head on, to communicate with it, to be one with it, and make it yours, as only that would eventually tame the monster. This was a time of deep self-contemplation for my father, and it overflowed into our relationship. In his letter, written to me overnight as I slept upstairs, he emphasized this need to remain true to one's vision no matter the difficulty or the outcome because to do it fully as oneself in all honesty was the only way to get to the other side of the nightmare, something he counted on in his current struggle. "What I am doing in the department ... my last act and I can leave," he wrote, "is trying to force us all to re-establish the base ... the integrity of our program ... by finally going fully through the horrors."

So what if parts of the house disintegrated? Ultimately, it was the foundation that mattered. It was the support, the common ground, the *heart* that sustained the blows and the shocks and the questioning. And from that place of cognizance, his advice to me was this:

> Time does not always conform to our desires—what we want to know and when. But this does not mean time is not working with us in conjunction. For everything is preparing itself before we recognize it. Often, we must flail about blindly, even if not especially blind to what is preparing in ourselves. Of this I am certain. We must do blind flying to know ultimately our mission, and from each and across all blind flights, do we get clues, intimations, not easily recognizable directions, if we listen as we fly.

My father became very good at flying blind—and if anyone ever rode as a passenger in his car, they might very well wonder if he drove that way, too. He had a remarkable, sometimes frightening, sense of trust in the world and in others. Although he understood consequences in any given situation, he trusted that things and people were as they should be and that you had to meet them where they were. Starting from this place of innate trust in the other drew people to him. Whether in class, in the hallways of the university, in the waiting room at the doctor's office, in a café or restaurant, on the platform of a train station, or just standing on the street, people approached him. As a child, I came to understand that I was going to have to share my father with the world because people loved him and wanted to be near him. Often, as a young and apparently invisible bystander, I listened to complete strangers share personal confidences with him, share ideas and visions. They must have felt in him a non-judgmental ear, an acknowledgment of their existence reflected back at them. Even those with whom he disagreed found a friend in him as long as the lines of communication remained open. He understood that if you engaged those who opposed you or your thinking from a place of shared humanity, you had a better chance of having them see your side. For example, my father would have two large departmental parties a year at our house, and often these involved large bonfires, drumming, and a long line of cars parked up and down our backcountry road. Needless to say, our very conservative neighbors did not appreciate the crowd and all that came with it. The police were called a few times, until my father had the brilliant idea to walk up to their house, knock on the door, and offer to pay their teenage son to help the guests with parking. We never had any issues after that.

Those who knew my father also know that he was very politically outspoken. His letters to the editor were frequently published in newspapers around the state. He thrived on debate and, even though he prodded and nudged his adversaries, he managed to remain friends with them if they were coming from an authentic place. Before he died, he was planning to attend the Conservative Political Action Conference (CPAC) with some of his former Republican colleagues from the history department. My father was a staunch liberal, so this made little sense to me, as did his frequent viewing of Fox News, which he justified as very important to understanding the other side's perspective. I could not believe how excited he was to go to this conference, but I also understood that being the outsider was, in fact, his comfort zone and that the prospect of being around people so different than him was compelling. Unfortunately, he became too sick to attend, and his disappointment was palpable.

My father had an endless capacity to be present with people. Looking back, it almost feels like he had a supernatural ability to spread himself across people and places while still giving himself fully to each one. Maybe this was because he had the uncanny gift of leaving a piece of himself with you to carry around forever. I am still approached by strangers to this day who share how my father changed their lives in one way or another. This is one of the very reasons I believe this book is so important. His writings and his vision should not be lost, and perhaps his words can still have impact.

His journey to humanistic psychology is laid out in his writings, but some may question why he never wrote a book. Although my father was an educator and was able to successfully pioneer a humanistic psychology department in the Bible Belt that attracted people from all over the world, he was not a traditional academic. His goal was not personal advancement through the system, as seems to be the case so often in the present academic culture. His purpose was teaching and learning and healing, and his position as department chair was not a step up to something greater but, I believe in his mind, a way to secure a safe and open space for his students and faculty for years to come. His almost inexhaustible energy was centered on his students, on his exchanges with colleagues at West Georgia and around the world, on building a strong foundation, and on my mother and me. For him, the genesis of the department goes back to before his studies at Brandeis, before meeting Maslow even. It goes back to a *choice* he says he made in the early 1960s while hitchhiking from Paris to Mâcon, France.

While still living in France, my father—who had not yet completed his doctorate—and mother worked together with Michel Siffre (my father's roommate) on the perception of time. This experiment, which involved Siffre living alone in a French cave for several weeks with no light while my parents took notes outside, was the first of its kind and allowed each of them to study time perception from their own unique perspectives. My father describes this as a pivotal moment in his life where he consciously chose his personal vision over what would have been instant fame as a psychologist specializing in time/space perception. In fact, soon after their experiment, Siffre created the French Institute of Speleology, and his subsequent research notes on time perception originating from that study were used by NASA, which recognized similarities between his physiological and psychological experiences and those of their astronauts in space. But, as my father wrote to me many years later,

I made another choice than that offered by this successful experiment. At 31, at that juncture, I was at my best, creatively, confidently, vision-wise. So I was then, as I am now, certain that my life choice was the very best. Simply put, I chose truth. You might say, I chose philosophy. I chose to know myself and follow myself, wherever this took me. And I *knew* it would take me where I had to be and that would be good .... Our program at West Georgia is the product of my decision, hitchhiking from Paris to Mâcon.

Even while understanding that my father embraced his calling to connect with others on a more intimate level, I sometimes felt personal disappointment at my father's complete indifference to elevating himself and his work for a larger audience. It wasn't until the last years of his life that he became inspired by new research on the psychology of the upright body posture and began a book that he never had time to complete. Until that point, this simply was not his priority. He was a doer, not a planner. I often sensed him as floating around in his head, embroidering thoughts and insights into a strangely beautiful order that reflected a sense of harmony that could be felt in any one of his lectures. For someone as organizationally challenged as my father in his day-to-day life—as evidenced by his desk piled with papers, empty soda cans, ashtrays overflowing with cigarette butts, and a car that looked like an extension of his desk—he had an extraordinary capacity to organize thoughts and express large concepts in a manner that unexpectedly fused logic and intuition. His lectures began with large questions, meandered through unexpected and wild territories, sometimes seeming like maybe he had lost his train of thought, to finally leaving the listener not only in a state of intellectual understanding, but with a visceral apprehension of the subject. This is what makes a great professor.

As I reread his papers for this book, it dawned on me that he was researching, contemplating, and writing those papers while the two of us were simultaneously living a profoundly magical father–daughter relationship. Looking back on those years now, I can't decide whether he was consciously preoccupied with being a fully present father or if it simply came naturally to him. Either way, he was a gift to me. To understand what kind of man he was, I believe it helps to know what kind of father he was. The energy and thoughtfulness he put into his teaching was similar to that he put into parenting.

At every stage of my life, my father made time for me in whatever ways I needed. When I was a young child, he was the ideal playmate. I am not sure how he was able to teach, write, do research, and chair a department with all the time he also dedicated to me. With all the attention and time he gave to others, I never felt that our personal time was lessened. And perhaps the book he didn't write was the tradeoff for our time together. He left me with an infinite collection of memories, like a treasure chest.

Our adventures were endless. I recall so many afternoons playing in the creek near our house, learning to balance steadily along the slippery rocks, hand in hand and laughing as we tumbled down into the water together. We took long barefooted walks through the forest, often off the beaten path so we could explore new areas together and blaze new trails. In his playfully sadistic way, he would remind me to keep an eye out for the wolves or convince me that he was pushing down trees with his superhero strength. Later I understood that these were dead trees, but the effect he knew it would have on a small child was as expected. My dad, in my eyes, was the strongest dad in the world. Who else's dad could fight off wolves and knock down trees? I felt a complete sense of security with him that continued throughout my entire life.

At night he loved putting me to sleep with bedtime stories. These were his stories, made up in the moment, full of detail and wonder. When he began, I never knew what journey he was going to take me on, but I knew it would be a journey like no other. Most often they were frightening stories filled with unsavory characters with foreign names. There were ghosts, abandoned houses in dark woods, monsters, and scary animals (always lots of wolves). When I think about it now, I believe this goes back to the notion of confronting what is uncomfortable; back to facing the monster and "going through the horrors." By bringing out of the shadows the scariest cast from a child's vivid imagination, he was teaching me to face my fears because on the other side was certain safety. When the story was over, I was still in my room, in my bed, and in his loving embrace.

Our weekends during my early childhood were spent ice skating, roller skating, or going to Six Flags, where he rode all the roller coasters with me. Our last roller coaster ride together was in 2004. He was 75. When we stepped off, he looked at me and, with an air of disappointment, said, "Sandrine, I don't think I can do this anymore. Makes my head spin too much." I laughed and said something to the effect of, "I don't think I can either!" I was 34.

I would not describe my father as a thrill seeker, but as an experience seeker. If I ever wanted to try something, he was willing to give it a shot. And this attitude gave me the courage to try new things. My father was not fearless. Sometimes he could be considered a worry wart. But from him I learned that fear should not be an obstacle. It should instead act as a whisper to keep moving. My mother, on the other hand, was the pragmatic one in our family, which is exactly what he needed. She could pull him back down when he started floating too high. If things looked too dangerous, she was the levelheaded voice of reason. She was his perfect match. She was like the earth that kept him grounded while giving him ample space to roam. And, like him, she was always ready for an adventure. I think this is what made their relationship so strong. Soon after meeting in Paris through a mutual friend, they left for Spain, and not long after that my mother had the idea to teach in Gabon, Africa for the French Ministry of Education. To be sent as a couple they would need to get married, so they did. Their adventures continued for 47 years.

Later, as I grew older, my father and I took longer excursions together. We went camping, canoeing, fishing, and generally spent more time outdoors further away from home. These were the years that launched deeper conversations. There was an unspoken agreement that either of us could call on the other as needed for a respite from the rest of the world. It wasn't unusual for us to meet in the middle of a busy day because one of us needed to talk, or we just hadn't seen each other in a while. We would often meet in a park and sit with each other for a short time, soak in the other's energy, share what we needed to share, hear what we needed to hear, and then go about our day. I loved talking to him about life, about finding purpose, about the beauty of the world and the ugliness too.

Those who knew my father well would also recognize that he was a bit of a klutz. In my teen years, I walked a fine line between embarrassment and pride when it came to him. My friends adored him and found his quirkiness amusing. For the observer, his clumsiness was endearing, but I understood later that my father still held onto some of the childhood trauma he endured when he was labeled "retarded," "incorrigible," or "unable to educate." These labels were, in my opinion, defining moments for him. As you will read in the following papers, he frequently brings up his childhood because his peak experience was recognizing that he was more than those designations, that he was misunderstood, and that he learned differently than others. Recognizing that is what motivated him to understand, speak to, and speak for those like him.

Mike and Sandrine, circa 1976. The family frequently vacationed in Florida, visiting Mike's mother in Fort Lauderdale every winter break as well as Sidney Jourard in Gainesville. (Photographer unknown. Contributed by Sandrine Arons.)

To say that I miss my father today is an understatement. The emptiness left by such a large presence is indescribable. I was living in Paris when he was hospitalized and, for the first time in my life, he refused to speak to me over the phone. He did not want me to worry. I knew from his silence that something was profoundly wrong. As soon as my mother told me, "Come home," I was on the next flight back to Georgia. I was astounded by his strength to the very end. He accepted that our roles had shifted. Now, I would be the one to put him to bed, I would be the one to comfort him, I would be the one to summon my superhero strength as he had done for me my entire life. As with every life transition, he accepted it. With my mother, we moved through it gracefully together. He left this world in the most peaceful way I could imagine. Never a complaint. Never any resistance. He embarked on this journey like he did a new roller coaster: curious, determined, and unafraid. But this time I could not go with him.

My father died in February 2008, and since that time I have continued writing letters to him. I guess in some ways those letters replace our meetings in the park, our excursions in the mountains, our travels abroad. They are as close as I can get to him now. He was a beautiful man, a wonderful thinker, a caring friend, and a child all in one. He lived his role of educator fully. His writings are such a small fragment of what he gave to the world. It was what he gave to the people he met that was the true gift. He planted seeds in people's hearts, and so many of those people are still creating beautiful spaces and sharing what they've learned in *their* way. As a conclusion to this preface, but as an opening to what follows, I would like to share this passage from a letter I wrote to my father a few months after he died, once I had returned to Paris:

> It's strange how the days pass and images of you pop up like images of a sea filled with laughter. You make me laugh … and as the echoes of your laughter recede further into the distance, my tears come in to replace it …. But I'm ok swimming in this sea of my own sadness because it brings me closer to your laugh and your warmth and your gentle touches and words. But there are days when I feel you are far or close …. I can't distinguish …

but there is a change. And I just cry and cry and cry. I want to call you and talk to you. I want to make sure you're ok ... that you're happy. I want to know if there is another time, another side, another "being." Am I with you??? Are we still linked? Being is nothingness. Nothing in being really is. There is just this strange entanglement of activities that create energy that we call life and one part of us defines that while the other disregards the activity inside ... I know that I could crawl so deep inside myself that I would come out and meet you on the other side of the self I have created in my head. I could meet you on the other side of myself that doesn't know myself. I would undo myself and come back to you. Because I still want to see you dance. I want to walk with you along the creek and tell you how good the breeze feels and how much I love you and how the love you gave me still envelops me like that breeze that pushes through the tall pines above our heads where I hear your laughter echoing in the crackling sound of the branches.

Introduction

by Andrew M. Bland

"The humanistic vision is the space we must always return to as the starting point, this ultimately irreducible wholeness and diversity of human being. What is the good human life? No other psychology can answer this question."
~ Mike Arons (in Elkins, 2000, p. 126)

This volume commemorates the life and works of Dr. Myron Milford "Mike" Arons (1929–2008), beloved psychologist, philosopher, existentialist, scholar/researcher, discussant, artist, educator, mentor, and friend, recognized internationally as one of the founders of humanistic psychology. Described by Stan Krippner as "a force of nature," by Louise Sundararajan as "the most authentic person [she] ever met," by Maureen O'Hara as "a man fully alive!" (quoting John Donne), and by Ruth Richards and Howie Whitehouse as an "advocate of open inquiry, authenticity, and truth," Mike "urged us all to live authentically in the moment—beyond distortions and limitations—and fearlessly see what life would reveal" (Richards & Whitehouse, 2008, pp. 268, 264). Consistent with humanistic psychology's emphasis on paradox (Rowan, 2001), which Mike embraced via his hermeneutic negotiation of dialectics, Chris Aanstoos (2008) portrayed Mike as "ever the organizer/disorganizer, leader/anarchist, serious/playful" (p. 375) and as "Socrates and Zorba, Apollo and Dionysus, an elf and a wizard" who was "ever-ready to encounter life, to embrace alterity, replete with dialectical contradictories, available to every possibility, every nuance. Where others would meet with disaster, Mike's openness discloses unforeseen opportunity" (Aanstoos, 1989, p. 77).

Mike, who had worked as a cab driver in Detroit before becoming a psychologist, was a strong proponent of narrative and its empathetic implications. He once remarked, "Cabbies, like bartenders and barbers, listen to and tell stories. The storyteller and listener are somehow personally implicated in these life stories, even when they are ostensibly centered on others" (in Aanstoos, 1991, p. 170). Once Mike entered psychology, he strove to employ narratives as a vehicle for interdisciplinary and methodological integration in the interests of broadening and deepening the field's scope and of legitimizing rigorous intersubjective approaches to understanding and contextualizing human experience in psychological science. He "cared deeply for others and for the trajectory of the future, far beyond his own lifetime and ours," imploring "us [to] be richly present in our lives, our work, our research, our relationships—and [to] use our gifts, for heaven's sake!" (Richards & Whitehouse, 2008, pp. 268–269).

Background

I first met Mike in 2001, during my first semester in the humanistic psychology master's program at the University of West Georgia. Though he had retired the previous year, as founder of the program and then emeritus faculty, he still regularly attended departmental events and facilitated Philo Cafés (see Café, n.d.) in the area. He also presented an early rendition of his *Standing Up for Humanity* project (see Arons, 2007; Chapter 7 in this volume) during a faculty colloquium series early in 2002, which I summarized for the department's periodical, *The Crucible* (Bland, 2002). Later that year, the psychology department changed buildings, and I assisted with sorting and moving materials. In a closet was a stack of mimeographed typewritten manuscripts of Mike's that I volunteered to convert to electronic documents and post on the West Georgia Psychology website (see https://www.westga.edu/academics/coss/psychology/mike-arons.php). That moving day also inspired me to begin work on a history of the department and to serve as curator of its artifacts. As part of the history project, I interviewed Mike at his home on several occasions, which often evolved into conversations that lasted well into the night.

During this time, I was getting to know Mike through two simultaneous channels: (a) the then-present-day Mike whom I encountered in the flesh and (b) the Mike of the past who spoke to me through his writing as I transcribed his papers into Word documents. After I graduated in 2003, Mike and I continued to meet regularly. One day he asked if I would serve as editor of his collected works. He left me with a box of additional papers—some published, some not; some from decades earlier, others from the previous month—and I set about the task of thematically organizing them. Meanwhile, I spent several afternoons with Mike by the fireplace in his bookshelf-lined basement or on the deck he built behind his house (the basis of his "platform experience," see p. 28 of this volume), dialoguing, debating, reminiscing about the past, musing about the next installment of his *Standing Up for Humanity* project. I also remember witnessing his e-mail discussions about psychology and science with Zeno Franco and Harris Friedman (compiled in Franco, Friedman, & Arons, 2008) as they took place on a list-serve, as well as his playful competition with Tom Greening over which of them rightfully deserved the title of "Emperor of China."

In 2007, I left Georgia to begin doctoral studies in Indiana. By this time, Mike's health was beginning to decline. I saw him for the last time that December, when I visited during winter break. He and his family stopped taking guests shortly thereafter. That February, I received the call from a fellow recent West Georgia alum that he had died "peacefully with his wife and daughter by his side" (Aanstoos, 2008, p. 375).

Having just started a doctoral program, for better or worse it was necessary for me to put Mike's collected papers on the backburner. Unfortunately, due to my own family and career obligations, they remained there until 2018—which marked both the 10th anniversary of his death and the 50th anniversary of his arrival at (then) West Georgia College to pioneer, per Abe Maslow's recommendation, the third humanistic psychology program in the United States. As both a tribute to his memory and a gateway to reflection and scholarship by future generations of humanistic psychologists who did not have the privilege to know Mike, I prepared an annotated bibliography of as complete a collection of Mike's writings as possible. It was published in *The Humanistic Psychologist* (Bland, 2018) and is included here (with additional material added) as an appendix. This volume, published in 2019 to commemorate the 90th anniversary of Mike's birth, provides readers an opportunity to revisit or to acquaint themselves with Mike's work in more depth and trace the trajectory of his thought as it evolved over about three decades, from the 1970s to the 2000s. In addition, Mike's daughter, Sandrine, has joined me as co-editor and has offered memories of her father in the preface. The title of this volume, *The New-Old: Recollections, Reflections, and Reconnoiterings of Mike Arons*, was coined by Mike himself. He also participated in the initial selection of the papers, and he prepared an autobiographical account specifically for this project that is presented here (as Chapter 3) for the first time.

Mike Arons' Scholarship

Mike identified his line of scholarship as entailing the exploration of "creative and intuitive processes, human science research, psi phenomena, and humanistic and transpersonal education and psychology" (in Aanstoos, 1991, pp. 170–171) as well as "mythology, history of psychology, cultural and cross-cultural psychology, and Ricoeurian hermeneutics" (Arons, 1999c, p. 1). A summative content analysis of Mike's vita (Arons, 2000b) indicates that between 1967 and September 2000, he delivered 192 presentations (throughout the United States as well as in Canada, the Netherlands, Germany, Iceland, Belgium, Russia, India, Thailand, Japan, France, Denmark, Sweden, Italy, Mexico, South Africa, England, and China); published 18 articles in journals and 6 in professional newsletters, 7 book chapters, and 8 other publications (book reviews, magazine columns, the *Directory of Graduate Programs in Humanistic–Transpersonal Psychology*, etc.); participated in 2 radio/television broadcasts and 4 film presentations; and facilitated 9 experiential workshops. This count is somewhat incomplete. During the process of compiling the aforementioned annotated bibliography, some publications were discovered that were not included on his vita. Plus, Mike continued to extensively write and present between his retirement in 2000 and his death in 2008 (years not included on the vita), and some additional material was published posthumously.

Mike described his delivery style as an "excursion" (Bland, 2002, p. 1). Accordingly, the papers included here possess the flowing, hermeneutic attributes of a quality lecture, often embellished with personal storytelling, more so than a formal written treatise—but anchored in rigorous interdisciplinary discourse all the same. Ever open to the transpersonal and the postmodern while remaining firmly grounded in the existential, phenomenological, lived experiential, and practical, Mike seamlessly integrated traditions in the style of his mentor-turned-colleague, Jim Klee (1982). As just a few examples, these included references to and/or dialogues with Maslow, Rogers, May, Watts, gestalt psychology, Ricoeur, Heidegger, Merleau-Ponty, Husserl, Straus, Kuhn, Jung, Hellenic and Gnostic philosophies, Plato, Pascal, Bergson, Einstein, early creativity literature (Barron, Guilford, Getzels/Jackson), Taoism, Buddhism, psi research, cultural anthropology, Greek mythology, and evolutionary science.

Nary a paper in this book fails to include an intellectual history of whatever broadly humanistic topic Mike was addressing—personal growth, intuition, holism, creativity, compassion, moral development, authenticity, choice, values, responsibility, experience, embodiment, mindfulness, time orientation, East-West integration, hermeneutics, etc.—and the relationship between that history (old) and then-current issues (new). He also frequently incorporated inductive, interpretative analyses of everyday language and its connections to greater macro- and chronosystemic issues. Accordingly, to read Mike's writings in sequence is to witness the unfolding of his thinking and experiencing, his ever reflecting and reconnoitering (his word), his way of being present to his surroundings and to developments both in and around psychology, over several decades.

Several motifs were explored and revisited throughout Mike's writings, but never in the same way twice. These included: (a) humanistic psychology as a third option to blind faith and to science that "plays dumb" to that which it cannot measure; (b) Barron's (1963) description of the creative person as "at once naïve and knowledgeable, being at home equally to primitive symbolism and to rigorous logic" and as "both more primitive and more cultured, more destructive and more constructive, occasionally crazier and yet adamantly saner, than the average person" (p. 224); (c) the dialectics of progression– regression, absolute/singularity–relative/multiplicity, and distal– proximal; (d) the wisdom of the body and the wisdom of insecurity; (e)

Panofsky's interpretation of Dürer's engraving, *Melancholia I*; (f) Maslow's (1968) self-actualization and his conceptualization of creativity as distinct from talent; (g) Ricoeur's (1970) dialogue with Freud and re-sacralizing hermeneutics; (h) *originality* having two vectors, one toward the *origins* (that which is already there) and the other toward *beginnings* (the new and unique); (i) multi-vocal symbols in creative work (e.g., *Gulliver's Travels* interpreted differently at ages 10, 20, and 40); (j) Merleau-Ponty's (1962) phenomenology of the body; (k) the riddle of the Sphinx; (l) Bergson's (1940) conceptualization of his many moods, sentiments, and interests as points–counterpoints in a life symphony as illustration of principles from gestalt and existential psychologies; (m) Socrates' method of selecting students on the basis of whether they still could blush; (n) the relationship between creativity and intelligence; (o) detached engagement in creativity and science; and (p) the problem of applying a linear conceptualization of technological progress to art.

Taken together, a principal leitmotif throughout Mike's work was: *How have we—as individuals, as psychologists, as a global human species—arrived at our current steps along our journeys through time, history, art, science, and life?* And, *what should we be sure to pack for the next leg of the trip?* To aid in this pursuit, Mike demonstrated the value of (a) starting with the big picture and *then* zooming in on the parts to prevent tunnel vision and (b) employing negotiation of dialectics to approach multiple truths without engaging in nihilistic deconstruction or one-sidedness. Broad-minded as Mike was, he also acknowledged the limits of human potential and creativity (à la May, 1975) and cautioned against free-for-alls. Thus, he delicately integrated the pre-modern with the modern and the post-modern (or -rational, or -scientific).

Mike Arons' Biography

Mike was born on October 17, 1929 in Detroit, Michigan. His family was of Hungarian Jewish descent; Mike's father emigrated to the United States at age 9, and his mother was first-generation American. Growing up, Mike was "tabbed retarded" (Arons, 1994b, p. 374) by the standardized tests of the day and "classed as what we now call a behavior disorder problem. The less kind and gentle term then was 'incorrigible'" (Arons, 1990a, p. 124). On the other hand, he also had a natural inclination towards and passion for "guiding" (p. 124):

> I spent years of my middle childhood ... walking, biking, or bussing up and down [the] streets [of Detroit] ... over and over, hundreds of times. I went to the top of buildings and looked down and around from each vantage to all the others and then went to the ground and looked up. I dressed up like a rich kid and sat in the posh hotel lobbies. I dressed to be saved and served on Michigan Avenue's skid row soup kitchens. I came to know Detroit inside and out and upside and down. I was the unpaid guide who understood Detroit as no paid guide ever knew or presented it. ... [Later] I took a job ... as taxi driver. I was not your typical taxicab driver. Sometimes I would pay the meter bill just to complete the tour I was giving. Sometimes the customer would pay for the whole day just to get the tour.

Following several unhappy years spent working in auto factories and selling carpet and real estate (interpolated by a single year at the Chicago Academy of Fine Arts, 1950–1951), at age 27, Mike enrolled at Wayne State University and majored in psychology. "No enterprise could have stood more starkly in opposition to the narrative perspective on the world than the field of psychology at the time," he reflected (Aanstoos, 1991, p. 170). On the other hand, having independently perused writings by humanistic psychologists via a copy of Moustakas' (1956) edited volume, *The Self,* that he found left behind by a passenger in his taxi (Arons, 2004), Mike discovered "what [he] thought psychology was all about" (Arons, 2000a, p. 1).

Mike graduated with honors in 1961. Nonetheless, left with a deep sense of "personal dissatisfaction" with how "sterile [he] had seen psychology" of the day (Smith, Moerman, & Wertz, 1986, p. 52), he "turned down thousands of dollars of graduate fellowships and assistantships" from eight U.S. graduate psychology programs (Franco, Harris, & Arons, 2008, p. 196). Instead, despite knowing little French, he opted to "cross the Atlantic on a Holland-America student ship and hitch to Paris" (Arons, 2004, p. 4) for doctoral study at the Sorbonne, "where existential phenomenology was blossoming .... I made this 'irrational' leap because I intuited [that] there was much more to being a human than anything being taught [in American psychology]—and bet my life on it" (Franco, Harris, & Arons, 2008, p. 196).

In 1965, Mike defended his doctoral dissertation under the direction of Paul Ricoeur (cited by Université de Paris as "très honorable") on the topic of creativity research as an expression of the implicit story of American psychology. During the interim, he and his wife, Christiane (whom he met in Paris and married in 1962), served as teachers in recently liberated Gabon, Africa, where they rubbed shoulders with Albert Schweitzer.

Mike returned to the United States for postdoctoral studies at Brandeis University, where he served as Abe Maslow's teaching assistant in 1966 and also was mentored by Jim Klee and George Kelly. Thereafter, per Maslow's recommendation, he pioneered two humanistic psychology programs, first at Prince of Wales College on Prince Edward Island, Canada in 1967 and then at West Georgia College, now University of West Georgia, in Carrollton, Georgia in 1968. The latter was the third of its kind in the United States (Richards & Whitehouse, 2008) after Sonoma State and Duquesne. Aanstoos (2008) reported, "At that time, West Georgia was a rather inconsequential place. [Mike] quickly turned it into a destination school for students and faculty from around the world" (p. 375):

> Upon his arrival, Mike effected a tremendous, immediate transformation .... Thirty new courses were added, many never previously available anywhere in the country, and a humanistically oriented M.A. program established. It combined ancient Eastern and contemporary Western psychology ... quickly [making] West Georgia a mecca for students and faculty starving for a psychology that addressed their human experience. A deep awareness of the personal relevance of this vision of psychological life flourished in this setting. Students and faculty understood this was not a psychology of the

impersonal Other, but a psychology speaking to—and transforming—one's own Being …. The program aimed to be mind-blowing, its inclusion of the far-out a way of opening students to go beyond the presupposed, to the very ground of their existence. Nurtured by Mike's genius for fostering creativity by removing its obstacles, this atmosphere *was* the clearing, the haven, within which one could ask *any* question, teach *any* course, explore *any* crevice of human existence …. Phenomenological, existential, hermeneutic, transpersonal, dialogal, experiential, perceptual, Jungian, Gestalt, parapsychological, [Asian], and body psychologies all were not merely welcomed, but integrated, each cross-fertilizing the others. (Aanstoos, 1989, pp. 78–79)

Although it is beyond the scope of this introductory chapter to further elaborate on the extraordinary story of the development of the West Georgia program, richly detailed accounts are available in Aanstoos (1989, 1991, 2008, 2017) and in Bland (2003).

Mike served as chair of the West Georgia psychology department for 25 years and as professor for 32 years until his retirement in 2000. Aanstoos (2008) recalled that "Mike was a singular teacher, and it was his inspiration of generations of students that is his greatest accomplishment …. Dialectically, hermeneutically, intuitively, whimsically, lyrically, magically, Mike called forth … in his students the best they had yet to discover in themselves" (p. 376). In addition, Mike served as associate faculty to the Institute of Liberal Arts doctoral program at Emory University in Atlanta beginning in 1977, was a visiting professor of psychology at Aarhus Universitet in Denmark in 1985, co-created humanistic educational programming in Mexico and France in the 1990s, and collaborated with Francesco Palmirotta to develop the International University of Humanistic Ontosophy in Bari, Italy during the 2000s. During the fall semester of 2007, Mike returned to West Georgia to instruct his last course, on embodied creativity.

Further, Mike's daughter, Sandrine, recalls him assisting adults with intellectual disabilities at a farm-based center in the Appalachians during the late 1970s and "pointing out their creative skills (in their artwork) as well as their ability to grow and prepare their own food" (Sandrine Arons, personal communication, August 25, 2018). Mike also served as president and director of the Papillon Life Enrichment Center in Whitesburg, Georgia, and in 1999 received an award from State University of West Georgia "for [his] service to the handicapped" (Arons, 2000b, p. 15).

Mike was an active participant in the institutionalization of humanistic psychology. He served on the executive committees of— and, in some cases, helped found—the Society for Humanistic Psychology (SHP, Division 32 of the American Psychological Association [APA], of which he was co-president [1975–1976] and member-at-large [1977–1979, and 1986–1989]) and its Transpersonal Psychology special interest group, as well as the Association for Humanistic Psychology, the Association for Humanistic Education, the Consortium for Diversified Programs in Psychology, the International Human Science Research Association, the Association for Qualitative Research in Psychology, and the Psychical Research Foundation. He also sat on the editorial boards of the *Journal of Humanistic Psychology* and *The Humanistic Psychologist*; chaired numerous conferences on humanistic education and human science research; introduced the European Philo Café (Café, n.d.) to the Carrollton, Georgia community, to the SHP Hospitality Suite at APA conventions, and elsewhere (for further description, see Richards & Whitehouse, 2008); was designated SHP's Oral History Archivist; edited the first five editions of the *Directory of Graduate Programs in Humanistic and Transpersonal Psychology in North America*; and advocated "using the Hospitality Suite [at APA conventions] to offer those 'off-convention' events that were more experiential, less formal, and offer us ways of engaging our discipline as whole (and not always buttoned down) persons" (O'Hara, 2009, para. 1).

Furthermore, Mike chaired numerous academic committees within the University System of Georgia's Board of Regents and was an active member of APA Divisions 24 (Theoretical and Philosophical Psychology), 49 (Group Psychology and Group Psychotherapy), and 52 (International Psychology).

Mike was the first recipient of SHP's Abraham Maslow Heritage Award "for an outstanding and lasting contribution to the exploration of the farther reaches of human spirit" in 1999. Additionally, he received the Charlotte and Karl Bühler Award "for pioneering work in graduate humanistic education" in 1993 and an honorary degree from the Humanistic Ontosophy University in 2005. "That Mike should have won all the awards [he received] should surprise no one. But that was never his aim. Indeed, the award with which he was most pleased" (Aanstoos, 2008, p. 375) was a plaque he received from the SHP Executive Board in the mid-1970s for his "undying devotion and ceaseless efforts to the plaqueless society" (Arons, 1988b, p. 382).

To do Mike's story justice is to hear it firsthand. Rich autobiographical anecdotes are embedded throughout his writings (especially Arons, 1978b, 1990a, 1991b, 1992c, 1994b, 1996, 2000a, all but one of which are included in this volume)—which taken together form a cohesive narrative of the first 40 years of his life. In addition, a recounting of Mike's memoir by Chris Aanstoos (2017; https://www.youtube.com/watch?v=-gvXpwSvqG0) is strikingly comparable both in detail and inflection to my recollection of Mike's own delivery.

Organization of this Book

Following Sandrine's preface and this introduction, 13 of Mike's papers (about two-fifths of which are rare, out-of-print, or unpublished) are presented thematically in four sections: (a) his inspiration and influences; (b) creativity, consciousness, and culture; (c) humanistic education; and (d) two of Mike's hermeneutic explorations (on the topics of intuition and the nature of self). Each of the four sections opens with an editorial summary. The book concludes with my remarks about the contemporary implications and applications of Mike's thinking as well as the accuracy of his predictions about the future of both psychology and society. Finally, an annotated bibliography of Mike's complete writings is included as an appendix.

Andrew and Mike at Mike's home in Carrollton, GA, 2004.
(Photographer: Christiane Arons. Contributed by Andrew Bland.)

Part 1:

Inspiration and Influences

Mike barefoot on cliff, circa 1966–67.
(Photographer unknown. Contributed by Sandrine Arons.)

Mike readily acknowledged, reflected on, and expressed appreciation for his mentors, influences, and colleagues. On the first page of his vita (Arons, 2000b), he included a list of 20 "teachers to whom [he owes] a special debt of gratitude": (a) his homeroom teacher during grade school; (b) his high school English teacher; (c) an instructor at Chicago Academy of Fine Arts; (d) five professors at Wayne State University; (e) "Hans" in Paris and "Andre" in Gabon; (f) Paul Ricoeur and Claude Lévi-Strauss in Paris; (g) Jim Klee, Abe Maslow, George Kelly, and Min Chiang at Brandeis; (h) Sidney Jourard; (i) the Dean of Education and a history professor at West Georgia; and (j) his wife, Christiane. During his career, he also prepared heartfelt obituaries for Frank Barron (Arons, 2003b), Duncan Blewitt (Schor & Arons, 2007), Earl Brown (Arons, 2003a), Carmi Harari (Serlin & Arons, 2004), and Jim Klee (Arons, 1997a, 1997b).

This section includes three autobiographical accounts of Mike's formative encounters with influential teachers and other sources of inspiration. In Chapter 1, Mike sketches his journey from childhood to chairing the West Georgia program and reflects on having been drawn to humanistic psychology via a sense of resonance with its universal, eternal qualities. In Chapter 2, Mike reminisces about his encounters with two professors who "spoke to a part of [him that he] was yet to discover": Roberto Giammanco at Wayne State and Paul Ricoeur at the Sorbonne. In Chapter 3, Mike traces the series of events—sometimes synchronous, sometimes serendipitous, often both—that constituted his excursion out of existential frustration in 1950s Detroit into a classroom with Maslow in the 1960s.

Chapter 1

Recognizable Paths of Humanistic Psychology (1994)[1]

Editors' note: This paper was part of a series published in The Humanistic Psychologist *in which psychologists reflected on the movement's personal significance by describing the ways that it had called to them.*

My own way into humanistic psychology was by the doors of recognition. And this path of recognition opened has been central to my own life's passage. I think many who came to this kind of psychology passed through these doors in themselves. That is, they recognized themselves more fully in this psychology, and this psychology spoke to a more recognizable model of human Being. This was true for the three historically opened phases of humanistic psychology—the existential, the humanistic, and transpersonal. All were a timely prod to personal and social consciousness. This suggests they were ideas that are socio-temporally bound, implying by this that they are relative visions. This is certainly true. They spoke specifically to a period and as reactions against it. But, for me, they have been a crack in our times, a timely expression in psychology which rejoins that field to the humanities it divorced—allowing us, in this new form, to see what others have seen and recognized about full humanness, across times and cultures. In this sense they speak to and are consistent dimensions of the universal.

Let me speak first to the historical path of recognition humanistic psychology joins, then speak to the cultural milieu in which I first encountered phases of humanistic psychology, and then to the personal

[1] Arons, M. (1994). Recognizable paths of humanistic psychology. *The Humanistic Psychologist, 22,* 371–378. doi:10.1080/08873267.1994.9976960 | Copyright © 1994 by the American Psychological Association. Adapted with permission from the American Psychological Association.

experiences of it which so affected my own life directions past and present. And by these experiences I think you will see why I have little patience with those amongst us who would fractionate the whole humanistic perspective. Less with those who feel they have undermined its essentials by a deconstruction of self. And much optimism about its future.

The Gnostics used this same term, *recognition*, to speak of the internal means by which they came to know God, the "Kingdom Within." Socrates, before them, spoke of *reminiscence* to indicate the interior path to the invisible reality of the forms, presumed by Plato innate to us. Freud's path of psychoanalysis is one of inversely following the "road signs" of resistance, those painful indices of the ultimately recognized psychical realities blocked out. Jung's *individuation* is the mutual recognition and reconciliation of alienated functions within ourselves. The Buddhist meditative path brings us to recognition of the way things are—not for us alone, but for everybody and everything... for nobody. In all cases, a reality (partial or complete, personal or cosmic) is waiting to be discovered by recognition from within.

I have been doing a series of videotapes on the oral history of humanistic psychology. It is remarkable how many of the long-timers of this movement were "seminally turned on" by just a few books, such as Maslow's *Toward a Psychology of Being* and Rogers' *On Becoming a Person*. That is what we mean by seminal texts. They are seminal, rudimentary, in the sense that they speak to us of basic realities which, by recognition, ring profoundly true. Such books as May's *Existence*, Frankl's *Man's Search for Meaning*, and Moustakas' *Loneliness* brought recognition in me of my humanness beyond those psychoanalytically induced ones that I recognized during five years of therapy. As Maslow insisted, it is not that Freud or the behaviorists were wrong; they were incomplete. Most of our field has now come to recognize that. But we also should not also forget that our field, psychology, in its 19th century ambition to join science, divorced itself not only from its humanities origins of this quest for fuller humanness, but from a value-laden perspective required to ever really understand this. It is here—in its rejoining with the humanities at the essential value level, as I indicate at the end—that I can foresee the humanistic psychology perspective taking wider root, serving to solve today's problems and prevailing into the next millennium.

Recognition requires a state of preparedness—a readiness, openness, a prescience of the desired missing. Socrates understood that, choosing his students on the basis of whether they could still blush. Things had to get emotionally bad enough for psychoanalysis and the Twelve Step program to click into recognition mode. The Zen novice's cup must be empty before it can be refilled with fresh insight. Or the reverse of all of this. One's cup has to "runneth over" to recognize the dullness of the typical life drone or notice what has been missing. In all, a person or society—as Hegel spoke of *collective consciousness*—had to be brought to the state of a readiness for recognition. And 1960s America was ready for humanistic psychology.

In the 1950s, America's cup "ranneth over" materially while its owners thirsted for authenticity, touch, and spirit. These were to be supplied by the existential, the touchy-feely ends of humanistic, and the spiritual ends of both of these but focused more thematically in transpersonal psychology. But, also, the economic opulence enjoyed at the period provided material support for exploration of the fuller reaches of our humanness spoken to by this then-newly emerging psychology. In this double sense of what was lacking in the times and what of its benefits supported the search for the missing, we can say humanistic psychology was time–space bound, thus relative. But, paradoxically, it was also opening up recognitions which others across times and geography had experienced—thus making it universal.

The 1950s was a post-war period of resettling into normalcy, psychological "normality" being monitored by the normative indices of "social adjustment." At its worst, all that didn't meet the standards of a single norm were being rounded. The harsh edges of life, experienced as war during the preceding decade, during this one were being smoothed out by the discovery and application of plastics of all sorts— symbolically, socially tinted in the inoffensive pastel colors of conformity and depersonalization, ultra-specialization, role and game playing, all housed in the sameness of "ticky-tacky" suburbs sprouting up across the land. Consistent with all this, the central axiom of psychology was its "tension reduction model." One could see what had been "smoothed over" all come out in such literature as *Who's Afraid of Virginia Woolf?* and later in the encounter groups which, following the suburban movement, came to spread across the land. It was a period when the destiny of happiness and fulfillment were confidently consigned to the value-free, impersonal forces of science, technology, industry, and a burgeoning economy. Yet, in contrast to these remarkable productions of the human mind, our psychology of the period was showing our fate to be fully determined, passive, will-less, and without consciousness. All the movements associated with humanistic psychology put into question these "helpless," "unconscious," "non-responsible" premises (an early version of our recent stress on victimization?) and, in this sense, their insights began to bring us back to life, showing the inner journey to be at least as adventurous as our scientific one while giving us recognition of what had been missing in our lives.

This landscape view—that my own recognitions within about humanistic psychology were part of a social *zeitgeist*—I see in retrospect. But I and others first experienced it individually. And based on my own experiences and the oral history tapes I've been doing, it is ironic (and hard for me to judge otherwise) that while all shared the social *zeitgeist*, each must have done this from a quite unique personal situation. My own path to recognition of humanistic psychology began in a very special personal state of preparedness, which included deficiency, pathology, and the supernormal. Each of the three phases of the humanistic psychology movement—existential, humanistic, and transpersonal—was instrumental in both understanding and the transforming of my life.

My four years as an undergraduate literally passed for me in a state of prolonged—which I only had the word then to describe as— "mystical" experience. And those were the pre-psychedelic days. And when "mystical" was the dirtiest word in the positivistic–rationalists' lexicon, worse even than consciousness. I was older, twenty-seven, when I started as a freshman at Wayne State University. Earlier, I had completed five years of psychoanalysis, and this educational experience was particularly special for me—and generally remarkable to everybody else who had known me—first, simply by the fact that I had been accepted to any college and this because I had spent much of my primary and secondary school years in a class for the slow learner. I was, in fact, by I.Q. scores, tabbed retarded. At fifteen, diagnosed with what later would be called "behavior disorder," I had been booted from the Detroit Public School system and, by my parents, was sent away to a military school in the South, an alternative to reform school. Even as I tried to enter college, my entrance examination scores were at the bottom of the applicants. My reading scores—at age twenty-seven— were put at the third-grade level. These scores never changed throughout my undergraduate years, even as I graduated with honors.

While at Wayne State, a new research area into creativity was just opening up, parts of which quickly merged into the humanistic *zeitgeist*. Getzels and Jackson, Guilford, Barron, Moustakas, and so many others all at once, were pointing to cognitive and related emotional capacities that our objective tests—particularly the I.Q.—were missing. And here particularly I recognized myself in the missing. Indeed, I was in fact retarded and had a behavior disorder from one dominant observable and measurable perspective, but from this new one opening up in psychology—the creativity perspective—these observables took on a quite different internal understanding. So, even more than all my years in psychoanalysis, like my experiences in the humanities and the other humanistic psychology literature, I came to recognize myself through this creativity literature—a literature which in the United States and especially via Moustakas and Frank Barron was beginning to merge with the existentialism that had arrived from Europe.

Nothing in psychology at the time—but bits of the creativity literature and Maslow in his noting of "peak experiences"—spoke directly to my ongoing altered state of consciousness. If I were mad— and that was the only explanation given me at the time—then I could not imagine how anybody would choose not to be in this state. By some magic neither I nor anybody else understood, without basic skills such as reading, writing, mathematics, or pre-college foundations, I was intuitively grasping all the college materials—the more advanced the easier—and managing to articulate these with great success. It was as if I had been placed in some state of grace where everything became immediately clear to me through words on a page I didn't understand

and by writing I saw appear on paper which didn't seem to come from my own hand. My empathetic and psychic abilities were heightened to a frightening degree. I was popping with epiphanies. I was passing from one synchronistic event in my life to another. All my previously chronic illnesses disappeared: carbuncles, headaches, bronchitis, pleurisy. I felt I could have composed all the great music I was listening to, written the novels, grasped the meaning of any philosophy.

What was this miraculously blessed state I was in? Beyond Maslow, I was getting furtive glimpses of recognition in such fiction as Hermann Hesse's *Siddhartha* and *Demian,* Somerset Maugham's *The Razor's Edge*, and through some religious works, such as Saint Augustine's *Confessions* and biographies of Joan of Arc. But I was not religious. As my school and family history indicates, I had never been a "good boy." I had never prayed other than what was required of me as an infant, by my mother, to get to sleep. I had never meditated (nor understood the meaning of the word then). Nor had I ever heard of pot or psychedelics. I had no relationship to God. Our family was slipping out of the Jewish religious tradition. Jesus was, by conditioning, an enemy alien.

After receiving my B.A., I decided to go to France to do my doctorate. It was the inspiration of existentialism—certainly not that of rationalism—which led and encouraged me to take this bold move. With no money beyond that for passage, no acceptance to the Sorbonne, no pre-communication with a professor, and no background in the French language, I set sail on a student ship. I planned to write a dissertation on creativity and had hoped this would be directed by Maurice Merleau-Ponty. He had died the very summer I arrived, in 1961. As a substitute, I was led by a total stranger I met in a café to a professor whom I had never then heard of: Paul Ricoeur, a giant scholar and gem of a human it turned out, who—in retrospect, I am amazed that I was not astonished by this—accepted me as his doctoral student on the spot and who was at that very period exploring the sacred dimensions of experience. Half a decade later I completed my dissertation, in the French language, under Ricoeur. Now I was on a full search towards understanding what seemed to be an endless state of "peak experience" I was enjoying. I returned to the U.S. to study and work with Abe Maslow.

On my return to the States, the psychedelics movement was in full bloom. Leary and Alpert had become heroes of the "New Consciousness." Maslow was writing *Religion, Values, Peak Experiences* and *The Farther Reaches of Human Nature*. At Brandeis, I encountered Jim Klee, who had the remarkable ability to transform the most banal matters and events into an endless string of sparkling insights. Courses under Klee gave the sense of recognition its fullest meaning for me. It was about that same period that a literal basket case, Tony Sutich—a man of extreme brilliance, yet his body so shriveled and twisted they had to carry him to the speaker's platform—was beginning, with Maslow, a journal and organization called "transpersonal psychology" and here unrolled the maps of my state of consciousness.

The path of recognition I once followed alone to understand my own experiences which nobody seemed to share or could explain to me was now congested with fellow travelers. Each in his or her way was feasting off the several-course meal being served up by existential–humanistic–transpersonal psychology. Maslow got me my first job, as chairman of a little department on Prince Edward Island, Canada. We created a humanistic–transpersonal program there in 1967 and I cannot remember an educational environment so completely turned on. In fact, the whole little college became a model centered on creativity, personal growth, and transformation of students and faculty. So much so that the government soon amalgamated it with a Catholic college, reset its mission towards technological training, virtually killing its spirit—and I left.

Maslow recommended me to my next job as chairman of the Department of Psychology at West Georgia College. There, in 1968, under the orientation existential–humanistic–transpersonal, we established 45 new courses and an educational ambience which began to draw students from all over the world. The program continues, joining some 35 others of similar orientation around the country, and the students keep coming for this in record numbers.

Yet times have changed. The optimism of opulence is gone from the national spirit. It has now turned mean and particularly reactive to much that represented the 1960s. Splintering claims for diversity and the chaos likely endogenous to a social transformation from a modern to postmodern paradigm leaving a wide ethical void—rather than bland conformity—characterize the current social climate. The humanistic orientation has had a broadly philosophical but not focalized influence on the field. And its transpersonal offshoot has yet to be accorded independent recognition by APA. Doubts have come to beset the national organizations representing this orientation. Accreditation, licensing and other credentialing standards, and professional ethics codes do not speak to what our graduates do best. Post-structuralists, like Gergen, have been deconstructing the self and everybody seems to be looking with some trepidation to what the future might bring.

I am optimistic, especially about what the future of humanistic–transpersonal psychology might be. This optimism is grounded in two points of basic recognition. First, that whatever its particular form of expression—that which I fully concede is culturally and historically relative—the humanistic psychology model has brought to light in its times a structure of humanness consistent with those of other times and cultures. Unlike either the scientific models or the post-rational ones, which share at heart an iconoclastic disposition—in the case of post-structuralism, a nihilistic one—humanistic psychology is from start to finish value-laden and holistic. It starts from an unassailable phenomenological and logical premise that despite all impersonal realities and especially through all the diversities one can enumerate, people want to be happy and fulfilled. This is the value that generates everything else. The ancient Hellenists demonstrated by both common sense and logic that these were the uniquely human ends. One does everything—health, wealth, relationships, etc.—for happiness. One does happiness and a sense of human completeness for nothing else, and this in terms of an optimal view of one's life as a whole.

Second, more practically speaking for our times and future, our current problems are largely ethical and spiritual. Maslow's *self-actualizers* were models of both these realizations as were the eudaemonic models of the Western Ancients and those drawn out of Eastern philosophies. The project of self-interest, personal fulfillment, ultimately and necessarily joins the project of other-concern, other-interest, and collective fulfillment. The self-actualizing spiritual trip is essentially an ethical and moral one. It is out of this recognition that a currently self-doubting humanistic psychology movement can begin to envision ways and vehicles for serving our current social needs and as a model for re-visioning our future. Practical steps in this first direction are now well underway as we consider a special sphere of service beyond the "fix-it" medical model practice in which our humanistic–transpersonal students can both serve the public and serve their own vocational needs—*vocation* used here in both the professional and spiritual senses. Likewise, initiatives are now underway to look to a human-centered value model around which community revitalization might be envisioned and reconstructed. Put more succinctly, how can the Constitutional guarantees of the Enlightenment rationalism, the great abstract principles (i.e., "justice, equality, life, liberty, and the pursuit of happiness") be recognizably grounded for their existential and spiritual realization? It is notable in this regard that Chancellor Kohl of Germany recently called for a humanization of capitalism.

I know the term *humanistic* has come to mean many different things; that, even within humanistic psychology—like *happiness* itself—it holds quite different meanings for different individuals; that it is easy to get caught up in the means; that these means are often conflicting. But for me, and I think for our times, humanistic psychology has set the right value itinerary. And I am deeply appreciative to have been on its voyage much of the trip.

Chapter 2

Two Suns of My Student Years
(1992)[1]

He Spoke to a Part of Me I Was Yet to Discover

Roberto Giammanco was a visiting professor at Wayne State University under whom I took an advanced undergraduate course called *European Intellectual History of the 16th Century*. An Italian Marxist–Renaissance historian, he was a solid man with head always cocked upward and slightly to the right, eyelids downward and slightly to the left, with huge prideful hands that seemed permanently glued to the extra-wide lapels of his thatchy wool sports jackets. He was the sort of intellectual I had never before encountered: fully stocked with extravagantly radical critical perspectives I had never before considered. His presence and presentations introduced me to the full compatibility of idea and passion—then and now, history and me.

He was disdainful of many things in America: "Arons," he chided me once when I cited a passage from Thoreau to support a philosophical position, "American pheeelozophy ees a contradiction in terms, eh?" And he was equally disdainful of most of the views I had taken to heart in the course of my general studies: "Arons, what ees zees exeeztential bullsheet, eh? Eet ees zee last dying gazp of zee bourgeois society." Yet the disdain was the sort of intellectual chiding that never failed to stimulate me to examine the certitude of my views and the solidity of their grounding assumptions, which explorations at paper-grading time he respected with such challenging notations as "Good, but where

[1] Arons, M. (1992). Two suns of my student years. *Journal of Humanistic Psychology, 32*, 46–50. doi:10.1177/0022167892321004 | Copyright © 1992 by SAGE Publishing. Adapted with permission from SAGE Publishing.

do you go from here with these thoughts?" He treated me much as he would a colleague with whom he would debate playfully. He spoke to a part of me I had yet to discover. I came to love the man.

When the time came for me to choose a graduate school, I was depressed. I had received fellowship offers from many programs around the country to study experimental psychology—about all there was at the time. However, my running dialogue with Giammanco as respectful interlocutor—in his office, waiting in line at his bank, browsing the bookstores on Woodward Avenue—had served only to whet my growing intrigue with existentialism. I came to his office one day in a particularly despondent mood. "Dr. Giammanco," I moaned, "everything rational indicates that I should take one of these fellowship offers, and my parents are certainly more than pushing me in this direction. Yet I feel I should be in France. However, I have no money. I'd have to reject thousands of dollars in offers. I don't speak French. I know nothing of the French university system. It is late spring. I've made no application and, then, how do I know I would be accepted? I would have to shift from psychology to philosophy, and my major advisor told me that would be academic suicide for a future career in psychology. Apart from my experience in the Navy, I have never left the American shores and, otherwise, have never left Michigan."

Giammanco looked at me with an air of impatience: "Arons, what are zees details?"

I completed my doctorate in philosophical psychology at the Sorbonne five years later under Paul Ricoeur. Here is how it happened.

"When You Are Ready . . ."

I drove my taxi double shift that summer of 1961 earning enough for passage on a Dutch student ship, with a few hundred left over. I arrived in Paris intending to study with Maurice Merleau-Ponty. He had died that very summer. By October, I had picked up the rudiments of French and, by appointment, met with Professor Paul Ricoeur in a vestibule of the Sorbonne inner courtyard. I spoke to him of my interests in relating existential–phenomenological thinking to questions underlying the American psychological research into creativity. Ricoeur took an interest and on the spot agreed to sponsor a doctoral dissertation exploring this relationship. "However, Monsieur Arons, we have no word for 'creativity' in the French language. But," he continued, "no matter. I am a member of *l'academie française* and will propose one to them, for how otherwise could you write your dissertation?" Thus, did the term *créativité* come to enter the French language.

Ricoeur had asked me for a 25-page prospectus of my dissertation. I was having trouble putting this together, especially as I had all that year been following philosophy and psychology courses that had pulled my thought far adrift from my own theme which, on my departure from the United States, had so neatly fit into my head. By the end of the year, I was running out of money. I had become attached to my future wife, a French student, and we decided together to go off to Gabon, Africa to earn by teaching in that just-liberated French colony. Ricoeur agreed that I could do my writing from afar and loaded me with so many books—authors including Husserl, Levinas, Merleau-Ponty, Gurwitz, and Levi-Strauss—that my baggage more than doubled the airplane weight limits then enforced. "But, Monsieur Arons," Ricoeur reminded me, "I would like that prospectus."

The climate of the equatorial village to which we were assigned could not have been more distant from those of cold and functional Detroit or of drizzly intellectual Paris. In that mountain village where we taught, the beat of music—life—was everywhere, always. The humor and quips, laughter and spirit were but playful variations of a grounding theme of moral and social certitudes. Our upper high school students, nearly all men, all future functionaries, danced hand in hand to class. I was teaching the likes of D. H. Lawrence in broken French to students whose native language was Fang, and my wife taught them math and chemistry. I couldn't have been farther in distraction or disposition from the existential ambience that had drawn me to Paris. Yet every night by Petromax lantern I read and wrote and, subsequently, despaired at my inability to fully grasp the thoughts or say anything much coherent. I ripped up over 2,000 pages intended for my 25-page prospectus.

By spring I was in daily despair. One day I hit our pet baboon. That night I wrote to Ricoeur telling him it was evident that I was incapable of the task I had set for myself, thanked him for his confidence in me, and resigned from the program. At school's end, I left my wife at her aunt's in the South of France and spent that summer wandering Europe in an attempt to run away from my failure. I returned to Paris in the autumn and checked into a tiny Latin Quarter hotel. Days later, I found a little enveloped note in my mailbox, the addresses almost completely blurred out by the "forward" stampings. The note had followed me from Africa and around Europe. Signed by Ricoeur, it read: "Monsieur and Madame Arons, it would be a pleasure if you would join my wife and me for dinner" on a certain November evening.

The French, especially at that period, invited almost nobody to their homes, especially for dinner, unless the invitees were intimately known. Ricoeur was one of the foremost professors of philosophy at the Sorbonne, part of the University of Paris, which at the time enrolled over 200,000 students. I had spoken with this noted scholar only three times to that point and then in butchered French.

Following the dinner, Ricoeur invited me to his den. Past some discussion of our experiences in Africa, he looked at me and so gently said: "Monsieur Arons, sometimes Americans can be a bit... let us say... compulsive." Then he proposed, "Why don't you forget your dissertation, go to the Latin Quarter and play... you do play chess, n'est-ce pas? Play for as many years as it takes: 5, 10, 20. And when you feel you are ready to present your dissertation, your doctorate will be waiting for you."

I spent 3 years in the Latin Quarter scene, attended what lectures intrigued me, read what was of interest, debated everyone about everything, and played lots of chess. I woke up one year and the dissertation began to write itself. The whole picture came together with remarkable ease, everything I had come to Paris with said within it but in a frame of reference completely unknown to me until it emerged through my writing.

I defended the dissertation that spring of 1965.

In the spring of 1990, in Québec, I told this story with Ricoeur at my side, as I introduced his presentation to the Human Science Research Conference.

Chapter 3

My Passage Through Maslow
(2004)[1]

Editors' note: Mike prepared this autobiographical sketch specifically for this volume.

In the summer of 1950, I reconciled myself to a life as a sweeper at Ford's Rouge Hot Roll Mill. In the summer of 1958, a passenger left in my cab a book of Maslow's writings. In the fall of 1966, I became Maslow's teaching assistant. Two years later, Maslow recommended me to head the psychology department at West Georgia College. In 1970, I visited him in California before his death.

I was spared the life sentence as sweeper by being fired from that job. It was the fourteenth job I'd lost since leaving school—a failure pattern going back to third grade. I became a commission-only door-to-door salesman for a home equipment company. Mocked and bullied daily by my crew leader, Fischel, swinging between suicide and murder I picked a psychologist's number from the yellow pages. He listened to my condensed life story, stopped me short of the fifty-minute session and said, "Okay, tell Fischel go fuck himself. $25.00."

A Detroit social agency referred me to a therapist of psychoanalytic bent. The ground rules included *don't change anything in your life* (meaning, continue working under Fischel). For nearly six years, my analyst and I excavated the under-hood of my "psychical apparatus"— no cruddy infantile memory left unscraped. Five years into therapy, almost as if awakening (perfect word), one morning my world began zooming both in and out in wondrous new experiences. Everything—

---

[1] Previously unpublished. Used with permission from Dr. Mike Arons.

nature, music, art; each leaf, note, stroke—became starkly, piercingly, yet softly, organically, hyper-present; pin-sharp yet vibrating, radiating, resonating in a lived paean to the majesty of being. I felt intensely what others felt, understood beyond words I could barely read, knew the said before the spoken. Diverse events gracefully coincided as if by pre-composed orchestration. I walked the daily world at oneness with everything—and more alone. I wasn't where anybody else was, but I didn't have the words to say where that was.

My tries at articulating this nameless state were taken by my analyst as obstacles to therapy—*defenses*, *resistance*, *fantasy*, *imagination* or *hallucination*. I knew fantasy and imagination—the sources of many of my failures. I didn't take drugs. And even my therapist didn't think me psychotic. This ecstatic state was *none* of the above. Against my growing protests—and my heartfelt efforts to express to her my gratitude—my therapist acted like an iron-minded ox-driver, obstinately prodding me back into the yoke of my past, to the "hard realities I won't face." Our tones turned taut. We agreed to terminate. As I walked out that last day—unlocked from my original oath to leave my situation unchanged—in our tearful parting hug, she whispered, "You might want to tell Fischel to go fuck himself."

I knew I was going to college. Like everything else then, I had no idea how—just certitude it would happen. It happened. I was the student of every teacher's dream. My childlike eyes were chasm-open, panting with thirsty awe. For me, Wayne State was Harvard, Yale, and Princeton combined. Class after class I near exploded with insights. Except in my major, psychology, where understanding rats and stats left me no closer to understanding my self or state.

At the time, in my late twenties, I lived free at my parents' home. They had no idea what was happening to me. My father deferred to my mother. My very wise mother—as she had through all my troubled and troubling years—continued to follow counsel of the nursery rhyme, "Leave them alone, and they'll come home." I drove my cab after school and summers. One evening, cleaning its rear seat, I found a book edited by Clark Moustakas called *Self: Explorations in Personal Growth* (Moustakas, 1956). I later opened it in a café. In it were two articles by Maslow. I knew I had opened the door to my new home. I think that's what Mother had in mind by, "They'll come home, wagging their tails behind them."

In the months following, buds then blossoming into the bouquet of Maslow's vision dropped their seed from everywhere into my soul's wide-open pores. By then, I was unsurprised by the convergence of *happenstance* by which this insemination evolved. My dentist, reading Sartre, left *No Exit* (Sartre, 1947) in the waiting room. Walking down Woodward Avenue, I heard a hardy verbal exchange burst from a church. I entered. The guest speaker, Victor Frankl, was debating a priest. His *From Death Camp to Existentialism* (Frankl, 1950) was for sale on the table. On a Bob-lo excursion boat plying its way between Windsor and Detroit, a Canadian girl I asked to dance introduced me to Erich Fromm. An exchange student cleaning up for his return to Afghanistan left a pile of Sufi and Zen texts atop a waste barrel. Buber, Bergson, May, Watts, Lao Tzu, the *Tibetan Book of the Dead* all attached themselves to my fingertips as I perused bookstore shelves.

And so it went. Within a year of finding Maslow, many of the ingredients being readied for the *third* and *fourth force* skillets—the neo-Freudian, existential, transpersonal menu—fell, extracurricular, onto my lap. Meanwhile, my courses—especially literature, art, philosophy—were providing an historical backhoe of this humanistic psychology spirit, vigorously churning up its insight-laden soil in the Ancients and Renaissance, providing inspiration and vigor in the old I found absent in the reductionisms and rigor in psychology's new.

One article I read through tears. It was about ongoing research being conducted by two educational psychologists in Chicago. Just as Maslow's papers had finally spoken to the state I'd been in for years, Getzels and Jackson's (1962) study of *Creativity and Intelligence* offered the first explanation I'd had for my consistent failures on standardized tests—notably on the I.Q. test—by which scores I had been diagnosed retarded and shunted for much my school life into *special classes*. Another book, Somerset Maugham's (1944) *The Razor's Edge* and its main character, Larry (cabby on a spiritual trip), set me on the next stretch of life.

On graduation in 1961, I passed up eight fellowship offers by psychology graduate schools and sold everything of value. With a trunk, a French–English dictionary, and several hundred dollars in pocket I crossed the Atlantic on a Holland-America student ship and hitched to Paris. A few months later I found my way to Paul Ricoeur, and four years after I defended my doctoral dissertation in philosophy at the Sorbonne. The ambience of Paris extended Mother's Little Bo Peep philosophy into my next stretch of life. Gertrude Stein put it this way: *It's not what Paris gives you, it's what it doesn't take away.* But it also gave me a new wife and twist of life.

Mike and Christiane's wedding, Paris, July 17, 1962.
(Photographer: Studio Lakonic, Paris. Contributed by Sandrine Arons.)

My first year in Paris, I lived at Cite Universitaire and found two French soulmates, my assigned roommate and a future wife. Michel Siffre, a young spelunk prodigy, and I (a late bloomer) got on perfectly. Christiane, a pert 4'11" student of math-chemistry, lived on the other wing of our pavilion. While the three of us were on separate academic paths—and despite the initial language barrier—that year, Michel and I conceived, and Christiane helped design, an experiment on *lived time*. Michel interested the French Air Force in the project and with its sponsorship it became a French media event that summer, as well as a pilot for later research (Siffre, 1963). In its execution, Michel spent two months in an Alps cave without access to time, reporting his subjective time estimations to clock–calendar time monitors above and as these related to his sleep–wake cycles, dreams, routines, and feelings and moods.

In mid-summer of 1962, while Michel was down under, Christiane and I—running out of money—married. We applied for a teaching job in Africa and were assigned to a school in Oyem, Gabon. I took with me a trunk of books Ricoeur had suggested and left with him my promise to mail him a 25-page dissertation prospectus. While gathering these books, I found and packed in another, the just-published *Toward a Psychology of Being* (Maslow, 1962). It would not be long before we spent a week with one of Maslow's models of *self-actualization*. Gabon was the home of Albert Schweitzer, physician, philosopher, and theologian. At Christmas break, we boated down the Ogoue River, across the Equator, to his remarkable hospital in Lambarene. On parting, he piled us up with his autographed books and others he recommended. But appreciative as I was, more books were not what I needed at that moment.

During the last semester, flattened for a month with hepatitis, overwhelmed by the books Ricoeur had recommended and underwhelmed by my progress getting out my 25-page prospectus, I fell into a state of despair. Maybe my therapist had been right: all that was happening was fantasy, illusion, a defense against reality. I needed touch. I wrote to Maslow—my first contact with him—and he wrote back. He invited me to visit next time I returned to the States. I did, when my father died in 1964. Then I returned to France, completed my dissertation, and in the autumn of 1965 came to Brandeis for postdoctoral studies. The following year I became Maslow's student assistant.

On the opening day of Maslow's course in Fall 1966, I distributed his syllabus reading list to the sophomores filling the amphitheatre. Their faces turned to stone as they perused the packet, thick as a town phone directory, that listed hundreds of books. A single student found courage to raise his hand to timidly inquire of Maslow: "Sir, did you have a particular schedule in mind for us to read these books?"

"Oh, no!" Maslow replied. "That list is for the rest of your life. Each of these books spoke to me when I was ready. Read any of them if and when it speaks to you."

Maslow was still adding to the list of those who spoke to him. At that period, it was particularly the writings of Michael Polanyi (*Personal Knowledge*; Polanyi, 1958), Marghanita Laski (*Ecstasy*; Laski, 1962), Douglas McGregor (*The Human Side of Enterprise*; McGregor, 1960), R. D. Laing (*The Divided Self*; Laing, 1965), and Colin Wilson (*The New Existentialism*; Wilson, 1966). Of Wilson, Maslow told everybody, "He's the brightest young thinker on the horizon." Maslow invited Wilson to speak on campus that year. He also invited Laing, and at his encouragement I invited Ricoeur.

Maslow's genius was to draw from polymorph sources and weave these into such a whole and vital picture of human Being that it couldn't help but to put new spring in every walk of life. His range of both source and sphere of relevance is starkly exemplified in the two books he wrote but a year or so apart: *Religion, Values, and Peak Experiences* (Maslow, 1964) and *Eupsychian Management* (Maslow, 1965). One inspired opening of a spiritual, transpersonal dimension; the other a business world's awakening to its human side—and in its own bottom-line interest. Even the military found inspiration in his *self-actualizing* theme ("Be what you are and all you can be") to create its most successful motto ever: *Be all that you can be ... in the Army.*

Largely because of this creative ability to find unattended unity in apparent opposites, it is not surprising that students would often puzzle over Maslow's lectures and their apparent contradictions. In one upper-division course centered on eupsychian social psychology, under the theme *The Good Society*, Maslow proposed a greatly expanded role for Wall Street. Some angry Marxist students virulently took issue with these ideas. "The good society?" they angrily implored Maslow, "How can you possibly defend and encourage a system centered on Wall Street greed that exploits the masses?"

"What I'm proposing," Maslow replied, "is that the masses take over Wall Street—from within." At that time, a tiny percent of the American population was invested. Currently, well over half the population is invested.

During the period I spent at Brandeis, Maslow's own investment was at stake. Both his life and department were under threat. It was, for Maslow, the "best of times and the worst of times." He had been elected President of the American Psychological Association but was unable to serve because of his first heart attack. The humanistic orientation he had pioneered in that department was now highly renowned and drawing the brightest students from everywhere. Yet, as he realized— by his own doing, by being so open—the orientation and department he had pioneered was then seriously under threat... and this, from within.

His emerging humanistic orientation (*third* and *fourth force*) was, in Maslow's words, "filling a huge, gaping hole" in the field. Yet he also realized and appreciated the valuable contributions that constituted the "conventional psychology" of his day, which he called the *first* (behaviorist) and *second* (psychoanalytic) forces. So while he had hired a number of scholars who shared his own pioneering humanistic– transpersonal interests, he also hired others who specialized in traditional interests. But these conventional specialists—in the name of need for sub-specialties—proliferated their number, and to protect their expanding turfs they built and kept thickening the mazes of requirements and prerequisite courses. At that period, by far most of the graduate prospects attracted to Brandeis were drawn there to study with Maslow and George Kelly. They would all come to discover the magic of Jim Klee's classroom. However, the requirement-prerequisite maze being built by the traditional psychologists had become so pervasive that students were systemically precluded from studying what and with whom they had come for. By 1967, Maslow sadly realized how bad the situation had become. He knew that seeds had to be planted elsewhere, and he encouraged his students to plant them. In 1967, at the invitation of its president, who had contacted Maslow, several of us—Min Chiang, Tiparat Schumrum, and I—started a full-blown humanistic program on Prince Edward Island. In 1968, the psychology faculty at another small school, West Georgia College, contacted Maslow in search of a new chair to develop a new orientation. Maslow recommended me. I interviewed and was hired.

That fall, on my way down to Georgia, I passed through Waltham to see Maslow. Of his own department's situation, he was clearly in despair. Of my future, he had this counsel: "Mike," he said, "Be a bastard." I understood what he meant. All of us had been fully trained in the conventional matter and methods of psychology. That's all there had been in our education. At West Georgia, we created a program that was outright humanistic and transpersonal in orientation, yet one that offered the range of traditional study areas. We solved Maslow's problem by hiring those passionately exploring the humanistic but who also taught the conventional. Within a few years, students from around the world were pouring to this little state college, attracted by its orientation. What they came for was an ambience-supported psychology curriculum fully fostering personal self-exploration and holistic inquiry into the *farther reaches of human nature*—from several decades of alumni feedback, *a kennel of wagging tails.*

George Kelly died in 1967. Jim Klee came to West Georgia to teach for the next twenty years. Abe left Brandeis shortly after my visit to Waltham, taking up a California Foundation's offer to continue his writings. By that time, he was beginning to see his seeds sprout up around the country. He died in 1970, a few months after my California visit to him. The night I returned from that visit, Christiane announced we were going to have a baby.

Part 2:

Creativity, Consciousness, and Culture

Mike reading a paper on the back deck at his home in Carrollton, GA, circa 2001. Mike built the deck with one of his former students, and doing so inspired his thinking on the "platform experience" (Arons, 1999c). Mike reflected that as he "crawled out to the end of the new frame to nail some planks, [he] saw [his] world—i.e., the world, the land, the home [he] had lived in for 30 years—as if totally new. These were new—not only to [him], but to anybody and everybody— because never before had there been that perch, vantage, overlook."
(Photographer unknown. Contributed by Sandrine Arons.)

These chapters explore the implications and applications of the concurrent infusions of the humanistic movement and of creativity research in American psychology, science, culture, and values during the mid-20th century. In Chapter 4, Mike proposes that humanistic psychology's orientation to process, potentials, meaning, and fulfillment offer alternatives to both science that "plays dumb" to subjective experience and fundamentalist religion built on blind faith. This thread carries forward into Chapters 5 and 6. In the former, Mike adds that, with creativity as its central value to well-being, humanistic psychology also both challenges and serves as a more sustainable alternative to the technocratic agenda of modern science. Then, in the latter, Mike surveys the contradictions of America's linear conceptualization of progress and the relationships between (a) creativity and intelligence and (b) mistrust of divergent thinking and social conformity. He also affirms humanistic psychology's accomplishments in its contribution to the legitimization of consciousness and experience in psychology via its focus on personal growth as a creative process.

Chapter 7 was Mike's last publication before he died. He had dedicated his post-retirement years to exploring the upright body posture as a platform for creative outlooks in human consciousness. Unfortunately, he did not complete the book he had been preparing. However, during his last year, he developed and published a succinct synthesis of this work, which examines the connections between humans' vertical platform, evolutionary history, consciousness and spirit, longing for balance and harmony, use of language, and notions of progress and originality.

In Chapter 8, Mike and Stan Krippner compare/contrast Western and Eastern approaches to creativity by considering their respective relationships with nature (conquering for the former, harmonizing for the latter). They recommend a research agenda that explores the interface of creative people and products (Western) and creative process (Eastern), which today remains ripe for further exploration in an increasingly global society.

Chapter 4

Transformations of Science and Religion Through Humanistic Psychology
(1976)[1]

Editors' note: Mike was among the first presidents of the Society for Humanistic Psychology (Division 32 of the American Psychological Association). As the result of a tie vote, he shared his presidential year with clinical psychologist Stanley Graham. This was Mike's presidential address, delivered in September 1976.

I would like to consider in this talk some of the transformations which have been occurring in the relationship of science and religion over the past decade or so. I speak here of science and religion, which have co-existed in the West over the past few centuries and which, as some philosophers have pointed out, have common origins, yet which have been characterized in historical recency by their opposition and their apparent incompatibility. It is my belief that humanistic psychology and the values associated with this and the new consciousness in general have been helping to transcend the historical opposition between science and religion and in the process have been helping to restore a basis of authenticity to both.

Furthermore, this restorative or healing process which I feel is underway, has far-reaching implications for most other domains of our socio-historical existence—just as the end of a feud between two

[1] Arons, M. (1976). Presidential address: Transformations of science and religion through humanistic psychology. *Newsletter: Division of Humanistic Psychology, 4,* 6–7. Adapted with permission from Dr. Nathaniel Granger (President of the Society for Humanistic Psychology, Division 32 of the American Psychological Association, 2018–2019).

members of a family alters the vision and possibilities of the entire family. In other words, our sense of ourselves, our sense of history and potential, of what is important, is due also to change as a consequence of this process of transformation. Our science should become more value-centered, but also infused with the energy of a subjectivity hitherto denied. Put differently, our science will no longer be conducted exclusively by those who feel they must play "dumb." Rather, the "objectivity" sought by a science through playing "dumb"—i.e., denying subjective experience—will actually be enhanced to the degree that science owns up to subjective experience and is conducted by fully functioning humans. On the other hand, our religion should come more to see itself in terms of enlightenment rather than in terms of blindness (as in the act of blind faith). Self-discovery, personal or finite awareness and realization, should be seen as not incompatible with Divine communion. Furthermore, the notion of process-centering, already accepted as necessary in the sciences, has also been centering the humanistic movement, but here relative to personal development. It is this notion of process orientation along with consciousness which could restore a freshness to religion.

It is ironic that in attempting to get a feel for the healing process which I propose is now occurring between science and religion, I am obliged to point to another polarity or axis along which I feel much of the action of transformation is taking place. What is ironic is that humanistic psychology and the new consciousness themselves risk being trapped in this polarity, just as they are helping science and religion to see how they can become "unhooked" from it. I speak here of the polarity of "direct salvation" and "indirect salvation." I suggest that humanistic psychology and the new consciousness have been lining themselves up on the side of "direct salvation." A notable trend associated with humanistic psychology is the refocusing or centering on the human. In general, we have seen a major shift in psychology, and in the society as well, away from the abstract and deferred kind of scientific psychology and towards the clinical, or human services. This trend extends at least to and through most of Western Europe where youth have come to value the direct helping fields—the direct helping of others and of themselves. I recognize that even behavior modification has benefited from this trend.

It is a general trend which I identify as the trend towards "direct salvation." But what has differentiated humanistic psychology from, say, behavior modification or medical approaches of the past is the focusing on consciousness. One of the clear-cut successes of humanistic psychology over the past decade or so includes the reestablishment of the term consciousness in the vocabulary of psychology. However, that term now finds itself at the very center of the social revolution as we speak of Black consciousness, social consciousness, women's consciousness, and so forth. In the trend towards "direct salvation" in general, I see something of an anti-scientific mood, at least to the extent that much modern science has identified itself with "indirect salvation" and has implied that "direct salvation" is mostly an illusion. On the other hand, with the stress on consciousness, I see a reaction against much of Western religion which has always offered the possibility of "direct" and "personal salvation," but at the price of apparent irrationality, or blindness—an act of blind faith—accompanied by images of meekness or sheep-like servility, or acquiescence to authority. Understandably, then, science as it developed had to oppose itself to much of what had become associated with Western religions. But by siding with "enlightenment" as opposed to irrationality or blindness, science came to see the only possible "salvation" as the bit-by-bit elimination of darkness and irrationality—i.e., of the subjective—by a concerted long-term approach of science and technology. The scientist sacrificed his or her personal considerations, even his or her life, towards the distant goal of salvation in the form of alleviation of pain and suffering; for greater liberty through reduced burdens and greater understanding of options; and, also, for the simple joy of being part of a social team and of questing and testing.

Scientific cynicism concerning the possibilities of "direct salvation" has tended, as science has succeeded, to be accepted as truths in the society at large; and, despairing of any possibility to achieve "direct salvation" or refusing to blind themselves, several generations have grown up developing their lives and values around the unique prospects of "indirect salvation" through science. Yet those same successes of science, unburdening and liberating as they were, also pointed increasingly to the greater failure at the level of human meaning. One lady, it is said, phoned the TV station during the broadcast of the third moon walk to bitterly complain that this boring nonsense was replacing the Smothers Brothers. Ludicrous, perhaps, but all the moon shots show little promise of relieving our everyday problems of meaning here in this life on this earth. Indeed, the successful shots which apparently sent the first man out into space revealed, at a more subtle level, the inability of humans to really escape their context, their environment. In fact, what was sent into space was a can packed with a man and his juices. The existentialists, those who provided some of the historical roots for humanistic psychology and the new consciousness, focused on the poverty of meaning even during a cornucopia of facts, knowledge, and understanding of the natural world and of humans to the degree that they are viewed as mere by-products of natural laws.

Camus, for one, never denied science or its potential value, only its relevance to his life here and now. Of religion, it offered him significance only to the extent that he bought a hopeful future on blind faith. That kind of meaning he refused. But he also refused the usual alternative, that life without meaning is not worth living—i.e., the alternative of suicide. It is hard to say what Camus did buy. But one has the feeling it was process, for one could only imagine, as Camus inferred, that Sisyphus, though condemned eternally to his rock, is nonetheless happy.

Whatever the particular route taken by Camus or the other existentialists, the existential shift was definitely again towards some form of "direct salvation." Existentialism rejoined us to this long but recently eclipsed Western tradition. Socrates, of course, had led his students to a domain of consciousness—recall—via which the student could come directly in touch with universal truths or essences. Socrates' approach is that of the guru, an approach highly favored today by many young persons as they seek something beyond the sterile, indifferent facts which constitute their normal academic curricula. Indeed, the students now seem to insist that what is taught comes from the soul or experience of the teacher, and in a dialogue of souls. This is another way of saying that the student wants knowledge and understanding to transform his or her own soul. Nothing is more demeaning as a prospect for today's youth than that they end up like engineers, understanding and pushing fact or knowledge buttons, without some personal transformation occurring. Of course, this tendency can lead to what Marin calls "narcissism." But evidently it needn't.

Returning to the tradition in the West of "direct salvation," revelation of course provided the possibility of receiving communication directly from the divine. Still, for those not in tune and who could not verify the authenticity of the communication, revelation led as easily to authority. And it was against such authority that the age of reason and subsequently the age of modern science developed as reaction. Indeed, to assure the elimination of all claims to salvation or understanding not verifiable by the common senses, the very existence of revelation or intuition and metaphysics was denied. Kant falls into the Western tradition of "direct salvation" in that he saved, against the attacks of the empiricists, intuition as a possible source of understanding and of transformation. Psychoanalysis is in the same tradition of offering at least a promise of limited "personal salvation" by the individual breaking through from illusion to reality—though as Freud pointed out, the reality of logos offers itself as a much more modest form of salvation than that promised by religion. Jung, of course, is a very good representative of the school of "direct salvation," in the Socratic sense, for his collective unconscious is the reservoir for greater universality which can be tapped by the individual as he or she expands out to the wider potentials. Jung provides the modern link to connect Socrates with the long tradition of "personal" and "direct salvation" found in the East. If the historical roots of humanistic psychology are in European existentialism, the field has been blossoming through its contact with Eastern philosophy. Not only does that tradition tend to stress "direct salvation," it often stresses it as enlightenment or of becoming fully conscious.

There are three points of transition that I would like to emphasize which have been inviting psychology, scientists, and others in the society in general to a more Eastern emphasis. First, I shall mention in passing, but certainly with no attempt to de-emphasize, the importance of the psychedelic movement and the kinds of experiences reported there which verge both on the religious and on expanding consciousness. Next, I should like to point to the body of research on creativity, which leaves the indelible message that the greatest strides in science, even science at its most objective level, are made not by denial of subjectivity or the so-called primitive experiences, including emotions, but via this subjectivity. The paradoxical nature of the creative experience, of which science is a major beneficiary, is well expressed by Frank Barron as he describes the creative genius:

> He may be at once naive and knowledgeable, being at home equally to primitive symbolism and to rigorous logic. He is both more primitive and more cultured, more destructive and more constructive, occasionally crazier and yet adamantly saner than the average man.

The creativity research suggests that some of the greatest contributors to "objective" knowledge serving "indirect salvation" in the arts and in science are also those who most consistently report creative, peak, mystical, or other religious experiences. The link between "indirect" and "direct salvation," between science and religion, seems to be in the way the person experiences, and hence the kind of quality of the experience.

Third, I would like to recall some of Maslow's contributions in this regard. By distinguishing between *deficiency* and *being* types of experience, he points to the possibility of two kinds of "subjectivity"— one, as scientists have always claimed, which is obstructive, in that the world is seen through the bias of "subjective" needs or, put more generally, through some form of narcissism. Of the *being* type of experience, Maslow calls this the potential for a Taoistic kind of science, a subjectivity which encourages the world to reveal itself *as it is* unconditionally, beyond the desperation of deficiency need where the world must be dealt with instrumentally. This defenseless sort of Taoistic subjectivity intrinsically rejoices in its communion with reality and hence is a fuller experience of it.

Maslow, of course, was encouraging this latter kind of science, which was the corollary of "personal salvation" or of personal development. Yet he recognized that not only was science the only way that knowledge could progress—i.e., lead to indirect salvation; he also recognized that by aiming at science or outwards in general and at "direct salvation," the individual was more likely to attain "direct salvation." Here Maslow was warning against salvation becoming a goal or end in itself, one which would then be pursued instrumentally. Under such circumstances, God, or all the symbolism of the struggle for salvation, becomes rubricized—i.e., are turned into idols, or graven images.

If humanistic psychology has helped to re-spiritualize science (Leary speaks of "sensualizing scientists"), then what has it been offering to religion? There is above all the prospect of religion giving up playing dumb by seeing salvation as quite compatible with greater understanding and insight, just as science can give up its act of playing dumb by denying all subjectivity. Religion has tended to specialize in some abstract spirituality, as science has specialized in hard facts. But existentialists like Camus, humanistic psychologists like Maslow, and Eastern philosophers have all stressed the discovery of the infinite in and through the finite. The "here" and "now" is already the "afterlife." This soul is, or is a portal to, the infinite. Again, it is a matter of how the finite is experienced. Existential, humanistic, and Eastern philosophies have all stressed experience as process. Hence, humanistic psychology contributes perhaps even more greatly to religion by not itself *becoming* a religion. All humanistic psychologists have pointed to the anti-spiritual quality of religions when they become fixed and then defensive even to the point of killing to save the faith.

Ricoeur has been making a particularly subtle study of the path from waking or dawning of consciousness to the other end, the reified consciousness, which he calls evil. The sacred and the evil being dimensions of each other, just as the sacred is experienced in ambivalence. It is in the tolerance for ambivalence, or what those studying creativity called tolerance for ambiguity, that something beyond the definable may be discovered. This indefinable Ricoeur sees as the "Wholly Other," discovered in our own ambivalent, existential condition, between our determinisms and our meanings. This "Wholly Other" is experienced as a call, or *kerygma*. I do not think that Maslow was referring to anything much different when he used the less religious, more psychological term, *potentials*. The call, or the sense of potential, is not a goal or end to be attained, but rather a sense of direction signaled by meaning and fulfillment which through diversity ties one to all. It seems to me that it is at this level, the call, that humanistic psychology ends and differentiates itself from religion. The call is heard, experienced. But the caller remains unknown.

Chapter 5

At the Juncture: Creativity, Humanistic, and Transpersonal Psychologies[1]
(2000)

Editors' note: This was Mike's keynote address at the Conference on Humanistic–Transpersonal Psychology *at Central China Normal University, Wuhan, China, in July 2000.*

I recently visited a university in my state to present a lecture. The psychology department there is quite conventional—behavioristic–cognitive–statistical—with the exception of one faculty member who invited me, who is a humanistic psychologist. I was surprised at how many students showed up for this event, nearly the whole psychology department and the counseling department. Nearly all of them were taking courses with this professor. I asked some of the students why, and they said, "Because this is what I thought psychology was all about."

Those were the exact words I had said to myself in 1957 when I was a psychology student and, outside of my requirements, first read Abraham Maslow, Carl Rogers, and others who were to form a *third force* called humanistic psychology. Since there was no school in the United States at that time dealing with the matters raised by humanistic psychology, after graduation I went to France to complete my doctorate in philosophy, where such existential and transpersonal views were then being discussed. I wrote my dissertation on creativity, which at that time was just becoming an interest in psychology. I then returned to the United States to study with and assist Abraham Maslow.

How could I, an average student who had never produced any

---

[1] Previously unpublished. Used with permission from Dr. Mike Arons.

recognized creative work, be writing a dissertation on creativity? How could I, who had been a taxicab driver in Detroit after working in the auto factories for years, be studying self-actualization with Abraham Maslow? In fact, I had been such a poor student in the public schools and had such a low score on intelligence tests that I had spent many years in a class for the retarded. How could I recognize in myself what others were writing about creativity and self-actualization? How could I have said—like the students I recently visited, and like all the students who now come to humanistic psychology programs—that "this is what I thought psychology was about"?

I now have some historical perspective on why, at least in Western and particularly American psychology, such topics as creativity and self-actualization have been excluded. And I now understand that both creativity and humanistic psychology were speaking to what it means to be fully human—and not only about eminent creative geniuses and superior human beings such as Maslow's *self-actualizing* examples.

Let me begin with some historical perspective. First, a large perspective of how Western psychology came to be what it is. Then, developing out of this, a recent historical perspective of the challenges that the study of creativity and humanistic–transpersonal psychology have posed to psychology and to us all as humans. In asking about the power of these three forces, I would like to try to pinpoint a juncture at which research into creativity, humanistic psychology and human science research methods, and transpersonal psychology overlap. And finally, I would like to point to a paradox—that the unity of the sciences ideally sought after may be taking place not at the level of the method, but at the level of the human subject matter. Creativity, humanistic, and transpersonal psychologies may be bringing psychology to the edge of the physical and biological sciences' most advanced discoveries, such as chaos theory and mind–body health.

I begin with a larger picture of the Western history of ideas in which to place Western science. But you may recognize in your own historical and cultural context, and in your own forms, some of the points this history is making. In fact, much of humanistic and transpersonal psychology has shown what our cultures can learn from each other about what it is to be fully human.

The Big Historical Picture: Science, Psychology, and the Western History of Ideas

Approximately 50 years ago, a critical line was passed in American psychology. Both its subject matter and its methods were radically challenged by a new field of research into creativity and a third force of humanistic psychology. These became revolutionary forces in psychology and the society. Both these initiatives, especially as they came to overlap and merge, were reassertions of the richness of the human subject matter over the rigidity and narrowness of the methods and theories of a psychology trying very hard to be a science. But let us return to this revolutionary period in a moment. First, a brief review of the history of Western psychology to see where the points inherently clash between psychology's human subject matter and its attempts to become a science.

Psychology Becomes a Science: "Fitting the Subject to the Method"

Western psychology—at the turn of the 19th century, then mostly centered in Europe—had chosen to be a science, rather than art or philosophy. Its model for method was the highly successful physical sciences. It was presumed that even the human subject matter would ultimately yield to these natural science methods. Of course, it was understood that as a young science, psychology would begin its inquiry dealing with the simple and that which could be observed and measured systematically and rigorously.

However, soon—and especially in American psychology—the tendency was not to start with the simple and move to the complex, but rather to deny all claims to humanness, which did not fit the method and other scientific presuppositions we will come to below. For example, behaviorists dealt only with what could be observed and measured. So they rid psychology and humans of consciousness. Creative genius became that which could be measured on a standardized I.Q. test. Excluding or denying what couldn't be measured was one way to make psychology a hard science. Another way of simplifying the subject matter was *reductionism*. That is, finding simple generalizable explanations for apparently complex phenomena.

Reductionism and Scientific Monism

Reductionism is a central concept in Western science. Modern Western psychology, along with its methods, had accepted the philosophical presuppositions which founded and supported the 19th century physical sciences. Central to the philosophy which gave this science birth was the belief in *scientific monism*—a belief that ultimately everything is one, material, and lawful. And science would come to understand nature's law and be able to manipulate and control it. By this scientific monistic view, all scientific understanding could ultimately be reduced to and explained by the laws of physics. Psychology would ultimately be reduced to physiology, physiology to biology, biology to chemistry, and chemistry to physics. This materialistic philosophical understanding of the ultimate unity of the sciences depended on method. But what did the method depend on?

This question presents at its heart the contradiction between the human subject matter of psychology and the method for studying it. During the 1950s creativity revolution, Bronowski proposed that the scientific method was probably the most creative human discovery of the Western world. But by that same date, in the name of that method, human creativity was being reduced by behaviorists to a conditioned response, or by applied psychologists to a high score on a standardized I.Q. test, or by the Freudians to a defense mechanism called *sublimation*. The greatest creative product of the Western mind, science, was thus almost completely denying the existence of creativity and mind. It was denying its own origins or was claiming those creative origins to be pathological.

Science and the Pre-Sciences

There were other interesting clashes between psychology's attempt to become a hard science and the human subject matter raised by the creativity inquiry and humanistic psychology. One of the presuppositions built into the scientific philosophical package that Western psychology adopted in the 19th century was a negative—i.e., *what science was not*. Science was *not* religion, myth, philosophy, or art. These were *pre-sciences*. Science had progressed beyond these. It was the superior way of knowing. Thus, it no longer had to hear what the humanities were saying.

And, above all, science would replace the ancient superstitious beliefs of religion. It would replace God's unifying laws—and the method of faith—with the unifying laws of nature, gained through reason and experiment. The battle between *faith* and *reason* has preoccupied much of the Western history of ideas. Little wonder, then, that science and religion by the 19th century were seen as stark opposites. Little wonder that any topic that even smells of being spiritual—such as *unitary*, *peak*, or *transcendent experiences*, or even *intuition*—is presumed to imply religion and is so strongly resisted by mainstream psychology and science in general. Yet, such experiences are consistently reported by the great scientists, as with artists in their personal creative process—persons who are religious or not, persons who are intelligent and rational or not. Studies into creativity and humanistic and transpersonal psychologies suggest a spiritual dimension that is not necessarily associated with religion but seems to be essential to being fully human.

Value-Free Science

By separating itself from religion and seeking an *objective* explanation of the cosmos, the Western scientific ethos adopted by psychology came to dismiss the importance of *values*. It calls itself a *value-free* science. But can a value-free scientific psychology ever fully understand its human subject without considering human values? Or the role of ethics and morality? These spheres, in the West, give over to religion. Humanistic and transpersonal psychologies, by contrast, make values central to the understanding of the human. Isn't scientific inquiry itself a value? And to what end? Let's return to this question in a moment. And is that scientific psychology really value-free when it proclaims its supreme value is *prediction* and *control* and the *manipulation of nature*?

Maslow and other humanistic psychologists were to show, as did the ancient Greeks, an intimate relationship between ethics and fulfillment. His *self-actualizing* subjects were also ethical models—and this because they more intrinsically identified themselves with humankind.

The Cosmological and Anthropological

What about this strong antagonism between science and religion in the West? Are these really opposites? Despite the strong opposition of contemporary science to religion, in the longer view of history of the West, as Cassirer pointed out, both science and religion share a common philosophical tradition which he called *cosmological*. That is, they both share the search to understand the relationship and lawfulness of everything. Seen in this philosophical context, scientific monism is just the other side of the same coin of religious monism. In the religious cosmological perspective, everything could be reduced to God and his laws. But there is something missing in both these views— let us say, metaphorically, the coin itself—the human interest in both inquiries. That human interest inquiry is the other side of the Western tradition. Cosmological inquiry for the Ancients, that out of which both Christianity and science grew, had its own opposite, which Cassirer called *anthropological*. That is, in that same ancient (mostly Greek) Western philosophical tradition there was another kind of inquiry— starting with and centered on the human—and an impulse for self-understanding, happiness, and fulfillment. If Democritus (in the 4th century B.C.) and his proposal that all reality could be reduced to atoms represents the cosmological side of Western history, his near contemporary Socrates' claim that "the unexamined life is not worth living" represents the anthropological side. This is the origin of a humanistic tradition in the West, which would repeat itself in the 16th century Renaissance and now again in humanistic psychology.

Moreover, Socrates talked much about his own creative process and his personal source of inspiration, which he called *Daemon*. This he described as a little supernatural indwelling force which prodded him to ask the right questions at the right time and provided him insights into the best answers. Today we would call that *intuition*. In fact, the

Hellenists, following Socrates and Plato, always joined intuition with logic in their inquiries about *the good life*. Democritus would have said that Daemon could be explained away as a certain arrangement of atoms. Until the studies on creativity and the development of a humanistic–transpersonal psychology, mainstream psychology might have agreed with Democritus. Today we would think of Socrates' intuitive approach, related to reason in the quest for self-understanding, as humanistic—and Democritus's approach, aided by such technology as the microscope, as scientific.

The 19th Century View of the Physical Sciences Adopted by Psychology: Homeostasis

The 19th century newborn scientific psychology not only borrowed its methods and meta-scientific views from the physical sciences—including its ultimate criteria for *validation* and *reliability* of prediction and control—but it also incorporated into its constitutional foundation the great discoveries of that science of its day. For instance, 19th century physics had discovered the laws of conservation of energy in a closed mechanistic system. Energy seeks a tensionless state. This mechanistic model would become the presupposed ground for much of psychology. If the psychology that used 19th century physics as its model wanted to understand why people learn or how they can be conditioned, or to understand why they have psychological problems, or to understand what is psychological health, they went to the *homeostatic* or *tension/anxiety-reduction* model. After all, if you are hungry, you have a drive to eat; thirsty, a drive to drink. Both hunger and thirst are tension increases. And reducing those drives, or tensions, leaves us peaceful and in a state of well-being. So, naturally, if a behaviorist wants to condition a subject, he uses as motivator something that will reduce the tension. That tension reduction becomes associated with the conditioning stimulus. And if a patient complains of anxiety, the psychoanalyst tries to find the cause of that anxiety in pathological unresolved conflicts.

The trouble with this homeostatic model—which makes everything nice, neat, symmetrical, and potentially predictable—is that it doesn't apply to recognized creative individuals or to what Maslow would call *self-actualizers.* In fact, they often seek out tension-creating, anxiety-provoking, and chaotic and non-symmetrical situations, and even see internal conflict and turmoil as necessary phases of their creative or self-developing process. Moreover, by definition, neither the eminent creator nor self-actualizing individual are closed-energy systems. In fact, they are known for penetrating the walls of any given system and for creating new ones, either through their original ideas and the external transformation of materials or by their insights and the internal transformation of their lives and meanings. The creative minds gave us the new worlds of quantum and open system mechanics, and self-actualizers gave us the penetrating, uncommon insights of Lao Tzu, Socrates, and Buddha. The word *originality* in English means, by definition, that which is *new and unique.* By definition, the new systems and ideas created are not predictable.

Originality: Paradox of the New and Unique and the Origins

But the term *originality* also has a paradoxical and apparently contradictory meaning implicit to it. It refers, on the one hand, to the *new and unique.* But on the other, to the *origins*—to the beginnings, to that which was and is. What kind of origins? The origins of science? The origins of that new idea? The process, conditions, and existing materials which gave it birth? The origins of myself, my birth, my mother's womb? Her origins and all that is human, the genes, or perhaps God? The origins of everything, all reality known and as yet unknown?

Those inquiries we consider to be the most uniquely human (such as in art, philosophy and science, or the religious, or the explorations of consciousness)—which we consider the most significant and which employ creativity and the insights and truths they reveal—all these start from some origin point, use the materials of that originating context, and are typically explorations into the origins of our lives, meanings, and reality. As are our personal dreams and collective myths—the former referring at least to our childhood experiences, the latter to the origins of mankind and the universe.

In most cases, that which we call *monumental creativity*, this search for the origins is associated with human *salvation*—happiness and fulfillment. Religion would restore the original order by returning us to the laws of the Divine Creator. Science and technology, by understanding the laws of nature, would bring us the products of knowledge to create and establish our own order and happiness.

Given this double and apparently contradictory notion of originality, it should not be surprising, then, that the very word *creativity*—which gives us all these wonderful new insights, products, and systems—should refer to an original creative source, either the Divine Creator (as in Judeo-Christianity) or the creative processes of nature (as assumed by the natural sciences). Yet, have any of these creative productions given us a sense of fulfillment or happiness?

Happiness and Fulfillment

I think we can all agree: This is the most important question for all humans, those who benefit from all the creative products and those who do not. We in America ask this question. I'm sure you in China must ask it also. The question of happiness, fulfillment, and the good life was central to the Western Ancients, as it is now central to humanistic and transpersonal psychologists. The ancient Hellenists spent six centuries, from the 3rd century B.C. to the 3rd century A.D., devoted to this question of happiness under the name *eudaemonia*. They recognized a very simple logic. We do everything—wealth, health, friendships, even life longevity—for happiness. We do happiness for none of these. As then, today we often confuse the ends with the means, and the products of creativity with the source of creativity within us. Just as the ancient Western philosophers posed this big question of ends and means towards happiness, artists and philosophers of the 16th century Renaissance posed the same big question.

Dürer's *Melencolia I* is in the public domain. Retrieved from the collection of the Metropolitan Museum of Art, New York, NY.

Consider this woodcut by Albrecht Dürer, an artist who lived in Germany from 1471 to 1528. The work is called *Melencolia I*. Notice the unhappy human figure crouched down in the lower right. Notice that he is surrounded by all the most advanced tools and technology of his day—from domestication of animals to navigational devices to tools and instruments. The sad figure in the picture represents the creative human. Notice how all of these advances of human science and technology, human creative products, lie heavy on or towards the ground. By contrast, notice that the vanishing point—that which represents the ideal, the ultimate, the complete, the union and fulfillment sought as the goal of all these works—remains far off in the distance.

The creativity literature tells us something about this question. Eminent creative individuals, even those deprived or who are suffering from pathologies, very often choose *not* to go into therapy when they feel that this therapy may relieve their suffering but also take away their creativity. That is how important their creativity, not their creative products, is to their well-being. At the very minimum, this fact suggests that there is something more important, more valuable than suffering. And it raises the question for those who seek happiness in products alone. But it does not suggest creative individuals would not be happier with other needs satisfied and suffering curtailed. Humanistic and transpersonal psychologists will take up this issue of happiness—not in the simple terms of, "Does prosperity and the products of science and technology make us happy?" but rather in terms of, "How are these benefits and products experienced and lived in terms of fulfillment values?" with creativity being a central value.

Chapter 6

Creativity, Humanistic Psychology, and the American Zeitgeist
(1992)[1]

This paper focuses on one "moment" of historical development in the United States, when two independent but overlapping movements emerged within the field of psychology: humanistic psychology and a surge of research interest in the subject of creativity. Both eruptions were reactions to that psychology's perceived limitations of psychology and the social climate of the times. American psychology—ostensibly and self-proclaimed to be objective, value-free, and socio-culturally independent—has revealed itself as quite value-laden and bound to the paradigms of its society and times.

There has always been a spiritual quality to creativity, rooted as it is in the Judeo-Christian West, to the notion of "Original Creation." Here, God did all the creating. The mode of reaching God was blind faith. This spiritual sense was again felt strongly during the European Renaissance—known for its bountiful individual creativity, but then connected with a philosophical linkage between Spirit and Nature. During the age of Enlightenment, it was science, particularly the physical sciences, which grabbed the torch of creativity to guide the Western imagination towards an understanding of the mystery of our sources, now presumed to be potentially disclosable exclusively in the regularities of nature. The mode to reaching the laws of nature was reason. Science was, Bronowski (1958) proclaimed, the greatest

[1] Arons, M. (1992). Creativity, humanistic psychology, and the American zeitgeist. *The Humanistic Psychologist, 20,* 158–174. doi:10.1080/08873267.1992.9986788 | Copyright © 1992 by the American Psychological Association. Adapted with permission from the American Psychological Association.

creative product of the Western mind—and as even Maslow (1962) added, "Only science could progress."

Post-war America held an almost total faith in scientific progress and its potential to reveal or offer the ultimate meanings of our lives. Yet this faith in science increasingly contrasted with the spiritual sterility of materialistic life characteristic of that period. At this paradoxical juncture, experienced aridity in the midst of apparent progress, the creative processes themselves came to center a quest for a fuller sense of humanness. This in post-war America: rich, unscarred, unhumiliated, and triumphantly naive. It is no accident that both creativity and humanistic psychology drew much original inspiration from the existential writings of post-war Europe. But much of their destiny—the directions in which these movements would evolve—was towards the consciousness and spiritual-centered traditions of the East. Like the creative process itself, the movements of both creativity and humanistic psychology have been simultaneously progressive and regressive. After all, the term "originality" has two vectors, towards the new and unique and towards the origins: the source.

Creativity *Zeitgeist*

The outbreak of interest in creativity in American psychology was ignited by J. P. Guilford (1950) in his presidential address before the American Psychological Association. In that address, he lamented the fact that for decades practically no research interest had been shown in an area so humanly significant as creativity. He then offered four reasons why he felt such an interest had been retarded: 1) *excessive preoccupation with I.Q. tests*, 2) *the domination of learning theory*, 3) *prevalence of excessively rigid methodological standards*, and 4) *the inability to find agreement on criteria for researching creativity*. The first three reasons cited propose that the directions that much of American psychology had taken were in some ways incompatible with the study of creativity. The fourth reason suggests an inherent difficulty encountered at the problem level—a heuristic one we will consider below.

The common link between all the American psychologies at the time of Guilford's address was their lack of vitality. They did not lack activity. Indeed, as in American factories of the time, "production rates" were high—in the laboratories, in the diplomas issued, in the journals, and on the therapists' couches. Productivity was impressive, as it was then in the society as a whole. And, while Guilford had made only inferential reference to this point, productivity was at the time being uncritically (and, soon to be demonstrated, quite mistakenly) identified, both in psychology and society, with creativity. This distinction between productivity and creativity was a key one to emerge from the creativity literature.

Lacking at that period was vitality at the theoretical and methodological levels. Theoretically, in different forms, both learning theory and classical psychoanalysis—grounded in mechanistic and Darwinian functionalistic preconceptions—held as basic a homeostatic model of the human by which "it" is "driven" toward the least amount of unpleasure, tension, or anxiety. This Darwinian stress on biological adaptation—through a social Darwinism—was translated in much of psychology and the society as a whole into an almost singly valued notion of social adjustment. Norms of social adjustment were essentially equated with psychological health. At the extreme, particularly at the applied and popular level, "social adjustment" (hence "psychological norm," hence "psychological health") was frequently interpreted to be little different from social conformity.

The applied level encompassed more than business, industry, and education. It included psychology itself, as a field of work, where there came to exist inordinately narrow standards of proper behavior. Many of these were dictated by the apparent urgency for psychology to become a science, in the sense that science was interpreted by psychology. The methodological rigidity (positively construed as rigor) of this image of 19th century physics worked to grossly narrow the range of personalities permitted into the field or who would choose the field. It worked to preclude any interests—individual, gender, racial, or cultural—which were not amenable to the methodology, regardless of how relevant these were to understanding humans. The stress on the external, formal accoutrements of 19th century physics—laboratories, equipment and apparati, control and certification down to the white lab jacket—required that psychologists conform to an almost laughable stereotype. The atmosphere clearly worked against risk, exploration, and speculation and towards safety, compulsive repetition, and rigid exactness. One can find here, as a necessary reaction, some seeds to the study of creativity.

The value on social adjustment had been built into the testing movement almost from its inception. While such testing was developed in the name of distinguishing individual differences, a tendency away from conformity, the growth of the testing movement in America owes much to its relationship with social institutions such as the military, business and industry, education, and governmental social agencies. It is obvious that testers are employed by institutions to serve their interest. And it would have been difficult for the testing movement not to have been biased by these interests. But, further, the relationship of the testing movement to the prevailing scientism of American psychology meant that no findings could be considered reliable or valid which could not pass the rigors of this methodology. Psychological tests, whatever their recognized or unrecognized limits and deficiencies, were applied to masses of people in many sectors of the society. Since these were often used in selection procedures, tests came to take on values by which critical life-affecting judgments were made.

Like Ford's standardized car, the standardized I.Q. test is largely an American product. When imported from France in its early individualized form, where it had been used in a limited and selective manner, it was given a standardized form to meet both the exigencies of scientific certification and the expediency needs for mass application within the institutions. Standardization removed the instrument from a context where interpretations of test results which might have revealed originality could be evaluated in individual context. The impetus for popularity of the standardized I.Q. test came largely from the work of Lewis Terman at Stanford University. Above all, Terman (Terman & Olden, 1947) pointed out, nothing more characterized his high I.Q. subjects than "a drive to achieve and their all-around social adjustment."

Because of what he saw as their intellectual superiority, Terman went on to call his highest scorers "genius." Thus, a new link—consistent with the rationalistic-utilitarian bias of the times and the American image of "melting pot" and its dream of itself as a haven for material success—was created between genius and social adjustment. That link ran counter to traditional stereotypes which offered the image of the genius as psychologically unstable and socially non-adaptive. Some psychologists, holding to the more traditional presumptions, took strong exception to Terman's view in this matter. They pointed out—and Terman was obliged to acknowledge this—that few of Terman's "geniuses" had accomplished any major creative breakthroughs, though they had indeed "succeeded" in traditional vocations and occupations such as law, military, etc. Further, according to the Lange-Eichbaum studies (1932/1962), which Terman strongly disputed, the recognized creative geniuses of the Western world had shown a much higher proportion of emotional instability and social maladjustment than members of the population at large; in fact, the greater the genius, the greater the maladjustment.

If the more romantic image of "genius" persisted in the public mind, this utilitarian, Terman image of "genius" began to dominate in the institutions, notably in formal education. Terman's studies had shown, at least at the extremes, correlations which linked this educational mission to utilitarian productivity (vocational–professional) and psychological successes. In a mass movement not followed anywhere else in the world except in Great Britain, where the "11+" (I.Q.) exam came to determine a child's future, feeding on the utilitarian social *zeitgeist*, it reached the point where in most American school districts all students were required to be tested and were often cursorily judged and academically slotted in terms of test scores. Possible limitations and biases of the I.Q. test were first ignored, then forgotten, as the instrument gained ever-wider popularity. The abuses of I.Q. testing reached such major proportions that by the 1960s many of the major cities in the country, including Los Angeles, had banned the test. Certainly, much of the rebellion in the United States—aimed at education and expressed in psychology by the creativity movement—was directed, if not exclusively at the I.Q. test, at the values which correlated so well with this test. It is not coincidence that the earliest studies on creativity after Guilford's talk focused on the limitations of I.Q. tests and showed, by implication, the extent to which these instruments and their use were reinforcing the most conservative devitalizing and unoriginal dimensions of the society.

Getzels and Jackson (1962) were able to demonstrate that I.Q. tests did not measure originality and that there was no necessary correlation between originality and intelligence as measured by the I.Q. What's more, those scoring high *exclusively* on I.Q. tests tended to share the traditional values of their teachers and parents. They were highly goal-directed and achievement-oriented in terms of socio-economic goals, lacked originality and a sense of humor, tended to be organizationally efficient and to have little time for idle inquiry and exploration, and tended to show minor interest in self-understanding. By contrast, those scoring significantly lower on I.Q. tests but high on measures designed to tap originality manifested considerably greater independence of judgment, considerably more awareness of their emotions and experiences; they permitted themselves to express greater emotional instability, accepted ambiguity, and tended to value self-exploration and philosophical questioning over efficient and success-oriented thinking.

Guilford (1950) had himself pointed out one key to this difference between the original thinkers and the high I.Q. scorers inherent in the I.Q. test itself. The standardized I.Q. test required, always, one correct answer. Evidently, this was an answer taken from existing public knowledge—hence, by definition, unoriginal. He called the thinking leading to success on these tests "convergent" and differentiated this from original or "divergent" thinking characteristic of more creative individuals. An original answer could not have been designed into a test without diminishing the capacity for standardization of scoring.

Expressive Role of Creativity Research

The major scientific weakness of the research on creativity during the 1950s and 1960s can be attributed to what Guilford (1950) cited as the fourth problem leading to retardation of the study of creativity: the problem of criteria. There had never been agreement on just what creativity was. Could a child's doodles be called creative, or even potentially creative, and hence, comparable to the great and recognized works of art? This is a question more centered on values than evidence. Therefore, this very scientific "soft spot" in the creativity research serves heuristically to intimate the importance of these studies when seen as social expression. So viewed, these studies expressed largely by implication the perceived problems in psychology and the society at the time. Hence, as one might expect, this research taken as a whole had a particularly American flavor to it. For example, American psychologists showed a much greater, more concentrated interest in "creativity" at that juncture in history than did their colleagues in other cultures.

But the concentrated American interest in creativity shows up more clearly as a social expression when we consider the: 1) type of variables researchers tended to select as relevant, 2) normative implications built into traits or variables diametrically opposed to those seen related to creativity, and finally, 3) implications of some cross-cultural studies which had a bearing on creativity research.

A number of studies, as indicated earlier, tried to differentiate creativity from other constructs which had, in psychology and the society, become confused with creativity. High scores on I.Q. correlated with "convergent," efficient, goal-directed problem solving, etc. By contrast, creativity correlated with "divergent," open-ended cognition, old problems seen in new ways. The research on creativity—certainly the earlier phase of it—implied value judgments, with creativity being very "desirable" (the "good guy") and that seen in opposition as "less desirable" (or often the "bad guy"). This reflected a strong, if indirect, form of reaction against that which had been given such high value status in psychology and the society.

Examples of commonly cited traits or adjectives correlated positively with creativity were: originality; affective surprise; humor; the unpredictable; metaphorical thinking; intuition, impulse or "inner voice"; formal appeal; psychological regressing in the interest of progression; risk; moods; openness to childhood perceptions and conflicts; complexity of perceptions; the ability to experience freshly, to transcend polarities and apparent incompatibilities, to seek truth or beauty beyond expediency and needs for tension reduction; independence of judgment, whole-part integration, growth-centering; preference for complexity, ambiguity, asymmetry, mystery—and doing this playfully with spirit and humor; incorporation of apparent polarities such as the affective with the logical sides of one's nature, etc. These traits or characteristics that typically correlated with creativity offered a picture which was alien or threatening to values dominant in psychology and the society at the time, exemplified by: stress on predictability, repetition, and compulsive discharging of duties; progress viewed as linear; expediency values of socially recognized achievement, popularity, productivity; stress on external authority, neatness, precision, consensual validation; disdain for intellectualism; fixed social patterns and sentimental traditions; suppression of "unacceptable" emotions as well as ideas which deviate from accepted norms; preference for finished product over process. Other characteristics which seemed in opposition to creativity traits were reductionism to the unequivocal, stress on a "maturity" which fails to distinguish childishness from childlikeness; failure to distinguish the simplistic from simplicity; preference for a judgmental attitude over existential awareness (Barron, 1963; Flanagan, 1963; Getzels & Jackson, 1962; Ghiselen, 1963; Sprecher, 1964).

Cross-Cultural Comparisons

Very few cross-cultural studies showed up in the early creativity research, but three such studies are revealing. They suggested a need in American psychology for what was lacking in that society at that period. At an early phase of the creativity focus, social psychologists such as Asch (1952) and Crutchfield (1963) had become interested in the problem of conformity. The results of these studies were surprising in that they revealed that conformity, seen as non-independence of judgment, was a dominant mode of behavior even where it might be the least expected, at the better American universities. These results contrasted with results of like studies with students in Sweden and France where far greater independence of judgment was reported. Frank Barron (personal communication, 1972) and his colleagues found that second-generation Italian children living in Boston did more poorly on his Barron–Welsh test than did children of the same families born and still living in Italy. D. Lee (1959) pointed to this lack of originality related to conformity among Americans at the period relative to a variety of cultures she had studied.

These cross-cultural studies suggest, again, that the lack of creativity—and those characteristics correlated with this—had been a serious American problem. And this, again, moves towards an understanding of why American psychologists so intently focused on this area. The creativity *zeitgeist*, although seen as isolated at this time, was one related dimension of a much greater reaction swelling up within the American society and particularly through and against its psychology.

The Greater Reaction

The American studies on creativity, both in their investigative and expressive aspects, paralleled and helped predispose the shift towards a humanistic psychology and a radical shift in American consciousness. Psychology has never been the same, nor has its society. The creativity *zeitgeist* challenged a psychology defined by its ability to predict and control behavior with a vital, conscious human subject whose mark was originality—which, by definition, is neither predictable nor controllable. It obliged that field to confront a greatly expanded and more complex picture of the human subject, one coinciding with that coming from the existential philosophers of post-war Europe. Philosophy, in the eyes of American psychologists, had already been dismissed as merely "pre-scientific." Barron (1968) well forewarned the field of the complex and paradoxical potential of the human in his description of the creative genius:

> Thus, the creative genius is at once naive and knowledgeable, being at home equally to primitive symbolism and to rigorous logic. He is both more primitive and more cultured, more destructive and more constructive, occasionally crazier and yet adamantly saner than the average person. (p. 224)

The other movement, largely American and largely inspired by the insights of European existentialism, was humanistic psychology. These two reactions from within, separately and in tandem, helped set the stage for major transformations which came to characterize the field and society in the 1960s and 1970s. Over those two decades, the field of psychology expanded enormously. The definition of psychology—now seen in a growing number of textbooks—reincludes the focus on experience and consciousness. There has been a shift from the purely academic research to a more person-centered focus, a shift which significantly influenced the unprecedented growth of clinical and counseling-oriented psychologies that first and most fully came to recognize dimensions of the humanistic model (Zinker, 1977). Even the academic-research wing—previously monopolizing the field with its 19th century model of science—has been, albeit slowly and grudgingly, forced to open to more ideographic and qualitative approaches to research, such as phenomenology, which have from the start been linked to the humanistic movement (Arons, 1987). Yet humanistic psychology has not become the center of gravity in psychology, nor have its values and construal of the human been anything but superficially assimilated into the soul of the society. Still, both creativity and humanistic psychology are reminders, often forgotten, of what else is possibly human. The 1960s and early 1970s were the period when that "possible human" was brought most fully to our collective consciousness. We are too close to ourselves now to know what the 1990s might bring. But at the end of this chapter we can throw a few brush strokes on the canvas of our own period in light of May's vision of history: Our Renaissance is still ahead of us.

Humanistic Shift in the Focus of Creativity

Within psychology, at the same time as the methodology was being challenged by the complexities introduced by the creativity research and the humanistic vision, the theoretical underpinnings of a behavioristic psychology were being put into serious question. Its reductionistic and deterministic model of the human was forced to confront a model of a creative, dynamically inner-directed human. Still, the general model of creativity was from the outset an essentially behavioristic one, a model inherently determined and limited by the methodology but also limited by traditional Western views of creativity. For creativity to be even considered present, it was obligatory that there be demonstrated some tangible creative product. It seemed self-evident to the Western mind that creativity would be product centered. Thus, preparatory to most of this creativity research, the creative individual was first identified by his or her productions, then studied in terms of how and by whom that product came into being via focus on the antecedent process or the predisposing personality traits.

A major shift of emphasis occurred with the onset of humanistic psychology. Maslow (1962) for one, distinguished two major kinds of creativity—one which was talent-centered, the other growth-centered: "I shall confine myself to a kind of creativeness which is the universal heritage of every human being that is born and seems to co-vary with psychological health" (p. 127).

This second type of creativity was more like a creative way of life, a way as one potential realized by those whom Maslow described as self-actualizing individuals. Many of these self-actualizers, unlike the renowned creative genius, could not be recognized by tangible, typically acknowledged, creative products. It was extremely difficult to identify or to study such persons with rigorous scientific methodology. And Maslow's new broader construal of creativity might well have been ignored completely had it not been for the wedge the creativity research had placed in the doorway of general psychology. Much that had been written of the creative process and personality of recognized creative artists, scientists, etc. correlated with traits of persons whose tangible productions were absent or not apparent or, perhaps as in the case of women (who rarely showed up in the typical creativity literature), whose characteristic products were not previously appreciated in light of this external product-centered focus on creativity. The humanists were beginning to offer a different kind of challenge to psychology—one of finding health indications, previously reserved for an elite, in the broader human potential. This, in the process of understanding the human subject at what Maslow would call humanity's best. And that best was not necessarily indicated by the tangible-observable, but rather more often by internal transformations and expanded consciousness. Maslow's self-actualizers were the very products of their own internally evolving creativity.

In the meantime, humanistic psychology was becoming an umbrella for a wide variety of ideas, theories, interests, and approaches which shared (sometimes only this) a centering on psychological growth, or a new psychology focused on psychological health. This popularization of the "health model" was also abetted by Guilford's (1950) urging for a broadened definition of creativity, i.e., transformations from a special gift type (the Mona Lisa) to a humanly endowed (child's doodles) supposition of creative potential. This redefinition, added to the views of Erikson (1959), Maslow (1962), and Bühler (1968, pp. 127–168), now indicated the path of self-actualization as a lifelong one. Much of the American public had little trouble identifying with this broadened model as speaking to their own personal potential, a fact exploited in:

"Be all that you can be... in the AAAArmy."

Humanistic Transformations within the Society

While Maslow was an academic psychologist, and while most of the early theoretical positions leading to a humanistic psychology came from academic psychology or philosophy, some of the first and most enduring insights into what was later to be identified under this name were developing in business, industry, and social organizations. Maslow and others like Rogers and Combs, in the Dewey tradition, were re-inspiring education—and this abetted by considerable inspiration from researchers like Torrance (1964). It was in the society that the problems of alienation, mechanization, and inauthentic personal relationships had become the most pressing. These problems were adequately portrayed in such literature of the times as *Who's Afraid of Virginia Woolf?* or *Rebel Without a Cause*. Goodman (1960), among a growing band of others, was articulating the conformity and alienation being widely experienced across the nation. It was mandatory that this broadly based social pathology, articulated by the existentialists, be addressed—and this most appropriately by psychology. In light of the new personal growth model, Wilson (1966) offered a new way of looking at classical neurotic symptoms, seeing these as "the rust which forms on a non-moving organism."

Maslow's (1965) writings were first taken seriously in economics and business, where success at the profit end of the enterprise had not correlated with success at the level of human relations. In fact, Maslow had theorized that profits could actually be increased if a "being" rather than "deficiency" model of motivation were effected. The National Training Laboratories in Bethel, Maine had for a long time been operating an institute based on developing more authentic human relations in the business and industrial field. An array of direct experience techniques had been evolved for this purpose. It was out of this experimentation that problems of alienation, mechanization, and inauthentic personal relationships had revealed themselves as so deeply embedded in the social structure of the times. The Bethel model of "T" Groups, largely inspired by gestalt theory, came to support a broader model of the encounter group which burgeoned into popularity at centers around the nation, the best known being the Esalen Institute. These growth centers—and a wide and rapidly expanding array of approaches, theories, and techniques, all centered on the "growth model"—seemed to speak forcefully to people across the land as no psychology had previously done. A large disaffected segment of American society in the 1960s was more than ready for a humanistic psychology and the new vision of the creative human it fostered.

Meanwhile, in line with this new vision, the newly revitalized term "consciousness" began to take popular hold. A series of social movements sprouted up around the land, each focusing on consciousness and each speaking to the fuller actualization of individuals or groups. Thus, the movements called "New Consciousness," "Black Consciousness," "Women's Consciousness," and "Gay Consciousness" evolved.

Transformations within Psychology

Other developments in humanistic psychology, particularly those approaches opening individuals to the resources within themselves, began to make the natural scientific psychology less palatable as a potential answer to human concerns. The shift in emphasis towards inner development and personal understanding predisposed a shift in emphasis from indirect (associated with collective rationality and science) to direct (associated with spiritual) understanding and realization. If for several recent centuries it had been believed that humans could gain "salvation" only through a collective scientific understanding of natural lawfulness, which knowledge could then be reapplied through scholarship or technology, the new thrust in psychology seemed to open up the possibility of direct understanding (Arons, 1976b). Personal growth and self-understanding could be—in fact, were—intrinsically combined and best gainable through direct experience. Increasingly, compatible with the evolution of the writings of Maslow and others, personal growth centers began to evolve into centers exploring dimensions of the human which purportedly extend "beyond" personal—to the transpersonal.

Transpersonal Psychology

Maslow and the third force had already sketched out, in speaking of "self-actualizers," dimensions of human potential—some of which were familiar to everyday personal experience and some quite unfamiliar to most people. Beyond those needs which he considered basic to survival (maintenance) and to which any kind of an "adjustment" or "coping" psychology might legitimately address itself, he elaborated a variety of "higher" level needs, all of which still fell within the range of human potential. Many of these higher-order needs, such as appreciation for aesthetics, had for a long time been culturally acknowledged. But Maslow (1966) also went on to speak of experiences, or potentials, which were quite alien to that society. He spoke of "peak," transcendent, mystical, and "plateau" experiences which also, but very rarely, were experienced or culturally acknowledged dimensions of that postulated human potential. Nothing could have been more alien or more antagonistic to any conventional American psychology at the time than mystical experiences.

Maslow's was not the first recent introduction of such experience in psychology. However, none of these previous intimations had really gotten off the drawing board in the positivistic climate of the times. Freud had alluded to, but shunned dealing with, the "Oceanic Experience"; Bergson and Jung's influence on American psychology was slight at the time. Ironically, Fechner, "father of experimental psychophysiology," was forgotten or forgiven for his trespasses into the mystical. James (1902/1985) was far better remembered for the first laboratory he began in psychology, and soon abandoned in disgust, than for his *Varieties of Religious Experience*. Sharing a like fate, Murphy whistled a lonely tune in this area. But reports of mystical experiences were not uncommonly reported in the research literature on creativity. Something akin to such experiences appeared with a certain regularity as part of an artist's or scientist's creative process. Of his ideas, Mozart wrote, "Whence and how they come, I know not, nor can I force them" (as cited in Ghiselen, 1952).

Something as bizarre as the mystical experience had been knocking at experimental psychology's front door for some time prior even to the studies on creativity. This was the all-but-rejected pocket of research in the area of parapsychology, directed by Rhine at Duke University and concerned with "the supernatural." There now exists a clearer distinction between parapsychology and transpersonal psychology— yet even in the ancient Veda texts these are seen at points as related, and individuals involved in one of these spheres are often involved in the other.

There was yet another point at which experimental psychology had been introduced to what is now being called transpersonal psychology. This is the research pioneered by Leary and Alpert at Harvard on psychedelic drug experiences. Reports of drug-induced experiences which bordered on, simulated, or were, in fact, the mystical were so prevalent in this project—and the research and drugs so controversial at the university, in psychology, and in the society—that those investigators were obliged to leave their institutions. Indeed, both

Leary (1990) and Alpert left science—the former seeking direct "salvation" through the drug, the latter ultimately seeking direct "salvation" through naturally-induced mystical experiences developed in the East.

The general stress held common to all the above became roughly merged under the heading of transpersonal psychology. And here, perhaps as nowhere else, did a reintegration of psychology with philosophy, theology, and the arts become a historical necessity (Klee, 1982). From Gudjieff and the Western esoterics to the vast spiritual literature emanating from Eastern psychology, the transcendental writers and poets of the West, the Judeo-Christian-Islamic mystical tradition, Shamanism of the Native American tradition, and classical Hellenic metaphysics, all became relevant to the new kind of psychological experimentation which was rapidly developing entirely outside the academic sphere. Transpersonal psychology has found no home in the American Psychological Association except with some delay, and with much reluctance on both sides, in the Division of Humanistic Psychology.

Creativity and the Humanistic–Transpersonal Revolution

Linked in their historical evolution, humanistic and transpersonal psychologies are now sometimes treated as different dimensions and destinies of the same human potential and, by some, are even seen as oppositional. Some transpersonalists—presupposing as Westerners perhaps a linear construal of the Chakra system—view the "transpersonal" as a quantum opening to the "higher" or "spiritual," while some humanists such as May pejoratively dismiss these transpersonalists as airy-fairy New Agers or as escapists from the existential, personal, and social realities of this historical age. Few, thus far, have looked at this distinction as two destinies branching from a common experience in the creative process—i.e., the tapping of the intuitive, one disposition favored in the West with its stress since the Renaissance on tangible individual creativity, the other favored in the East with its stress on internal self-development.

One juncture at which Maslow touched the line between humanistic and transpersonal psychologies was the distinction he drew between two types of creativity. The new type—not talent- and product-centered, and not recognized by Western researchers or Westerners in general—implies an internal growth-centered creative process characteristic of his self-actualizing subjects, but also of Eastern mystics. It may be instructive to reflect on the distinction made by Ferren (1953):

> Both artist and mystic, at the time of insight, experience a deep sense of personal fulfillment. But the mystic works gratuitously for revelation alone. The creative worker is predatory; he grabs the insight for a filled purpose, he is far less than divine, and the Promethean fire snatching symbol seems very apt.

Substitute "artist" for Western "destiny" (or path of "salvation") and "mystic" for Eastern "destiny" (path of "salvation"), and perhaps we glimpse in Ferren's description a bridge in human experience which links two apparently different outcomes at the level of "insight" (in French, "prise de conscience," the taking of consciousness)—both of which can be called creative paths but one taken by the West, the other by the East. Western creative individuals acknowledge the great role intuition plays in their creative success. By not totally different processes of initial arrival (e.g., suspension of ego dominance), transpersonal psychologists focus on opening to a greater collective source of all understanding—a "unitary consciousness," a universal energy—which expresses itself through everything: that is, anything which can be conceived of as separate, as *individual*, and in the case of people, *personal*. This consciousness/energy is ever present for "tapping," which speaks through persons "tapping": it is sometimes referred to as "superconsciousness" and is otherwise known as intuition.

Creativity, Humanistic Psychology, and Now

The popularized inner search crested in the late 1970s, effectively terminating at Jonestown and in narcissism, almost immediately and symmetrically replaced by Heritage U.S.A. and greed. The Age of Aquarius, by astrological birth signs, turned out to be the Reagan era. Creativity came to be explored in safe computer-simulated models where, under the control of "cognitive science" (Sternberg, 1985), it was viewed as a step-by-step process no different from "problem solving." Or it was avidly practiced as entrepreneurship, risk management, and the "vision thing" now worshipped by the conservative Right—i.e., yesterday's radical Left and the former Evil Empire. Self-actualization was recast in "upscaling" activity terms. We may, in the 1990s, be beyond even this. Mirror, Mirror has been discretely silent. But our current times here in America are unsettled and unsettling. Something unpleasant is oozing from the edges of "artificial time" (Rifkin, 1987) and our artificially injected bosoms of self-esteem. Now an entire society is feeling Camus's (1955, p. 4) "worm at the heart": "the undermining." The forth and back meanings of the 1960s through 1980s, which had replaced the meaningless 1950s, are dissolving, often, into meanness. We reach for our deepest myths (Houston, 1992) to hold things together—or for "Virtual Reality" to put us back in charge. Our stewarted earth-in-pain bites its master. The ghost of McLuhan taunts that of Gutenberg. The ideals that served us for centuries are postmodernly melting into some transmuting species of irreal reality which feels to many awfully foreboding and which is experienced as squiggly and chaotic. Psychedelics are back, replacing the "uppers." Our physical scientists (Bohm & Peat, 1987) now explore "Chaos Theory"—and some of our humanistic–transpersonal psychologists, who yanked psychology from the old physics, are feeling right at home in this new one, recognizing in it familiar and exhilarating messages from the creative heart—viz, chaos is pregnant with order.

Chapter 7

Standing Up for Humanity: Upright Body, Creative Instability, and Spiritual Balance
(2007)[1]

"Our body is not in space like things, it inhabits and haunts space."
~ Maurice Merleau-Ponty

"When he is up, I knock him down. When he is down, I boast of him,
Until he realizes he's an incomprehensible animal."
~ Blaise Pascal

The term *originality* implicates two opposing yet paradoxically related vectors: to the origins and to the new and unique. Perhaps one new view of human nature and its transformative creative spirit comes from reflection on our species' oldest distinguishing mark: the biped upright body posture. Can attention directed to this lived high-rise platform provide new insights into human being and potential?

This chapter explores a postulated linkage of human creative capacity, values, and aspirations, with tensions inherent in the lived upright body posture. It considers evolved organic–anatomic links to an upright posture (e.g., cognitive, vocal, manual capacities) as well as value-implicating expressions (e.g., "upstanding citizen," "down to

[1] Arons, M. (2007). Standing up for humanity: Upright body, creative instability, and spiritual balance. In R. Richards (Ed.), *Everyday creativity and new views of human nature: Psychological, social, and spiritual perspectives* (pp. 175–193). Washington, DC: American Psychological Association. | Copyright © 2007 by the American Psychological Association. Adapted with permission from the American Psychological Association and from Dr. Ruth Richards (editor of the book in which this paper originally appeared). | *Author's note (Mike Arons):* I would like to thank Dr. Howard Whitehouse for insightful dialogue and general assistance with this paper.

earth"), which appear conditional to the lived experience of a physically challenging upright stance. These organic–anatomical inquiries are then viewed in light of traits and dynamics implicating both creative and spiritual endeavor. The chapter concludes by suggesting that human creative capacity may be both expression and mediator of the physical instability and disharmony inherent in the upright stance— fostering both survival and spiritual needs and implicating human strivings for balance and harmony.

Background

Revived Interest in Creativity, Consciousness, Values and Body

In the mid-20th century, psychology found itself refocusing on creativity, consciousness, and other specifically human capacities and qualities, including meaning and values. These qualities were largely being ignored by many mainstream psychologists, or else treated as epiphenomenal, or sidelined for methodological reasons (Arons, 1992a; Arons & Richards, 2015). At about this same time—even if only at its perimeter—psychology's interest in the body and somatic experience was also resuscitated, sparked by interest in such Western writings as those of Reich and Merleau-Ponty, and by a newly born interest in Eastern, shamanic, and other esoteric psychological– spiritual traditions. However, with few exceptions, such as Straus (1966) and Keleman (1981), the habitual human biped upright body posture remained mainly a concern of the evolutionary sciences, not of psychology.

Creativity can be defined broadly as encompassing originality and meaningfulness (Barron, 1969). This casts creativity as a human quality, potentially found in everyone—whether taking the form of eminent, talent-centered, self-actualizing, inventive, or everyday creativity (Arons & Richards, 2015). However, much early research into creativity narrowly emphasized elite examples. For instance, Roe (1951) studied living scientists and Maslow (1968) studied self-actualizing individuals described as exhibiting heightened states of awareness, "being" values, and having notable creative capacity. The issue remained whether eminent individuals are exceptions or represent everyone to an outstanding degree. Are creative capacity, self-actualizing values, and enlightened consciousness the potentials of all humans? The answer, when postulated in the affirmative, came to foster interest in *everyday creativity* (Richards, Kinney, Benet, & Merzel, 1988) and a universalized model of self-actualization.

Whether one subscribes to the elitist queen-bee and drone or universal model of creative capacity, scholars of evolution and creationist theologians likely concur on at least one point: *Homo sapiens* is specially endowed, among species, with a highly developed and self-reflective consciousness and an extraordinary creative and inventive capacity. What might be the relationships between these consciousness–creative capacities and the unique human upright body posture?

Unsteady Platform and Organic–Anatomical Links

Why we stand upright is a question not yet answered definitively by the evolutionary sciences or Christian theology. There is no specific reference in the scriptures, for example, to this unique human body architecture. Some evolutionary theories date the biped upright posture to a human ancestor called Toumai, as far back as 7 million years ago. There is a range of explanations for the postural rise, including changing environmental conditions that required appropriate adaptation, such as the "down from the trees out to the savanna" theory. None of these views is without contemporary critics (Stanford, 2001). Nearer to our times and present human form, science tells us that *homo habilus*, found at the boundary between early and modern humans, prospered between 2.3 and 1.3 million years ago, marked by an increasingly upright stance, use of tools, and more cooperative living. There was also a remarkable increase in brain size. *Homo habilus* was followed by *homo erectus* (upright human) with further and marked increase in brain size—before either organized society or the advent of language (Ornstein, 1991).

Despite the evolving distinctions between human and ape, recent DNA evidence draws a close genetic relationship between them, notably with the chimpanzee. This intimate genetic tie is all the more surprising given the observably radical distinctions in endowment and achievement that apparently separate the two species. This conundrum has inspired a renewed line of research (e.g., Goodall, 1986; Stanford, 2001; Steeves, 1999). On one side, it focuses on overlaps, postulating that behavioral, sentimental, and cognitive-related similarities between human and ape are far more pronounced than the common stereotype, and previous research, indicate. On the other side, another line of research—including this inquiry—seeks to understand the definite differences and their bases that at least comparatively, if not absolutely, distinguish and define human nature.

One marked, if still overlapping, distinction between modern man and ape is the upright body posture. For humans, unlike apes, the biped upright posture is habitual. Much that is organic and anatomical has developed in concert with this habitual human stance. Likewise, although researchers of what we might call the "overlap" school are coming to discover intimations of "creative" thinking in apes (e.g., symbol manipulation, meaningful gestures and utterances, tool making), all this, incontestably, has developed to a far more advanced level in humans.

To what degree can the incongruity of close DNA kinship and vastly distinguishing creative output between chimp and human be attributed to difference in habitual stance and walk? To start with a puzzle: How has *Homo sapiens* survived and thrived encased in a vertical anatomical architecture that challenges gravity and other natural forces? It is a puzzle, because this stance is tenuously balanced and is not in apparent harmony with the laws of nature. Would one buy a two-legged stool?

Look at the human body! We typically link consciousness and creative capacity to the large, complex brain, to our wide-ranging verbal capacities, to a rapport between freed-up hands and the invention of tools. However, all these handy, brainy, and talky human features are organically linked from an evolutionary perspective to the biped upright body posture. The biped walk frees the arms and hands. A raised body expands the perceptual horizon. And, the complex brain nestled in its large cavity replaces the massive front-loaded muzzle structure. Moreover, a combination of this diminished muzzle and a gravity-stretched vocal tract—both related to skeletal rise—helps explain human verbal agility (Straus, 1966). The large, well-developed human brain has a history of how it evolved. Of that history, it is important to note that living the world from a vertical rather than horizontal platform is not the same experience. As Straus (1966) points out, "Men and mice have not the same environment even if they share the same room" (p. 139). Thus, it is not too daring a thought to suggest that the human brain learned—and, by at least one mechanism, genotype-environment interaction, structurally incorporated—much from its lived world(s) of experience afforded by that vertical platform.

The Shape of Things

We look at some of these posture-related lived worlds presently. First, consider that standing biped—upright in a world in which gravity has a strong pull—is a remarkable accomplishment. Again, would one buy a two-legged stool? It is remarkable to the degree of provoking the question of why our ancestors did this at all. It is an achievement as puzzling as it is remarkable: This vertical human stance is an aberration and, in ways, an apparently costly one. Look around! Nearly all unrooted objects and creatures are horizontal. This horizontality, presumably, is not only a matter of complying with gravity's demands but also the best design to accommodate other of nature's elements. As with birds or planes, horizontality is better suited to navigate the air, roam the earth, or, like fish or submarines, to ply the waters.

Moreover, the top-heavy vertical stance of the human posture is not the only factor that sets it at odds with gravity. As artists will verify, the human body's anatomical shape consists of three inverted modified pyramids, set tenuously one atop the other. It is hard to imagine a less stable structure. When a pyramid is stood upright, broad bottom down, fine pinnacle up, it is a mythical symbol of balance and harmony—as used by Maslow (1962), for example, to symbolize his needs hierarchy, a matter we return to at the end of this chapter.

Straus (1966) enumerates some current costs to humans associated with the upright posture, beyond the lengthy evolutionary span required for developing adept balancing mechanisms. These costs, as the Riddle of the Sphinx (Sophocles, 1982) mythologizes, include the extraordinarily long developmental time required for a human infant to stand and walk (this is why we celebrate "the first step") and the consequent lengthy period of childhood dependency. There is also, later in life, the need for third-leg support. Across the life cycle there is a stature-linked proneness to a number of breakdowns (e.g., back problems, hernias, and even flat feet; Weidenreich, as cited in Straus, 1966). Overall, human life is exceptionally challenged to stay upright and balanced. This is while reharmonizing—on its own resourceful terms—with the lawful natural world. Think of the technological breakthrough of the Segway scooter, and its dynamic stability. For human or machine, this is a feat. Have we not signs of a defiant posture? What is defying nature compared with defying God, as Judeo–Christian–Islamic theology would have it? Might one speak, in both the corporeal and divine worlds, of a general species proclivity towards rebellion, or at least an assertion of achieving balance and harmony on human terms?

Uplifting Spirit, Embedded Values

Keleman (1981) makes a powerful observation that links posture to consciousness and spirit. The human body, already physically unstable, is not even held up by its legs. Consider that while the supporting columns of a disintegrating ancient temple may well continue to stand firmly erect, human legs may become shaky and crumble with the body, for example, when consciousness wanes or the mood gets too dispirited.

Put this way, the human body, legs included, is held up by its consciousness and spirit. All this suggests that if we did not recognize it in the evolutionary effort to stand upright, that *up* may carry a positive value for humans as indicated in such *up*lifting common expressions as an "*up*standing individual."

Indeed, Lakoff (1987) addressed this example in his "spatialization of form hypothesis." This involves "a metaphorical mapping from physical space into a 'conceptual space'" (p. 283). Hierarchical structure, for instance, can be understood in terms of *up–down* schemas, and foreground–background structure in terms of *front–back* schemas. Lakoff does not go further, however, in suggesting reasons for these particular spatial mappings and the values they may carry.

Here, however, I continue this argument. Let us note that *up* comes to stand for positive longings (strong desires), and longings can be linked to values and ideals. Powerful longings can be linked to deeply embedded value dispositions (positive, for example, progressively upward and negative, for example, avoiding one's downfall). Embedded in what? When some feeling is deeply embedded, one may say "I feel it in my bones," which is a figurative English expression. Perhaps, though, our bones do have something to do with values in terms of anatomical architecture and spatial mappings through and from which we experience and live the world.

Two Psychological Models of Balance and Harmony

Constancy Model
A great human longing is for balance and harmony. This paired duo reveals itself as such across a range of spheres, whether expressed in Platonic idealism or in the wholesome aims of Tai Chi, diet, psychology, politics, investment, aesthetics, or ecology. This merged value of balance and harmony was recognized by an earlier psychology under the related term *homeostasis*, a model it borrowed from biology, emphasizing restoration of a state of constancy from a state of psychological instability. This state is achieved by reducing destabilizing tension or anxiety (Arons, 1992a). Taken in its most mechanistic sense, this is a model following the principle of inertia, or an indisposition to motion, exertion, or change—that is, *stasis*. Homeostasis offered the psychology of the mid-20th century a coherent model for conceptualizing pathology and psychological health. (Let us also note here that in practical terms, inertia and gravity have much in common.)

Emerging Model of Complexity and Paradox
However, as humanistic and creativity research critics came to point out, the homeostatic model did not well accommodate the far more complex and dynamic—and often tension-engendering, even destabilizing—picture emerging from their own inquiries of the creative individual (Arons & Richards, 2015; Krippner, 1994). In fact,

they were notably disposed to motion, exertion, and openness to change, and prone to the toying with constancy and order in the interest of gleaning new and higher unities—a heuristic dynamic that also applied to those engaged in self-exploration. The creative individual would be best described in paradoxical terms—including more complex indices of health and pathology—as exemplified in Barron's (1963) famous description of the creative genius in his book *Creativity and Psychological Health* as "both more primitive and more cultured, more destructive and more constructive, occasionally crazier and yet adamantly saner than the average person" (p. 234).

The emerging model in psychology is not a full rejection of the old homeostatic balance. With the advent of complex dynamical systems (and chaos theory) in psychology, however, a precarious balance may be found instead "far from equilibrium"—one which at times can change in an instant, and with little provocation, to find new balance (Arons & Richards, 2015; Krippner, 1994). One example of this is the so-called butterfly effect. Hence the present model adds an expanded and—especially with regard to creativity—tensional, less predictable, more open-ended, and more paradoxical dimension to it. This includes an interplay of opposites that relate to the new model itself (e.g., tension-reducing–tension-inducing), as well as an interplay of what Maslow (1962) called "basic" and "being" needs and values. When basic needs are satisfied, only then is there a personal opening to as-yet unrealized self-actualizing needs. At this point, the earlier and relative place of the basic needs is seen against the larger scheme of optimally lived human possibilities.

High-Wire Human Condition and the Balancing Act: Eschatological, Existential, and Postural Finitude

This more complex vision of psychological health joins the adventurous to the quiescent, as it does the chaotic to the previous order. Here are co-constituting and, hence, co-valued determiners of human balance and harmony. The creative genius at the moment of illumination and the spiritual seeker who attains a deeper meditative state shares with the rest of the species a human condition. That condition, taken from theology or philosophy, is one of finitude. A finitude that is shared not only universally but also of which human beings—uniquely perhaps—are potentially conscious: an awareness of life's impermanence, and a sense of the underlying profound interconnection of all that exists. Yet, so much is unknown, unseen, and likely also unsuspected. The expanded perceptual horizon from upright posture might have abetted this finite–infinite consciousness. Yet, given the awe-inspiring, fear-inducing, open-endedness of this horizon, conscious humans stand homeless between the open-ended mysteries of earth and the heavens, amidst an infinite surround, betwixt their source and destiny. The term *originality* implies homage to this intermediate state in the vital interplay of its double vectors: to the origins and to the new and unique.

This eschatological alienation from origins and destiny—both ends grasped for through religion, meditation, philosophy, art, and science—led existentialists to speak of the *void*, in Sartre's (1943/1948) term, the "nothingness" out of which we are "condemned to choose." For some existentialists, this condition is experienced as angst. Yet, there is a condition, lived consciously and fully, that can lead to what Watts (1951), speaking for some Eastern traditions, called the *wisdom of insecurity*. Could the conditions of our tenuous existential state prompting such wisdom as how to best live it be incarnated in the upright body posture, both as the condition's symptom and symbol? Could that condition, as well, heuristically in forms of exploration, discovery, invention, and creativity serve both to satisfy survival needs and foster eschatological inquiry?

Talking the Walk

A Lived Orientation Geometry via Posture-Value Expression

It seems possible that the evolutionary process of standing upright has left impressions on the modern human psyche, especially considering the energy expended over many millions of years developing the organic balancing mechanisms. Are there meanings and values of these impressions revealed in the psyche's expressions? Using some common expressions and the values they imply, let us see if we can discern what might be called an orientation-value geometry of the lived upright body posture.

Our terms *up* and *down* are linguistic indicators of opposite lived spatial directions in a vertical orientation, having solely the earth as a solid reference. This is a fundamental point: Only the vertical up and down plane or direction has such a solid unequivocal reference as earth, *terra firma*. For *front* and *back*, on the horizontal, one can turn in any direction. There is a plane of infinite orientations. Let us call this the *all-around*. Experienced directions are referenced to the body with face and visual senses concentrated *up-front*. Front is wherever the body is facing, and back is its opposite. The sides and all-around lived spaces, similar to front and back, have no direct, fixed, and firm earthly equivalent. Rather, they are diverse reference points related to objects (including the body). Thus, to indicate an object horizontally tangential to the body, rather than saying "up or down, back or in front," we say, for example, "It's over there, next to the mirror and above the sink." Hence, the lived world(s) of the lateral all-around directions are both more other-dependent and relative to context. In sum, the up and down axis has an absolute quality to it (earth-referenced), whereas the front and back orientation is referenced to the infinity of possible front-faced postures. Are there meanings and values embedded in these orientations and experiences?

One can compare these directional indicators to commonly expressed Western values: In one sense, *up* joins *forward* almost synonymously, whereas *down* becomes a near-synonym of *back*. We value prosperity. Therefore, it is good for the stock market to be *up*, to move *forward*. Our financial prospects are *up*, we are moving *forward*; that is, progressing. Compatibly, our spiritual fortunes are *up*, in the heavens (we hope), not *down*, *below*. Intellectually, psychologically, socially, politically, we *progress*, we hope—not *regress* or *retrogress*, *return*, or *go back down*: that is, *back down* religiously to original sin, intellectually to ignorance, culturally to the savage, epigenetically to the child, phylogenetically *back* to the animal, microgenetically to the realm of the unconscious.

Even when our banker or friend says they will *back* us they mean back us *up* (the back being more vulnerable than the front), or support our good credit *standing*. For, we are *upstanding* citizens. Let us hope they will not let us *down*. To be honest is to be *straightforward*; to be frank is to be *up-front*. Whereas our worst fears and character weaknesses have to do with the *back* and *down*. For example, betrayal is characterized as being stabbed in the *back*. We cover our *rear*. Inability to sustain religious devotion is called *backsliding*. We are cautious about our tentative, many-sided (lateral) worlds: the conditional worlds of "this depending on that" or, for other matters, expressed as "a *side* issue," or "*beside* the point." We describe pathology (unbalanced) and criminality (crooked) as deviance from norms and "normal" folks as *straight*, implying also balanced and forward moving. Finally, we are also suspicious of politicians who speak from the *sides* of their mouths, and we disdain hypocrites who speak out of both *sides* of their mouths.

Melded Space-Time Directionality and Ambiguities of the Lived Body

Let us pinpoint an observation so far bracketed—that is, put *aside*. The spatial posture-value links between *up* or *forward* and *down* or *backward* meld into the temporal. Now, *up* or *forward* in space becomes *up* or *ahead* in time. "What's *up*?" is the semantic equivalent of "What's *new*?" *Forward* signifies ahead in time as well as in space—for example, "I am looking *forward* to meeting you." We physically progress along a footpath as we psycho-spiritually progress in our lives. Progress is *forward* and *up* while regress is *backwards* and *down*. Many of the opposites of the positives *up* and *forward* are in the temporal dimension *down* and *back*. "Our earnings are down because we are *behind* (schedule) in our work." Even when we speak nostalgically of the "good ol' days," we think *back* to them, to those many opportunities left behind. Sadly, they cannot be recaptured, as they now belong to the past. The only solution to our current dismay is to get *back up* (once again) on our feet and move on (*forward*) with our lives. Physically, to do this we reach for a branch or any solidly grounded object around, spiritually and psychologically, for a pastor or therapist or a healing practice.

Having suggested that lived body architecture can resonate with certain values, let us now consider, as did Merleau-Ponty (1962), some of the ambiguities and tensions such posture-linked values bring to the foreground. *Up* and *forward* often attach themselves to positives, yet too much of a good thing can be just that: too much. Being too *up*-front, in '60s slang, can also be a *downer*. Nobody likes a person who is *up*pity. Thus, it is not "more is better." In moving forward, the right balance is again sought.

Conversely, we laud certain individuals for being "*down* to earth" (solid, stable, grounded) and for kneeling prayerfully. Certain cultural groups, such as the Scandinavians (perhaps as a reaction to their Viking ancestors who got too *high* and mighty) seem to value a *lower* profile and socially attuned, or spread-*out*, consciousness. Or consider the message God sent to those overreaching constructors of the Tower of Babel as he leveled, spread out, and divided humanity using mutually incomprehensible languages.

Life's Ins and Outs
Let us look at another, the *in* and *out* plane of lived experience. Consider the role of proximity in the notion of objectivity. To take mainstream scientific inquiry as a case in point, there is a tension implicated along this *in* and *out* lived value plane. To make positive advances in science, a distance is needed to avoid subjectivity; that is, the body's needs and desires may obscure, confuse, and therefore distort an unbiased view of what is observed. From this perspective, the body—taken as unreliable interiority—is seen as a negative for inquiry.

However, our touch with the objective "real" world is often expanded and enhanced by *in*sights. Here the subject–object distance is decreased and may even momentarily disappear. Intuition has its place in all phases of *in*quiry. Many scientists, including Einstein (1934), have insisted that intuition is at the heart of all science in process (Runco & Pritzker, 1999). One might also add the following "*ins*" to the creative heuristic disposition required for science's advances: *in*terest, *in*trospection and *in*spiration. Also, if our thesis about the upright posture's *in*herent relationship to the value world is valid, let us certainly consider *in*cluding a skeletally evolved instinct. And these are distinct from the often-related terms such as *out*look, *out*come, *out*put, *out*flow, *out*wit, *out*standing, and so forth.

These posture-related metaphors and value-tensions, I suggest, manifest themselves in diverse forms and phases of human inquiry and, in fact, are implicated in the supreme values of balance and harmony towards which human inquiry ultimately strives.

Collective Inquiry, Balance and Harmony, and the Human Condition

Creativity at the Intellectual Macro Level: Tensions and Balance

Contemporary scholarship is often involved in a balancing act of debate; for example, when a relativistic postmodernist takes on modern rationalism, with its *up*ward bent towards unifying truths. This modern–postmodern dialog reflects tensions that, in a variety of forms, have repeatedly expressed themselves throughout the history of Western inquiry, under such polar terms as *idealism* versus *empiricism*, *realism* versus *nominalism*, and the *One* versus the *Many*. Are such intellectual balancing acts extrapolations of the anatomically disposed value orientations?

Such debates draw out tensions between the high and the low, the vertical and the horizontal, the far and the near, the in and the out. Are there universal truths that can be grasped by the human mind, or can we trust only the relative givens of our bodily senses? Or, as nominalists claim, can we trust only the diverse signs assigned to designate bits of reality? Theologically, is there, as Judeo–Christian–Islamic faiths hold, one absolute God *up* in the Heavens, a single *high* Creator of the infinite diversity—or, as some pagan traditions hold, a multiplicity of earthly deities?

As to our means of inquiry, we find similar tensions. Do we trust the *in*nards of *in*dividual *in*tuition, or only that which is collectively testable by detached methods of experimentation? Are detached facts our touch with reality? Or must these be grounded for logical and theoretical coherence and even more *in*timate *under*standing—for example, by means of a hermeneutic exegesis that, in its spiraling interplay of interpretations, brings the distant and multiple *in*tuitively home: an *inner* grasp; an *in*timate joining of the objective and subjective, *multiple* and *singular*, *distant* and *near*, *up* and *down*.

In, Out, and All-Around Pathways of Progress

These posture-related value tensions are expressed in virtually all inquiry traditions. Each has their ins and outs, as do the variations of history. Like China, who offered us the introspections of Lao Tze in one period and the engineering marvel of the Great Wall in another, the West has had its *in*troverted periods of soul-searching and *ex*troverted periods of science and technology, seen as a whole, as aspiring to both the more immediately practical and more distant eschatological ends. All this marks the unique progression of humankind.

Even the notion of progress—taken figuratively as an upward and advancing trip—takes on a different sense relative to inquiry spheres. Technological inquiry marks its advances by clear criteria. Hence, model TX-2 (say, of an airplane) is a progressive advance over the previous (*backward*) model, TX-1—according to, say, the criteria of greater speed, shorter landing distance, and greater fuel efficiency. Whereas, in the inquiry worlds of art, poetry, and much of philosophy— or the meditative traditions of the East—it is far more difficult to speak of progress in this vertical–linear sense. Is Surrealism a *forward* advance over, say, Impressionism, and Impressionism over cave art? (Technique-wise, this may be true; but as an art form, perhaps not.) Here, progress may be marked laterally in revealing a wide range of ways in which humans experience and interpret their worlds.

Yet, art can also reflect the advancing progress of deepening and unifying consciousness, just as science can move between the two modes of progress, expanding (spreading) and lifting (raising) human consciousness. All these creative vehicles, as an ensemble—like the double vectors of the word *originality*—stretch our consciousness *back* towards discovery of our mysterious origins while stretching consciousness *forward* towards realization of an equally mysterious destiny.

Creative Individual, Process, and Product

What can be said about those individuals who create advances across domains and disciplines? Are they involved in some sort of balancing act? Of such eminent creative people, Csikszentmihalyi (1996) wrote,

"If I had to express in one word what makes their personalities different from others, it would be complexity" (p. 57).

Csikszentmihalyi (1996), although specifying a range of paradoxical personality traits, like Rogers (1959) and others studying the creative individual, also adds the trait "openness to experience," the opposite of psychological defensiveness. That is, openness, in the sense of presence—engagement, awareness, and sensitivity. In addition— and this relates to presence—what these people bring of themselves to any sphere, domain, or discipline is what Csikszentmihalyi calls a *multitude*, or an entire range of human possibilities within themselves. Hence, for example, they bring to any creative engagement or everyday life not only their adult qualities—for example, seriousness, realism, logic, skill, knowledge, and responsibility—but also their childlike (not childish) qualities, of naivety, imagination, awe, wonderment, playfulness, and even a disposition for irresponsibility. All these dispositions are available to them as resources to call on in the interest of a dynamic heuristic interplay with life events or specific creative projects.

The creative process itself can be a dance of apparent opposites, such as "detached-engagement" (moving *out-in*)—or as in Kris's (1952) neo-Freudian characterization of "regression in the service of ego," where there is a *backing down* to what the ego put *aside* (i.e., to preconscious resources): All this is in the interest of deepening (*in*) and expanding (*all-around*) ego's grasp of reality. Phases of the process may call for opposing states of mind or ongoing tension, in particular, of both divergent–convergent processing (Richards, 2000). An embracing of complexity engenders an emergent result that Skolimowski (1984) refers to as a "higher order simplicity" (p. 47): a new form of unity that contains the earlier multiplicity, such as one finds in the elegant solution to a complex problem.

Creativity and Psychological Health
Pathologies of many kinds are found among eminently creative individuals who, themselves, are not cast in a single mold (Runco & Richards, 1998). Consider the bizarre life of Dali or the state of depression Darwin experienced for decades. Yet, even these

pathologies can take on a different, healthy meaning when viewed broadly in the light of the larger creative context and, specifically, in the light of our thesis. Paradoxically, imbalance, stress, and disruption, in the right holding context, can idiosyncratically serve the larger creative balancing and harmonizing act. In creative context, imbalances such as obsessive traits and hyperemotionality may serve both to ground and free the mind.

The very factors creative individuals tend to have in common, including openness and preference for complexity (Barron, 1969), foster the paradox of accepting—even thriving on—imbalance in the interest of ultimately greater balance and harmony. Drawn by life and project, possessing multiple resources, they can create a kind of overall—albeit flexuous—safety zone of balance. For instance, the childlike imagination that belongs to the same creative dynamic as the adult reality checks such as logic and caution can be permitted to expand all the more freely and playfully. Here are potential examples of divergent and convergent types of processing. One can he reassured by these reality checks that the creator will not eventually be carried overboard into insanity or wild and consuming fantasy. Similarly, focus and perseverance can be exercised more freely without changing into the uncontrollably obsessive. Some anxiety and ambiguity can be tolerated without these degrading into debilitating neurotic vacillation or procrastination. Consider the letting-go experience, for example; the need to put aside a heated creative engagement for a time, which might even result in depression. In this *fluid* center (Schneider, 2004) resides such a strong *in*ner sense of confidence that even such phases of let*down* have their place in the creative process. At times, the process may be somewhat like pregnancy, where pain and malaise may be (even joyously) endurable because they are inherent to a necessary period of incubation. The creative process, similar to pregnancy, has its own phase of incubation, and ultimately engenders something meaningfully new and unique, as well as being a fulfillment and extension of one's self.

This openness to experience combined with complexity represents, in the condition of open presence and engaged multitude—and despite some delays and false starts—an overall balancing and harmonizing act. At the product level, whether in the arts, sciences, or everyday life, a new human–world unity can be produced. At the individual level, a new and *in*timate connection is established between self and external reality as well as between self-as-known and its own expanding horizons of possibility. The creative process may be a portal to yet deeper and wider potentials of *in*novation and expression as well as a portal to self-understanding and expanding states of consciousness.

Considering this dynamic, it is perhaps understandable that certain creative individuals also report what Maslow (1962) called peak experiences—ecstatic, rapturous moments that can transform one's experience of self or world. These experiences can be accompanied by a profound feeling of satisfaction and may sometimes include a sacred sense of being, seemingly aided by a force beyond self—as in a gift of illumination, or a "guided hand" recognition that "the painting painted itself." The experience may be accompanied by a dual sense of humility and fulfillment, of having more than realized one's personal talents and calling while being at that moment in a supreme state of balance and harmony. The creator's life as well as receptive humanity may meaningfully be advanced. Here are moments to feast on, but also—if the creative individual or humanity should succumb to achievement-incited hubris—moments prone to get *up*pity.

Spiritual Paths to Balance and Harmony

Let us conclude our inquiry with a snapshot tour of some of the world's great spiritual traditions and take a speculative look at our directional themes. Spiritual traditions vary greatly but typically hold that "reality is not limited to the material, sensory world ... [there is] a spiritual reality ... be it belief in a supreme being or order, life after physical death, an ultimate reality, or supernatural beings like angels or demons" (Miller & Thoresen, 1999, pp. 5–6). In our worldly sphere, practitioners are in search of how to live in balance and harmony and towards a greater goal.

Let us begin with the notion of *up*pity, or when events directionally go too far. This might be magnified to eschatological proportions. Original sin marks, for Christians, the rupture with divine unity and harmony. Christ comes down, in body, from the heavens to save the multitude of souls otherwise doomed by their base and earthly ways, which averts the fate of hell *below* as well. The moment of grace (i.e., my cup runneth over) is one of sublime reunion with God, and leads to a new, balanced, and more harmonious way of living the mortal life. One may see aspects of a creative detached engagement by being in but not of the world.

Other spiritual traditions also begin with rupture from a harmonious origin. In the Judaic tradition of Kabbalah, during the process of incarnation from the unity realm, of which all are a part, into the separate ego and world of diversity, one is wounded—one's vessel (individual and the world) "becomes cracked." Once individuals are capable of negotiating the many challenges posed by this world of multiplicity, they are able to return to the unity realm in order to bring back (down) healing energy, the divine sparks, which can be used to repair or heal the cracks in the vessel. This process of return from peak to base in order to repair or heal, to reestablish harmony and unity in the world of complexity and contradiction, is called *tikkun* (Cooper, 1997; E. Hoffman, 1985; Matt, 1997).

A spiritual voyage that encompasses up and down, in and out, back and forward and the multiplicity of the all-around, in the interest of balance and harmony, expresses itself in different ways in other traditions. In the varied practices of shamanism (Harner, 1990; Heinze, 1991), shamans, acting on behalf of their communities and its members, are able to access altered states of consciousness so they can mediate between the sacred and profane. This includes ability to travel between the lower, upper, and middle worlds to obtain information necessary for healing individuals and their communities. Whether through the use of drumming, the ingestion of powerful psychoactive substances, or other means, activities disrupt practitioners' ordinary consciousness and open them to the liminal realm, which becomes a portal for many possibilities, including magical cures, visions of an extraordinary nature, and visits with ancestral spirits (Matt, 1997).

In the multiple traditions of yoga—"to bind together, hold fast, or yoke" (Eliade, 1969, p. 4)—students are guided in the process of refocusing their reactive, habit-bound, states of consciousness through the use of a variety of somatic and meditative practices. The ultimate goal of liberation presupposes a preliminary breaking of bonds, to transcend the world of suffering, for ultimate knowledge and self-mastery. Among many diverse practices, there are energetic techniques for moving energy (evolution, expansion, involution), upward, outward, and downward, to further harmony and balance within the individual and the greater cosmos (Chaudhuri, 1965, 1977).

In Western psychology, Maslow (1962) chose the ancient symbol of the pyramid to depict elegantly the process he calls *self-actualizing*, at the peak of his hierarchy of needs. There is movement *up*ward from the array of *down*-pulling basic needs, such as physiological and safety needs, most of these shared with other animals. When satisfied, one ascends through middle level (belonging and self-esteem) needs—to those more uniquely human, such as belongingness and love. One then ascends to a pinnacle of *being* needs developing fully to one's capacity. Attainment of this may be accompanied by *peak experiences*, moments of unity and deep insight, of experiencing the sacred in the mundane, the all in the particular.

The form of the pyramid expresses the need for groundedness before ascent. The four corners of this grounded base all join to the pinnacle. This is the point from which insights may be brought, geometrically and communicatively, down to the world of the base as a transcendent and prophetic message. The goal is to provide benefit, but not to get stuck (hung-up) *down* there. In pointing to Maslow's symbolic pyramid, we might also take note that one who meditates in the lotus position has formed his or her body into the shape of a pyramid.

Conclusions

The human creative capacity may be viewed as a mediator between body and psyche, and body and spirit. Also, as the double-vectored term *originality* implies, the creative process may represent a kind of revolving doorway between our mysterious human origins and equally open destiny. Resourcefully, this creative capacity converts tensions—some anatomically associated with the upright posture's lived values—towards individual survival and the remarkable achievements of the species as well as the farther reach of human possibility.

Seen in this light, the answer to our earlier question of whether creative capacity and the potential for spiritual development are reserved for the elite, or are the birthright of everybody, shifts in favor of the latter. Both appear embedded and embodied in humanity. One may then ask why some people do not exercise these human capacities more fully. Just as the work of upright posture may be taken for granted, perhaps we are not adequate recognizing potential for creativity and spiritual growth that are embedded in the activities of everyday life.

The nexus I propose between upright posture, creativity, and supreme values of balance and harmony helps us better understand how inspiring dancers or acrobats, stretching to their body limits in performance, can fall under the same creative label as the *in*sight-producing artist, and can evoke awe. Similarly, the architect or paradigm-shifting scientist can amaze us, drawing us to new heights of order and balance.

This raises a question for scholars of evolution, the sort psychologists have raised when their observations took them beyond the constancy hypothesis. Why did any of the earliest ancestors of *Homo sapiens* stand upright? How and why did this begin? The outcomes would seem to impose this question. For, given this creature's unique and remarkable accomplishments, not least among these involves coming to relative harmony with nature on its own terms, and thriving, to boot—all this given the vulnerabilities of the human posture—one wonders if whatever set that transformation in motion can be explained in survival terms alone.

Chapter 8

Creativity: Person, Product, or Process?
(1973, with Stan Krippner)[1]

Editors' note: This paper was originally delivered with Stan Krippner at the 20th Annual Convention of the National Association for Gifted Children in Des Plaines, Illinois, February 1973.

There are important differences between Eastern and Western views of creativity. As we learn to harmonize them, we may discover how to maximize creative growth among all individuals.

To inquire into the origins of creativity is as ambitious a quest as to inquire into the origins of the universe. Indeed, would not the two inquiries have the same goal, seeking to discover how we and everything we experience come into being? The English word "creativity" is linked etymologically and historically in the minds of men with genesis, or original creation, as well as with the concept of origin itself (consider the term "originality").

We could do worse as a starting point than to consider both the original term "creative" and the relative one "creativity" as being ancient dwellers in the forest of mystery. In fact, some of the most creative persons insist that as a fish does not long survive out of water, so creativity as we understand it would not exist without mystery. There has often been a resistance on the part of creative persons to attempts to gain a systematic understanding of creativity. Apparently, they either fear that some of their creative potential will be lost if some

[1] Krippner, S., & Arons, M. (1973). Creativity: Person, product, or process? *Gifted Child Quarterly*, 17, 116–123, 129. doi:10.1177/001698627301700207 | Copyright © 1973 by SAGE Publishing. Adapted with permission from SAGE Publishing and from Dr. Stanley Krippner (co-author of this paper).

of the mystery is removed or else that such attempts are simply futile because mystery is inherent in creating.

Origins of Creativity

The historical link between the creative experience and mystery extends back to our earliest ideas of genesis itself. An amazingly consistent theme is found in the mythology of diverse cultures. The familiar theme contends that from chaos order was born, from the obscure the earth took form. A naturalistic analogue to this theme still holds favor among many scientists who theorize that the earth evolved from nebulous clouds of particles which were floating about in space.

The idea of bringing into being new order out of non-order, new form out of the formless, a comprehensible out of the incomprehensible, is basic to the classic meaning of creation as it is implicit to our modern concept of creativity. When we think of the word "creation" we think of life, something being brought to life: an idea, an invention, a painting, an automobile, a woman's hat, etc. Each of these *could* be a creation. But we do not say that every hat or every idea or every car is a creation. We do not say that automobile #1,354,000 rolling off the Ford assembly line in a model year is a creation because it is just like the other 1,353,999. A pattern had already been established. It is not novel; it is not a surprise. We already know the plans from which it has emerged. We are more likely to term it a product, or a production. But the first model in that line, though it carries on a tradition, may be a creation—and the very first automobile, the first machine of that nature to start rolling around, definitely was a creation.

A theme compatible with the mythological concept of humans being estranged from perfect order has appeared in both Western and Eastern philosophy and religion. Socrates, for example, believed that all humans' search for knowledge was an attempt to recall a pre-existent state of truth and order. We live our normal lives in a state of confusion and illusion obscured from the truth which we have "forgotten"; we must rediscover or come to recall this pre-existent state through a personal search. Many Eastern philosophies and religions hold as basic that the states of consciousness which we consider normal are actually illusory, obscuring from us the fuller truth. In order for us to "wake up" or become "enlightened," we must pass beyond or transcend these obscurities and illusions. In this transcending process, we open ourselves to our origins and to the universal order of which we are a harmonious part.

Notice that in the case of Socrates and Eastern thinking it becomes possible to *re*-discover the pre-existent truth. The concept of *re*-discovery is applicable because, according to this common premise, we are uncovering, or opening ourselves to what is there within us and what we have been blinded to or obscured from recognizing. It means that now—this very moment, "in" every one of us—there is an infinitely greater awareness available than we are exercising. We come to know this truth, and the manner by which we became alienated from it, by learning how to experience the world correctly.

While there has been a persistent recurrence of the *re*-discovery theme throughout Western history it has, over the past 300 years, been something less than popular. At the origins of modern science, this belief was attacked by a heavy barrage of philosophical criticism. Empirical–positivistic philosophies which developed in the 17th through 19th centuries—and upon which modern science is principally grounded—refused to consider the possibility that there was any sort of "pre-existent" or innate truth. Rather, humans were viewed as a *tabula rasa*, or blank slate, at birth and all that they were to become or could understand was to be acquired through their sense organs and by the reasoning they applied to what they perceived in the naturalistic world. This set the task for science to invent ways of cutting through the veil which shrouded nature; though nature is to some extent perceivable, its underlying laws are not easily grasped. Following this premise of humans starting unaided and discovering the laws of nature, even humans themselves became a mystery of nature; they had to be studied in the same detached scientific manner as rocks or plants.

Starting from the premise that every person at birth is a blank slate—and that all the knowledge which one can ever have is acquired through one's empirical experiences in this world and his reasoning on these—the idea of cumulative or progressive knowledge became appropriate. Part of this learning experience could be the acquisitions which are passed down and added to from generation to generation. Thus, we see the emphasis on collective and cumulative knowledge where a public sort of creativity (e.g., the invention of a technique, the discovery of a new fact) could be judged relative to the collective scientific project. Creativity, from this vantage point, would have a tendency to be externally oriented; that is, it would be seen as a contribution to humans' continually expanding discovery of the hidden secrets of nature.

Given this tendency towards collective knowledge, it should come as no surprise that many persons interested in creativity, particularly Westerners, have tended to stress this more constructive, outgoing, individualistic (though collectively oriented) form of creativity. Some have gone so far as to claim that creativity as we now understand it originated with the early philosophical foundations of modern science, when humans turned their heads outward towards nature. Even art, according to these writers, became an attempt at searching for new ways of viewing the world and human feelings about it. This can be contrasted with the art of the Middle Ages, which made no attempt to understand humans and nature but which rather represented mere reflections on an inner personal search, or were symbols of currently held beliefs; that is, medieval art was simply a by-product of the temper of the times and was not itself a vehicle for discovery in the collective sense. Medieval art was expression but not exploitation and discovery. Contrasted with Leonardo da Vinci, one of the first of the modern creative artists, the artists of the Middle Ages were essentially craftsmen expressing, in materials, the common spiritual themes assigned to them (e.g., the construction of a cathedral) rather than, like Leonardo, searching to individually explore the structures of nature.

From our present values based on "exterior" discovery, our notions of progressive control of our natural environment, our stress on individual contributions to a cumulative collective understanding, and our consequent emphasis on history and the importance of our roles within the historical frame of reference, it is understandable that we look back upon those years preceding our own age of modern rationalism and science as the "Dark" Ages. By this we imply that there was very little in the way of the outward discovery and creation which characterizes our own period. "Dark," in fact, signifies to us the unknown and what appears to be the unprogressive. It behooves us to remember that our own emphasis has been on the "exterior," that which we can see, and that we are judging that period by our own standards, including our standards of creativity.

We could view such Eastern art and technique in the same way as we view that of the Middle Ages. There, also, centuries have passed with little apparent evidence of scientific or technical progress. Yet the danger of applying our standards to the creations of the East have become much more evident to Western philosophers and psychologists over the past few years.

Developing the mythological theme that humans have been obscured from a "pre-existent" knowledge and must *re-discover* the truth within his own psyche, the domain of consciousness and techniques for its exploration have been studied to a remarkable degree by Easterners. It appears that, far from there being a lack of creativity in those cultures, the creative effort has been turned inward, opening up an amazingly complex universe of consciousness which has been for the most part almost disregarded in the West over the past few centuries. This lack of inner direction has been very evident in psychology, which has strongly reflected the overall Western tendency to direct attention outward. Much of what now goes under the name "humanistic psychology" appears to be leading in a direction which is consistent with much of Eastern philosophy; in some instances, Eastern thought has become a model for a deeper psychological understanding of the human being. This is not because Eastern thought was imported into a vacuum and that it has become fashionable. Rather, the tendencies which have been evolving in Western and more particularly in American psychology of late have actually brought us to a point where a synthesis of sorts it possible. A synthesis is not a reduction of one to the other; rather, the two points of view appear to be saying much the same thing—if from different perspectives—in terms of human values, human growth, and human potentials. If we look at the viewpoints as complementing, rather than contradicting one another, the difficulties of each tend to vanish, just as for a child the mystery of the shape of his wrinkled balloon vanishes once it is blown up completely and seen as a whole.

Two Views of Creativity

The idea of the creative is universal, a deeply rooted and central concept in both the West and the East. Confucius stated, "Great indeed is the generating power of the Creative; all beings owe their beginnings to it. This power permeates all heaven." Yet such Westerners as the American philosopher Northrup do not view their type of creativity—that which seems to have characterized their cultures and history—as being identical with the Eastern modes. To this the Eastern sage would probably agree and disagree. He would set forth the possibility that Western creativity has been seen as one-sided rather than two-sided; that it has been characterized by breaking through the unknown to progress humans even further towards an understanding of nature and control over it. Thus, the Western creator is conceived of as one who risks, who is bold, who pioneers, who explores, who is even open to new possibilities, who breaks through existing order to establish the base for new order and whose goal is ultimate mastery.

Something akin to this view of creativity is expressed in the Chinese word for "sublime," also meaning "head," "origin," "great," and referring to "the creative one." Another concept which is coupled by Easterners with "sublime" is *"success"*—as when the *I Ching* states, "The way to success lies in apprehending and giving actuality to the way of the universe." It is particularly in the meanings of "success" that we find an apparent difference between the Eastern and Western concepts of creativity. The first part of the statement, "the way to success lies in apprehending . . . the universe," appears similar to the Western notion of creativity—i.e., to come to understand. The latter part differs from that of the West—i.e., "giving actuality to the way of the universe." This means that once the universe is grasped or apprehended, the creative person attempts to "further" creativity's natural development, helping it to grow along natural lines, preserving this orderly growth by establishing correct and appropriate rules.

It is this latter part of the quotation which seems somewhat out of line with our Western notion of creativity. Breaking through to the new is acceptable but becoming an agent of perseverance is debatable. The enactment of rules to preserve what has been discovered appears to us to be antithetical to creativity. How can the creative person also be an agent for the maintenance of the status quo?

This paradox can only be understood if we tune in more closely to the Eastern meaning of perseverance and, more important, grasp the basic difference in assumptions which are characteristic of Eastern and Western thought. One reason we cannot conceive of the creative person assuming the role of apparent conserver of a discovery is that we have tended in the West to dichotomize spheres of activity: The innovator bursts open order to discover new order, the dogmatist clings to the old order. We know from our personal and historical experience that it has been the dogmatists, and those holding rigidly to the status quo, who seem to constantly obstruct progress and serve as enemies of creative individuals. There are historical periods where the social "Establishment," in order to protect its own interests, seems to obstruct innovation through protective and legally instilled rigidity. Have not most of the old religious sects, in the name of doctrinal purity, prevented many individuals from moving towards an authentic spiritual quest?

We justifiably consider these forces to be anti-creative. However, our problem in understanding Eastern creativity is that we equate the kind of perseverance spoken of in the East with the kind of perseverance characteristic of the dogmatic forces mentioned above. Rather, the creative person, in the Eastern sense, attempts to maintain the growth process itself. An ancient Chinese philosopher wrote, "The course of the creative alters and shapes being until each attains its true specific nature, then it keeps them in conformity with the great harmony. Thus does it show itself to further through perseverance." This can be put more simply with specific examples. A flower grows more fully into what it is (e.g., a rose, a lilac) if it is given a certain kind of soil and a certain amount of moisture. Once one understands the nature of the flower, perseverance demands that one establish those conditions which will foster or further that flower's growth. An infant is created by its mother and father, who to continue their creation must do all possible to help the child develop to the fullest its human potentials. At some point this may require setting up rules and guidelines and perhaps enforcing them firmly. At another age this may require letting go, accepting that the next stage of development requires that the child leave home. The creative individual does not treat a flower like a child or a cat for he recognizes their different natures and attempts to further development along the lines appropriate to these natures. In the same way the nature of one child, or one flower, or one cat is not identical with the nature of another child, flower, or cat, and these individual natures are fostered by the creative person.

While this is not a difficult concept for us in the West to understand, it is a perplexing one for us to practice for several reasons. It is difficult for us to accept helping things to be what they are because we have been too successful in changing the nature of things. We have seen how our educational system has succeeded in acculturating people to think along similar lines. We have seen our parents attempt to channel us towards a particular profession because that vocation has a high status or a satisfactory income. Women have seen that by sitting in beauty parlors for several hot hours they could alter nature and adopt their current hair style. We know it is not our nature to die at age thirty, as people formerly did in the Middle Ages, because modern medicine can assist us to live twice as long. We also know that it is not in our nature to be Earth-bound, since our technology has enabled us to leave the Earth. In addition, we can splice two fruits and can produce a third, and we can divert the natural flow of a river to fertilize a naturally arid desert.

Creativity in the West has very often implied altering the nature of things to serve human needs. This process frequently obscures the simple understanding of what appears to be the nature of different beings. Instead we select the goal of gaining control and putting these things to our service.

Given the limited ends of forcing nature to alter itself to our goals, the West and its form of creativity has been an enormous success—as our goals have included satisfying our hunger, moving ourselves about at enormous speeds, making ourselves look physically younger, extending our actual life spans, etc. A question which has remained stubbornly resistant to all our creative efforts, however, has been the one concerning human purpose itself. To live to the age of 100 is one thing. To sense one's self as fulfilled is quite another, and Easterners see this question of fulfillment as identical with the question of the nature of humans or of any specific individual.

Some artists could be giving us a useful distinction between creative tendencies in East and West when they speak of the goals of both the creative worker and the mystic. Both artist and mystic, at the time of insight, experience a deep sense of personal fulfillment, but the mystic works gratuitously for revelation alone. The creative worker is predatory; he grabs the insight for a filled purpose, he is far less than divine, and the Promethean fire-snatching symbol seems very appropriate. Several examples of this Promethean behavior exist. Robert Louis Stevenson reported that he was able to control his dreams for creative purposes, his short story "The Strange Case of Dr. Jekyll and Mr. Hyde" being the best-known example of this ability. Louis Agassiz, the naturalist, attempted to solve a problem involving the location of a fossil in his dreams and succeeded on the third try. Kyo Izumi, the architect, took LSD in a successful attempt to work out the spatial problems involved in a mental institution he was designing. Any number of artists and writers (e.g., Ernst Fuchs, Allen Ginsberg) have engaged in regular periods of meditation in a deliberate attempt to bring creative insight to their work. Rather than having a product-oriented focus on novel perceptions and conceptions, a process-oriented creative person would use insight-producing states to develop themselves as people or to obtain "enlightenment." This orientation is closer to that espoused by Eastern philosophers.

Many significant works of art have emerged from the Eastern tradition, even though stress has been placed on the development of creative people rather than on what they create. In the East, the "product" is fulfillment itself, the sense of unity which creative people experience in that moment when they feel a sense of unity between themselves and the universe. Easterners' ultimate "product" is to penetrate their own deepest nature, which according to them is the reciprocal of an insight into the universe, and a unity with it.

As we have seen, some idea of creativity is present in the thinking of all cultures. In this sense, creativity as a basic experience of humans is universal. However, we have just noted that there are some important differences between creativity as it is viewed in the East and as it has been viewed in the West. We have suggested that this difference reflects a more basic cultural difference generally recognized between East and West—that is, that in the West over the past few centuries, there has been a strong tendency towards the conquering, or the domination of nature. In the East, the tendency has been towards merging with nature or harmonizing with it.

The Role of the Creator

Given this basic difference in underlying goals, it is understandable that creativity in the West would be more "product-centered"; that is, what would be considered as a candidate for the term "creative" would more than likely have to be of value to humans' dominance over nature. Such a contribution could take many forms. It could be a technological innovation which permits for greater productivity or comfort. It could be a scientific discovery which unveils a secret of nature, or a new theory, which offers us new possibilities to investigate. It could be a musical composition or a painting or a sculpture, which offer us new dimensions for perceiving. It could be a philosophy which offers us a new way of construing a situation or our relationship to situations.

To say that creativity in the West is primarily product centered is not to imply that the creator himself is of little or no importance in the West. In fact, how a creative person creates is of great importance—for if we value creative products, we certainly value that which makes a person creative. As you know, the creative person is held in extremely high esteem in the West. However, the value placed on the product has often meant that without some observable contribution, we have not generally recognized that a person is creative. In the East, a product-centered creativity often is less valued than what we might call a "process-centered" creativity. In process-centered creativity, the person's aim is to be fully "awake" and alive, the ultimate goal being personal "enlightenment." In such an endeavor, to become preoccupied with products can be seen as a "hang-up"; frequently, the process-centered person will actually forego the temptation to create a product. Many Eastern philosophies warn against the development of art or science or even certain powers such as extra-sensory perception, for these can "untrack" the growth-oriented person from his ultimate search for full awakening.

Many writers in humanistic psychology refer to the two types of creativity as "special talent creativeness" and "self-actualizing creativeness," adding that some people demonstrate both tendencies. However, those exhibiting "self-actualizing creativeness" often do almost anything in a creative way because "they live far more in the real world of nature than in the verbalized world of concepts."

In the West, the tendency of investigators has been to start with the product and then attempt to understand the person who created it. This has led to a certain amount of disagreement among Western cultures concerning just who should be considered creative. Not everybody agrees on what a creative product is; what one culture may consider to be a major contribution, another may ignore. This selectivity obviously depends on many factors. Consider, for example, the historical needs of the culture. One could say that during the early pioneering days on this continent, an ax, or he who wielded one with skill and vigor, was worth many meditative philosophers because there was a critical need to transform the wilderness into a livable environment. You can well imagine that the same value was not given to the contributions of the ax in aristocratic Europe. Even to this day, we in the United States tend to hold in greater esteem than do many Europeans those enterprises which require manual and technical skills. The French tend to consider many of our technical innovations as "inventive," or "clever," or "resourceful." However, they reserve the term "creative" for more "spiritual" innovations such as great art, philosophy, and theory. It is perhaps for this reason that the French have no equivalent for the English word "creativity." They still employ the word "creation," suggestive of a spiritual link with original creation. Our term "creativity" (a quite recent one, incidentally) permits us to consider as creative many products and persons which are only remotely linked with any idea of original creation.

Differences in traditions and values do play an important role within the West in defining what is actually meant by creative. In fact, such cultural and value differences play an essential part in determining why anybody should be interested in creativity in the first place, or in how this question should be studied.

The difficulty of defining "creativity" in a way that will find nearly universal acceptance among scientists will be with us for some time. Meanwhile, the student of creativity research must identify and understand the definition of creativity used either implicitly or explicitly by the author of each scientific treatise he reads. The student must also decide if the author is discussing the creative process, the creative person, or the creative production.

In general, humanistic psychologists define creativity broadly, feeling that it is the universal heritage of every human being that is born. They reserve the term "genius" for those with extraordinary special talent creativeness in the arts, sciences, etc.

It is this perspective that is helpful in harmonizing the Western and the Eastern concepts of creativity. If we regard creativity, in its broadest sense, as a basic human potential, we can modify educational, childrearing, and psychotherapeutic procedures in ways that will maximize creative growth among all individuals. At the same time, we can be concerned with the creative product—and can assist our culture in giving these products the proper reward and attention they deserve. In so doing, of course, we will reinforce this type of behavior and will encourage the flow of imagination and innovation. As for the link between the creative person and the creative product, psychology must pay further respect to the creative process and design research studies which will give us a clearer glimpse into its nature and development.

Part 3:

Growth and Potential in Education

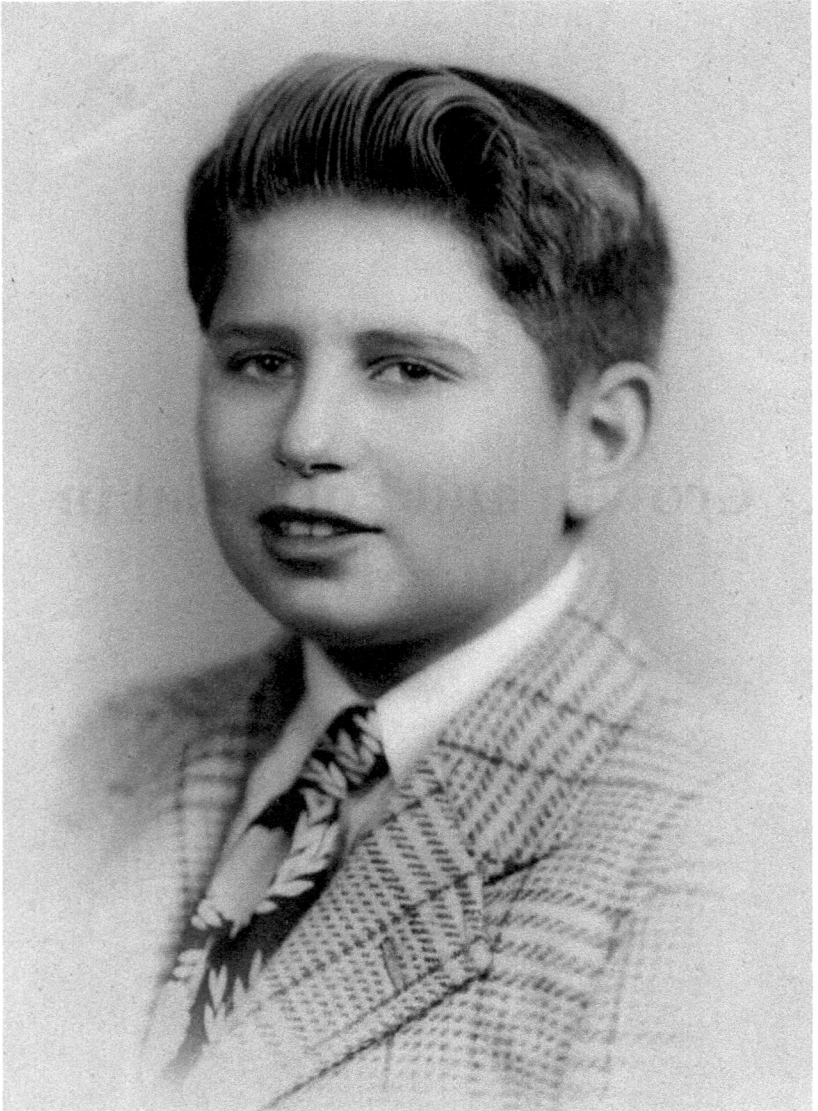

Mike as a child in Detroit, MI.
(Photographer unknown. Contributed by Sandrine Arons.)

One of Mike's students, B. Z. D'Elia, recalled that he "[created], through his great mind a spirit, an atmosphere in which we *are* the learning and the learning is us. Seamlessly combining the intellectual, the experiential—the mind and the spirit—Mike was able to offer his students ... a space in which to be" (in Richards & Whitehouse, 2008, p. 266).

This section features three of Mike's papers on humanistic education, all of which are embellished with personal storytelling to convey his points. In Chapter 9, Mike recalls his journey from public school to college and how his ability to apply intuitive and empathetic processes enabled him to be successful. He also proposes that teacher burnout is the outcome of feeling powerless in the face of preoccupation with testing and mechanical productivity that results in conflict between one's values and one's job duties. In Chapter 10, Mike further explores the role of intuitive experience in the learning process and, revisiting themes from Part 2, challenges the notion of linearity and convergent thinking as "the best or only way of conceiving of human progress." Then he emphasizes the value of the arts for priming insight in educational contexts. In Chapter 11, Mike critiques Carl Rogers' dichotomization of traditional and person-centered approaches in education, suggesting that doing so ultimately backfired and begat an anti-humanistic ethos. He proposes a middle-way approach for education to get back on track by focusing on universal values and transformation to promote "the opening, freeing, and revelatory experience of the student."

Chapter 9

The Growing Chasm Between Mission and Job
(1989)[1]

Editors' note: This was Mike's presidential address to the Association for Humanistic Education in Denver, Colorado, April 1989.

The Need to Share a Personal Experience

I would like to talk with you about something we do not speak of in teachers' lounges or faculty meetings. I am not even sure whether anybody here will know what I am talking about. Yet I have to take the risk. For while, in other times and places, what I have to say may be taken for granted, that which I find missing in our own current debate over education seems to me to be of fundamental importance to the dialogue amongst ourselves and between us as educators and the public.

I recognize that the personal experience I will share with you is probably very different from your own. Yet it is the sense of a "call" or "path" that you may recognize in your own experiences. If my personal experience can find company at the level of the call, then I think you may agree with me that this subject I am raising may be of crucial importance to education in our times.

---

[1] Arons, M. (1990). The growing chasm between mission and job (1989 presidential address). *Journal of Humanistic Education, 14,* 124–127. | Copyright © 1990 by the Association for Humanistic Education. Adapted with permission from Dr. Tracy Cross (editor of the volume of the *Journal of Humanistic Education* in which this paper originally appeared) and from Dr. Anne Richards (former executive officer of the Association for Humanistic Education).

The Call

I feel I have a call to be an educator. I have never seen God or the "burning bush." I have had in my life what are called religious, even mystical, experiences, but I am not even a nominal Jew or follower of any religion or sect. The call did not hit me at one time. In fact, most often it has been difficult for me to discern this call. I am still both hearing and doubting that I hear a call. The call seems to take place throughout my life. I do not even recognize this lifespan continuity until I recognize something in everyday experience which "speaks" to me, but in the sense of a feeling that "this is you" or of putting on the right shoes.

But the comfortable metaphor of feeling at home does not quite say what I mean. For when I hear this call in an experience, that experience seems also to be excitingly perturbing to the core. It lights me up, turns me on; it empowers me. I feel powerfully at home in the classroom, yet teaching is only one aspect of this call. The greater call is as educator. The sense of educator does not diminish when I leave the classroom. What I am doing now, speaking to you this way, I sense as my passionate obligation. I cannot be fully myself unless I speak to the best in education.

I know what is best in education because I experienced it, finally, as an undergraduate. I passed through four years of the most incredibly insightful and transformative experiences I had ever known. Those were the years—without pot, acid, health foods, or meditation—which were the most deepening and mind-expanding of my life. I understood what an education could be and could do for a person. But this undergraduate experience was not the source of my call; it was a step along the way of following that call. The navigational signs indicating this way for me flashed early in my life even before I entered school and during that period when schooling or teaching or educating seemed the most alien to my inclinations and abilities.

When I was a small child, no matter whether we were stringing a group of wagons together to make a train, or playing ball, I preferred the role of being outside of what I was in—feeling best playing the dispatcher or the radio broadcaster than driver or passenger or player or even manager of the team.

Another passion I had, later, was Detroit. I spent years of my middle childhood (often while playing hooky from school) walking, biking, or bussing up and down its streets, the same streets over and over, hundreds of times. I went to the top of buildings and looked down and around from each vantage to all the others and then went to the ground and looked up. I dressed up like a rich kid and sat in the posh hotel lobbies. I dressed to be saved and served on Michigan Avenue's skid row soup kitchens. I came to know Detroit inside and out and upside and down. I was the unpaid guide who understood that city of Detroit as no paid guide ever knew or presented it. My greatest joy was guiding. I took a job as taxi driver. I was not your typical taxicab driver. Sometimes I would pay the meter bill just to complete the tour I was giving. Sometimes the customer would pay for the whole day just to get the tour.

I was not only a bad student during my primary and secondary school, I was ultimately placed in a class for the slow learner. This was based both on performance and a measured I.Q. of 80. Later, on the advice of my shop teacher, and reinforced by the growing problems I was having at home, my parents sent me to a military school. By that point, I was being classed as what we now call a behavior disorder problem. The less kind and gentle term then was "incorrigible."

I managed to graduate from high school, but I messed up at every job, mostly factory work in Detroit, and was finally given a last chance as sweeper of lathe shavings at a steel mill. This was the only future I saw for myself. But I got partially reconnected to other possibilities when I took a door-to-door sales job. This led to other sales jobs and back to guiding. When I sold carpeting, for example, I guided people through the carpet from its variations of weaved backing to its tightness, ply, loop, or its unique materials, body, and style. I took the customer, in their minds, through the odyssey of rug and carpet creation at the mills in far-distant lands called Philadelphia or Dalton or Isfahan. I never knew where any of these lands were actually located.

It was at the end of seven years as real estate agent, at 27, that I knew one day, at one single moment, that I was going to college. I put my application together and took the entrance examination. The counselor tried as kindly as possible to inform me that I was the last person to attempt college: "This is the mean on the quantitative," she pointed to the first curve on what I later learned was a profile. Then her finger slid to the very bottom: "This is your score." She passed through the four categories. I had scored at the bottom of each. Nothing she said had any significance for me whatsoever. I simply sat there waiting for her to find the way I would enter college. I knew she would. Because I knew I was going to go through college.

Though right through to the end of my college education I scored at the bottom of reading and writing tests, I ended up turning down grant offers to a variety of graduate schools. After driving a cab the year of my graduation, I took the few hundred dollars I'd earned and boarded a student ship for France. Five years later I completed a doctoral dissertation in philosophical psychology at the Sorbonne in French.

It is not that the testers had been wrong. They were right about what they were measuring. They and all the "vocational" counselors simply did not understand the path I was on. I didn't know then, nor do I understand now, what was drawing me. But the path put me in touch with a string of people and events which seemed to be waiting for me. None of these heuristic encounters seem earned by me in any objective sense. Others more talented, more skilled, and more personally ambitious should well have had these encounters before me. The only quality I seemed to exhibit was being fully where I was.

My reading pace was no more than two pages an hour. It is not too much better than that today. I came to learn grammar, punctuation, and spelling by osmosis. Yet, I received a B in that first introductory English course where ten books, including the Bible and *Vanity Fair*, were assigned. I stayed with the page, with the word, until I felt myself at the inside of them and, finally, on the inside of the authors. I came to share the human space they were coming from and then knew what they were saying because I could see what they were seeing. It was then that I first met the existentialists with whom I later ended up studying in Paris, and Albert Schweitzer whom I came to meet in person when my first teaching contract with the French Government sent me to Gabon, Africa. That is how I came to meet Abe Maslow, in a shared space, well before we met in person, and it was Maslow, in person, who ultimately recommended me as chairman of the West Georgia psychology department where, over the past two decades, we have developed a humanistic psychology department to explore such mysteries as these of human potential.

The Confidence of Empowerment

This feeling of being on the right path, this fundamental sense of empowerment, precedes the actual definable facts or the nature of the experiences which await me on that path—and precedes, as well, skills and techniques. Put differently, I feel the power to be where I am to be before I encounter, let alone master, facts or learn skills or develop techniques. Nor when I speak of this path do I refer to talent.

What characterizes my particular call the best is the term "educator." This includes but is not encompassed by teaching. It is reaching out through and beyond what is taught to something that I see or think I see in and beyond these particulars which gives a fuller sense of life and meaning. Of those things seen and unseen, James Joyce put it, "Its whatness leaps to us from the vestment of its appearance; the object achieves its epiphany."

I do not want my students to take what I point to as truths. Nor do I want followers. I am constantly in doubt myself, just as I doubt that what I am saying to you will make sense or is even valid rather than vain. Still, I am not without certain internal checks. I feel right when I point as far into the hidden veins of the material as I can, as when I was selling carpet, or trying to make the ball game exciting, or guiding people through the steely plainness of apparent Detroit to its dazzling soul. I feel right when I do this. I feel not right when I do less.

From the heart of these internal checks, what I see in advance and how I show it—that is, doing the right thing at the right time—I call intuition. I feel I can distinguish this intuition from projection or inference or speculation because I only know it is intuition for sure when I validate it. The philosopher Henri Bergson said this, and I recognize it as valid for me: intuition lends itself to validation.

It is certain to me that this path or any given particular intuitions are not logical. But it is not certain to me that reason, even logic, and intuition are opposites in some absolute sense. If the final project is coherent, that coherence had its germ in the initial intuition and, likewise, intuition is ever present, like the sketch lines below the paint in the final product.

Great works of art or everyday experiences tell us that we've seen or done something right before we knew what it was we were moving towards or how we got there. A call or vocation is a big intuition. It is seeing something way ahead for yourself that, if you follow the path, comes to be validated along the way.

Bergson spoke to my experience when he wrote of this lifelong intuition of coming to know himself. Bergson said that when he was young, he was at one time this, another that; sometimes very high, sometimes very low; sometimes very mean, sometimes very good. He had a variety of interests which often seemed mutually incompatible. He constantly despaired because, though each role or temper or state or interest felt like him in part, he couldn't imagine what he was altogether. Then he came to see, nearly all at once, that all of these different and often contradictory tendencies were, in musical terms, variations: assonances, dissonances, points, counterpoints on a theme—his life theme.

Once he discerned this as variations on a theme, these differences and contradictions began to cohere, make sense—from his earliest childhood out towards his most distant future—and form the completion of his symphony. His moment of revelation simultaneously informed him that from that point on, he was the composer of his symphony, the theme of which he was just discovering. As he composed, created in tune with the theme being revealed in its variations, he would discover what his symphony sounded like—who he was. But to be "himself," he had to create what he was in process of discovering.

The Greeks spoke of this creative-centered discovery in terms of the internal relationship between fate and destiny. Fate is sometimes called determinants, or "givens." But fate reaches teleologically towards something important beyond. And in the struggles, both successes and failures (remember Oedipus was forced into discovery of his destiny by trying to escape his fate), we come to discern and realize our destiny—

which, as did Oedipus, we one way or another must "choose" to live out.

A call, in the Christian tradition, is a vocation. Where we are sent by this call is a mission. *Vocatus, Missus sum* = I am called, I am sent.

The Cultural Call and Societal Job

Let me now begin to draw out the implications I see for education in our times based on the type of experience I have just shared with you. I know I am not alone in having such experiences. My experience of a "call" has a deep strain of tradition in our culture. Because we live out the Hellenic-Christian tradition, this sense of call and mission are very much a part of our culture and are dreaming giants in its deepest reservoir of meanings and values.

This is why people who know nothing of Greek or of Christianity value two of the major vocations in our society, that of healing and that of educating. Deep down, there is something sacred about these. As sacred, it is expected that those following these vocations have a sense of mission. They are expected to be fully trustworthy and honest because they are following their call to where they were sent, which for the Christians is God's way and, for the Hellenics the path to health and truth.

In Jung's terms, these vocations and others are even more deeply grounded than in our historical culture. We recognize these calls and missions from out of our pre-historic, "racial," collective unconscious. While denying many of Jung's assumptions, the existentialists, exemplified by Sartre's "fundamental project," tend to see this oasis of transcendent meaning in the desert of absurdity obliging the paradox of "choosing to be who we are." If the Christians, Hellenics, Jungians, Bergsonians, and existentialists, as well as the average man and woman (at some level of their beings) all recognize, though rarely speak of, something like a call and mission, then how do we reconcile this widely shared belief and value with the state of education as we see it today?

For years, teachers did not unionize because they did not see their vocation as a job—that is, an avocation (Christ's carpentry was an avocation for him, not his call or mission.). But in this scientific utilitarian period, we don't cite our call or mission or even the art that educating becomes when it is realized as a great self-validating intuition. Rather, we say we are professionals.

True, there are dimensions of professionalism inherent to our field. But are we willing to settle for the classification as professional because that sounds like the best bargain we can come to in our times? Are we aware of the price we may be paying for such a compromise? People respect and trust a professional for different reasons than they trust one who has a calling. A professional will act in an expected social manner within a predefined set of ethics and standards. The artist is not predictable and dependable in these ways but is trustworthy in other ways—namely, by risking to go beyond the expected in order to make intuitions valid intuitions. The painting or original composition validates the intuition. The experience of the best of education validates the call.

The Split

I suspect that we educators couldn't trust our scientifically utilitarian-oriented society to trust us as artists. Given this double-edged timidity before challenges, we justify ourselves as professionals with official certificates of courses taken attesting to factually accrued knowledge and technical skills. Like any professional school, and unlike art schools, we who teach teachers came to convince even ourselves that we could teach the essentials of our art. Certainly we are not totally out of touch with other informal criteria. We feel some applicants to our professional education schools are good "teacher material," or "love children," or may themselves have had a good teacher who inspired them, or were inquiring researchers. But we have come less and less to ask of our novices the question asked of those who enter the priesthood: Have you been called? We have come to ask this question less and less of ourselves, while all the time sensing that educating is an art—prior to and beyond being a science or technology or even profession.

We write "mission" statements and state all the ideals engrained in all times or, more often, popular to our times and clients—and all these stated ideals ring true and good even to ourselves as they are transformed into our "objectives." Then we are asked to account for these objectives on a step-by-step basis, within each class session, over the semester of classes and over all the years our department and school will be teaching this curriculum and subject matter. We evaluate our success and vow to improve when we fall short according to one of our pre-established, shared criteria. Would an artist make such a commitment?

We assess and evaluate along the lines of each criterion according to the logical system we have devised to break it down into its elementary parts. We break down the tests we use for evaluation into even more discreet, isolating, elementary bits and apply a system of statistics to determine how meaningful (that is, significant at the .05 level) are our tests and other evaluation tools, and in order to distinguish one from another of us along one or another scale. We end up presuming to know quality via quantity. And then we form our judgments of good or bad, success or failure, on this presumption. Do we really believe quality is reducible to quantity?

That we feel we can do this bisection (or do this while doubting the quality-can-be-broken-down-into-quantity presumption) is a quirk of the scientific–utilitarian–technological times in which we live. For while our stated mission ideals include and may even be headed by our value of opening the human child to his or her fullest human potential, we do not really see how the sum of the parts equal, let alone exceed, the whole.

We certainly do not see how this value of a bisected-whole human child moving towards her or his full human potential ultimately coincides with what this utilitarian society really needs. What would our society really do with such a human? Or with millions of them? And stripped of this sense that the greater man and the greater society are, ultimately, identical goals, we find ourselves split—doubtful, militantly espousing abstract ideals or assuaging our cynicism in whatever the perquisite of body or vanity are afforded by the job. Our *raison d'etre* becomes "We love to work with children"; our personal goal is being good and acceding to the will of power or the majority opinion in the name of harmony. Anyway, we feel, at the end of our own education, disempowered. So naturally we then proceed to prepare the child for power somewhere at the end of his or her education. How easy it is to forget the power at the heart of education itself.

Our humanistic rebellion of the 1960s and 1970s was one manifestation of and reaction against this split between the call from the heart of education and the educational mission defined from without. We reacted against the actual and impending sense of conformity and depersonalization at the end of, and therefore in the process of, education—and stressed, rather, our individuality in the fuller sense than either Protestants, the demands of democracy, or Adam Smith economists understood. We reaffirmed our fuller humanness. But we humanistic rebels did so by ignoring or dismissing or reacting against those social needs and attitudes we saw as oppressive. We didn't see that the problem was not in the specific but in the anti-educational distortion into which it had been twisted.

We called for affective instead of cognitive education, because cognitive had come to mean just systematically learning what our society considered important without an insistence on an understanding of this, to borrow from Michael Polanyi, as Personal Knowledge. We became preoccupied with creativity because recognition of it previously had been so lacking.

Personally, I have a hard time distinguishing my call as either affective or cognitive; intelligence or creativity. That is why, today, I have a hard time dealing with assessments which divide educational matter into affective and cognitive components, as is our new way of "balancing things." When I look at the stories of the great artists and thinkers, I feel that they also would have a hard time responding to such assessment forms. Their genius is not measurable in either a Stanford-Binet or the Barron-Welsh scale of originality. Nor is their genius a special mark of being superhuman. Rather, it is a mark of being more human, more in touch with our common humanness.

The great visionaries are compassionate. Compassion in Eastern philosophies implies pain; for the existentialists, angst. It is from our pain that we feel and therefore see clearly (*clairvoyant*) beyond ourselves. For that is what our pain is, that recognition that our everyday ego identity is not all, nor even the most essential, contact with reality. We only come to see this reality in its fuller extended possibilities when we struggle with and, ultimately, surrender (*se rendre*) or render our narrower views to the greater ones which speak more fully to the struggles and potentials we all share. "Se rendre" is not joyless passivity or selflessness but, on the contrary, joyful passionate feeling at home with the very best in your "self." Compassion is spirit, spirit is heart; and when we come from our heart we cut through the bureaucratic realities of daily experience to the heart of life. We can see from the heart of our self to the heart of the child and settle for no education which cuts us off from our centers. We see further than most, and we are propelled by what we see. Seen this way, we can understand what Aristotle was getting to when he called touch the sense of validation. And the deeper meaning of our "touchy-feely" humanistic psychology—different but ultimately more life-engendering than the detached validation requirements of science, technology, business, and current education—hits home.

The Big and Little People

Children know this struggle between everyday "objective" reality and the heart of reality, though we rarely help them to recognize it for what it is. Much of what we, from our social–utilitarian frame of reference, call adolescent crises the French call *la crise spirituelle*. My daughter characterizes the struggle between the small and greater self in terms of the "big" and "little" people: "We little people are like marionettes through which the big people talk." To go further with her great insight, she does not need a psychology of adjustment to the little people, but a humanistic and transpersonal psychology, or a good humanities education where such things are spoken to us by poets, artists, and philosophers—which hearing invites her little self out towards her and our greater self. This is not the same as learning civics and social responsibility.

Like compassion and vision, though in a sense more personal to us, the call we receive and the path along which we are sent are intrinsically beyond us personally. Yet these link us to the beyond that implies the best for our society, perhaps even the best for our scientific society. For before science there was the vision of science, or what

Bronowski calls the greatest creative product of Western civilization. And before every certified act of science is, as Einstein realized, the creativity-engendering human intuition. Before every business there was the businessperson's vision. Is it less true that before the "great society" that politicians claim to be leading us towards, there is vision, call, and mission?

We substitute for these terms, motivation and incentives. The student is "not highly motivated." He or she will not be motivated, it is presumed, until given the right combination of positive and negative incentives. Certainly, this view is valid within its space. But nobody hearing a call or who is sent on a mission lacks "motivation"—nor does that term, "being motivated," fully describe that person's experience. We come closer when we say, "intrinsic motivation." But intrinsic motivation, as the lives of the creative indicate, rarely follows our curricular and course outlines, and is barely tapped by our complex of accountability instruments. If education does ultimately coincide with the ideals of our "mission" statements, it is likely that it will have passed through the inner and not outer path. But like intuition in our current *zeitgeist*, this path will receive none of the credit or even recognition.

Re-Empowerment

Are we ashamed to talk about this inner path, except perhaps in sequestered places and spaces such as this? Why? Is it that we do not believe that others in our current society's state of mind would understand such talk? Is it that we lack this trust in that society, even when we know that Jung calls this respect for and recognition of the vocation of Educator an archetype? Or do we secular educators feel this all sounds too religious? Or do we lack trust in ourselves? Do we doubt our own calling?

Today there is a great discrepancy between vocation and job; between mission and job description or task orientation. Perhaps much of what we call burnout or our sense of powerlessness before the social forces could be attributed to this experienced conflict. Perhaps the first step out of burnout and towards re-empowerment is to recognize this conflict as such.

Thank you for letting me join you in this space. I appreciate your hearing me out. Distinguishing your own from my personal experiences, nonetheless, do you, my fellow educators, recognize anything I have said?

CITIZENSHIP

Citizenship is one of the most important goals of the school. The card is checked (√) only where improvement is judged by the school to be necessary.

Will you please help us develop your child in the qualities listed below?

	First Report	Second Report	Third Report
Adaptability: being able to meet new situations well			
Co-operation: working and playing well with others, both children and grown-ups	√HR.		
Courtesy: being considerate of others, both children and grown-ups	√HR.		
Initiative: being able to see what needs to be done and to do it without being told	√HR.	√HR	HR.
Reliability: being dependable and truthful			
Self Control: being able to take care of one's self, to plan and direct one's own activities	√HR.	√HR	√R√

ATTENDANCE

	First Report	Second Report	Third Report	Total
No. half days absent	8	0	0	8
No. times tardy	0	0	0	0

SCHOLARSHIP

Scholarship is the child's achievement in the subjects taught in the school. Both ability and interest are important. Satisfactory progress is marked S. Unsatisfactory work is marked U. An unusually high quality of work is marked E for excellent.

SUBJECTS	First Report	Second Report	Third Report
Arithmetic	U	U	S
Art	S	S	S
English	S	S	S
Handwriting	U	U	S
Health Education	S	S	S
Literature	S	S	S
Manual Arts			
Music	S	S	S
Nature Study			
Reading	S	S	S
Social Science		S	S
Spelling notebook incomplete	U	S	S

Mike's 5th grade report card, Winterhalter Elementary School, Detroit, 1940. (Contributed by Sandrine Arons.)

Chapter 10

The Value of the Arts for Special Populations (1978)[1]

Editors' note: This was Mike's invited address to the Conference on Arts and Special Populations: A Beginning Look *in Atlanta, Georgia, March 1978.*

I feel a special kinship to this subject, Arts and Special Populations. So, this is not just another talk for me. Because the subject speaks to the core of my personal experience, I want to refer to that core. So, I will ask you to tolerate some of my autobiography. Because of some of these personal experiences, I find myself more than moderately upset by the current crusade to restore as the ground of education: reading, writing, and arithmetic—or what are worshiped as "the basics." I most certainly question that these are the basics of education, though I feel they are justly valued as one set of means towards *understanding* and full *human development*, which are what I do consider to be the basics of education. I do not think that the arts are the basic of education. But because of their nature they may in some ways provide better means to certain understanding and fulfillment than the "three Rs."

Special populations, as I am going to see these, are those which need or can benefit from something prior to, complementary to, in place of, or beyond the written word. The arts, of course, include that which depends on the written word—poetry, prose, theatre, and so forth. But when we speak of these arts, we are not speaking of acquisition of language skills, as so many see as the prime function of education today.

[1] Previously unpublished. Used with permission from Dr. Mike Arons, who also contributed the painting made by his student included at the end of this chapter.

We see in the arts a spiritual uplift, a spacing out of consciousness, a touch at the jugular of humanness.

We do not know whether the students of Socrates—indeed, whether the master himself—could read or write. More essential towards understanding than the literary skills, to Socrates, was personal sensitivity. According to Paul Goodman, the prospective student's ability *to blush* served for Socrates as an entrance tool rather than some ancient counterpart of the SAT, the GRE, or the Clep. Though he was certainly speaking of a quite different kind of understanding, Marshall McLuhan, who saw the historical limits of the written word, was in certain agreement with Socrates and did indeed help to prepare the ground during the 1960s for this conference. The psychedelic drug experience of the 1960s, ecological consciousness, indeed new consciousness—with its emphasis on self-realization, transpersonal psychology, and transcendent thinking of East and West—speaks to domains of potential human experience which are not denied to the illiterate, or guaranteed to the literate.

I have had some rather unusual educational experiences, and I would like to share some of these with you. I was functionally illiterate at the time I left high school and even when I entered college at age 27. My college entrance examination scores were well at the bottom, not only in the verbal areas but in every other area. These corresponded to my I.Q. scores, which on standardized forms never got above 80. I had spent the last few years of high school in a special class for the slow learner. Before that I had been sent to military school under the assumption that my school problems could be cured by discipline. Even before that, I had been placed in a general curriculum, centered around shop class, evidently based on the belief that students unable to succeed academically are only suited for manual labor. In fact, I failed as badly at military school and in shop as I had in the normal classroom.

I shall not stop here to speak of how I got into college ten years beyond the usual time. I would like rather to speak to the question of, "How could a person who was unable to read or write at better than a third-grade level manage to get through undergraduate school and then complete graduate studies and write a doctoral thesis in a foreign country and language?" It was not easy, but for reasons other than what one may imagine. What was required was the ability to translate understanding into language. Most of us "well-educated" understand only through language. Brahms put what I am about to say well. A music critic from the newspaper asked him to play his new composition. "It is fine," commented the critic. "But what are you trying to say in that music?" "Oh," exclaimed Brahms, "You didn't understand?" So he played the music again. I believe that that great master of the English language, Winston Churchill, was also saying something close to what I am about to say when as a child he handed in a blank sheet as his entrance exam to Harrow. "What does this mean?" cried the headmaster. "Sir," explained Churchill, "You asked me what *you* wanted to know, but you did not ask me what *I* knew."

In both cases, there was a resistance to use the language inappropriately. In the case of Brahms, he was suggesting that whatever was being said was better expressed in music; a discursive language would reduce or deform the reality. In the case of Churchill, he was saying that language was a part of him—like his sweat, his thoughts. Attempts to design language to express where he was were fine but that he could not use it to express that which was alien to him. Premature use of language is also inappropriate. We have all felt at times that in some way we wear long trousers before we grow into them. We listen to children who have acquired language skills but hear nothing of them through these, or when they grow up we hear a relatively good use of language but to express only common ideas. My own school experiences were the reverse of this. I could understand no language until I could first understand existentially what was being said. Then I would have to struggle to put this understanding into a conventional form. So in college I would read rather difficult texts—Plato, Hegel, Swift, Dostoevsky—and not really understand more than a few words in a paragraph. It would sometimes take me days to get through a few pages, and even then, I could not pass a reading test on what I had read. Since I could not understand the words which were alien to me, I had to understand the person who wrote these—enter his or her world by discovering it already there in myself. This I would do through a self-evolved form of meditation. Once I understood the frame of reference, the world of truth from within which the author was coming, the rest would follow; slowly at first, and then in a lightening array of insights the language would become clear—what it meant; why the author chose this way, rather than that, of putting it; the feel of the language, the images the author was grasping for; and, yes, the limits to language itself. For I could then understand far more than what the author could possibly have written on the subject. I was in the creative world, a creative soul among creative souls.

I can offer a specific example to you which serves not only to indicate how I came to understand writers whose words I could not initially read but also point to what I was doing in those classes in elementary and high school while others were learning reading, writing, math, history, and so forth. When I was around eleven, a social studies class discussion had turned to the subject of slave trade in the South. The teacher, and the class, quickly moved on, but I found myself fixed on a "fantasy"—which through doodling enumerable variations of the theme kept me preoccupied for months. This is its essence: A man purchased a slave. The slave worked the fields and, hence, developed stronger muscles. The master could relax, and he ate and got softer and fatter. As he did less for himself, he required more from his slave until the point when the slave could no longer stand the burden and thought of what before had been unthinkable: *revolt*. By this time, the soft master was vulnerable as he had not been when he purchased the slave, and the revolt succeeded. When we read Hegel in philosophy, I quickly recognized this simple but essential paradigm of the Hegelian dialectic. I understood the dialectic with no trouble and could easily think within that framework.

The next thing that I am going to say about this particular example is more important than the observation of how I had already dwelt on a Hegelian paradigm at age eleven. Having recognized this paradigm of Hegel, I entered into his world, but also the entire world of philosophy. In that world, I recognized in myself Plato, Spinoza, Descartes, Kant, and Husserl. Certainly, I did not recognize elaborate philosophies but the frame of reference within which their thinking made sense. Likewise, I was able to enter the world of poets—Keats and Yeats and Auden and Dryden and Emerson. They were not speaking to me through some language. They were speaking with me and I could understand and admire the language they chose but could also recognize some limitations, as we in psychology recognize the limits of Freud today while all the time admiring his brilliant treatise.

Indeed, the real talent or skill of the genius is to give form, through language or art or whatever, to the insight. The *insight*—that, I believe, is our birthright. Alas, our education makes us stand on the other end of language—assuming language to be the only vehicle through which insight can be gained—and in this belief, I feel, it actually creates a wall of separation between many children and the insights. They are asked to master the language forms before they are asked to get in touch with what may be understood by more appropriate means. The illiterate is not barred from the gates of heaven. Joan of Arc was not barred from her visions by illiteracy.

What of art, then? In our current technological–scientific frame of reference, art is pre-scientific. For Auguste Comte and the positivism he fathered, the human mind in its progressive reach for clarity and objectivity outgrows the artistic consciousness, just as the artistic consciousness was an outgrowth of religion and myth. We find in both Freud and Piaget psychological versions of this progressive development from the subjective towards the objective—from the irrational instinctual drives to ego control, from games of fantasy to games of logic and rules. By laying out reality (historical or psychological) as linearly progressive, art (as expression of the subjective), becomes merely a pastime of the modern age. The serious and important mission is now in the scientific. The language itself is learned scientifically, objectively. But is linearity the best or only way of conceiving of human progress? Or is the metaphor of linear progress merely a product of our current technological mind?

In technology, we do clearly distinguish stages of progress by indicating by clear criteria that the latest model is an improvement over an antecedent one. TX-2 is better than TX-1 because of longer wingspan, greater speed, increased maneuverability, etc. *But what of art?* Can we say that Impressionism is an improvement over Flemish art and that this is an improvement over cave drawing? Surely, in the case of art the same statements as in technology do not hold. We can say only that Impressionism is different from the art of the Flemish masters. Yet does this mean that we cannot speak of progress in the arts? Not only can the arts progress technically, but each new form of art opens our consciousness to the universe in a different way. Art expands our awareness without one form superseding and rendering obsolete the previous ones.

So there does exist a form of progress which is not linear. Indeed, modern phenomenology and much Eastern philosophy is based on a voyage through and around consciousness which *moves always back towards its source*. We can put this differently and speak of "spacing out of consciousness." By contrast, much of our modern emphasis is on thinking that is convergent—outgrowing, as we said, the subjective in ourselves and hastening to scrap that which is obsolete in the world of objects as we stretch towards the correct. But what is the most correct part of a painting? Surely, the background is not to be scrapped because our eyes more easily fix on the foreground. There is no foreground without a background. In music, is it the purpose of the conductor to arrive with the greatest speed possible at the end of the composition?

Art—as painting, music, or metaphor—does not, in the subject, render everything obsolete save the intelligence. *We* are called upon as a whole in art, just as the object calls us to *its* whole being. And yet art is not without its criteria of correctness. If there is a point at which our consciousness smiles and locks in it art, it is there where the human soul feels right—heightened—as we are pulled beyond the immediate to the universal, beyond ourselves to an experience shareable with others in our space.

Nothing is left the same—our senses, our feelings, or our intelligence. Each has grown by the feast. We are deepened and prepared for insights at another level. So the archetype or gestalt form is not a once-and-for-all experience, but we are prepared by each to encounter another level of correctness. For instance, as children we may share the insight in *Gulliver's Travels* of little and big men. Although the book has not changed over the years, at 21 we are disposed to discover more through and beyond the initial insight. Indeed, at best, we come to see ourselves as a work of art, recognizing our common stages of passage through life. Henri Bergson likens consciousness to a musical composition. We recognize at some point the threads of our theme of life through the variations, and choose then to play out our symphony as fully as possible. *We choose to be what we are*—a convergence of creativity and discovery, choice, and destiny.

In speaking of those who potentially have these experiences, are we really speaking of a small and special population, an elite group? Perhaps. Yet consider that the archetypes of Jung are characterized by their universality—as are the forms of Plato and those of the gestaltists, which are not reserved for special groups but for all of us. The master–slave relationship of Hegel is archetypical. If these universal forms are inaccessible to most in our modern education factories, we must then see its human products as the special population which is out of touch with that which is inherently human, even if this group constitutes the large majority of us.

I wonder sometimes at the way we handle those whom we do call our "special populations"—among them the behavior disorders, the dyslexics, the autistic, the retarded, and a variety of racial and ethnic groups. From our lofty perch in modern reason, we assume that if these persons cannot function adaptively, they most certainly cannot operate at the so-called higher human planes. Note how we make these planes of universal understanding "special." We are charged with using special methods (special education) towards the sole aim of functional adaptation. Even the arts—music, dance, play, and paint—are used instrumentally, as means to get the pill of functional adaptability down the child's gullet, not for their own sake. We rarely stretch our own search to find the artist in the child.

Nine years ago, a young student was sent to me by the college reading clinic. She could neither read nor write and it was certain she could not remain in school. She was sent to psychology because we had a class called *Personal Relationships* which primarily involved group encounters and discussion rather than reading or papers. I tested the young lady myself and found, indeed, that she could only make out a few words in every paragraph. Her writing was poorer than her reading. She spent the quarter in the *Personal Relationships* class, and it became evident that her own insights ran deeper than those of the other students. She saw well beyond the tangible details to the hidden obvious. She was encouraged to express herself in art during the class.

The next year she joined the art department, and I have here a painting she exhibited at the end of the year. She received a scholarship to an art school abroad. I have not seen her since. She is one of those people, however, that I have always known very well.

Identifying information has been removed by the editors.

Chapter 11

The Politics of Education, A Critical Tribute: From the Heart of Rogers to the Heart of Education (1991)[1]

David Ryback, then our coordinator of educational psychology, came into my office one day to gleefully announce that Carl Rogers had agreed to be our guest speaker for the Second National Conference on Humanistic Education. Rogers' talk was given on April 24, 1975 here at West Georgia in the School of Education where a year earlier the organization had begun. Bright days for humanistic education seemed just ahead.

Two years after Rogers' talk, West Georgia's School of Education was "reorganized." The dean, who in 1968, via psychology, had brought the humanistic orientation to the college had "resigned." The psychology department was forcibly split. One part, kicking and screaming, was shipped off to Arts and Sciences where, after years of struggle, it has rebounded to prosper on its own. Little of vital significance remains of a humanistic influence in the West Georgia School of Education.

Nationwide, about that time, other significant humanistic inroads into education institutions such as that at Boston College found themselves in trouble. Previously prospering humanistic psychology programs around the nation, many cited by Rogers in that 1975 talk as

[1] Arons, M. (1991). The politics of education, a critical tribute: From the heart of Rogers to the heart of education. *Journal of Humanistic Education, 15*, 6–17. | Copyright © 1991 by the Association for Humanistic Education. Adapted with permission from Dr. Tracy Cross (editor of the volume of the *Journal of Humanistic Education* in which this paper originally appeared) and from Dr. Anne Richards (former executive officer of the Association for Humanistic Education).

models of the "coming" positive shift in values, began experiencing troubles of their own. The social and political winds in this country had radically shifted. Soon, it was not just humanistic, but all of American education that found itself in crisis.

Politics of Education and the Socio-Political Context

I have been asked to write this paper as a reflection on Carl Rogers' talk here in 1975. I cannot help but view his thoughts in the shadow of humanistic education's unhappy fortunes during the years following that talk—but also in the more optimistic light of the future prospects for the humanistic paradigm of education. I revisit this paper with a decade and a half of hindsight. And so I feel required not only to revisit but to revise or attempt to extend the core of Rogers' thinking that day to what I feel has always been the core of the broader humanistic paradigm in education. This is a core which I feel speaks to the unique mission of education at large and can and must be found even through that which Rogers "the politician" opposed.

In 1975, Rogers was introducing to educators ideas which largely had taken root in psychology and philosophy. These were ideas new to many educators and he spoke to them in functionalistic terms, as indicated by his choice of the political idiom—i.e., how could these approaches do better for the teacher than those which were then being practiced? As with all new ideas, in the interest of their clear articulation, Rogers rhetorically set up clear oppositions—i.e., the new or person-centered politics vs. the old or traditional-centered politics of education. The term "traditional" was implicitly defined only by what he opposed. If humanistic psychology is to have a significant future, I think it is now necessary to broaden the politics and move beyond the oppositions. Educators today—maligned from without, doubtful within—are seeking their soul. And I think that humanistic education speaks to that soul. But it does so only if it speaks to the soul of education, and by finding and recognizing in itself what is good and valuable in that which it opposed.

Rogers' Politics of Education:
Person-Centered vs. Tradition-Centered

The topic Rogers chose to discuss at West Georgia was the politics of education. By this, he did not mean "political parties" or "government organizations." His talk seventeen years ago focused on "politics" as used when we say, "the politics of the family" or the "politics of psychotherapy" or "sexual politics." He set out to present "as clearly as I can two sharply differing approaches to education" and the different politics which are implicit to each approach. He added, "In this present-day sense, I believe the word 'politics' has to do with power or control in interpersonal relationships and the extent to which persons strive to gain such power...or to relinquish it."

Rogers looked at the characteristics of these two modes of education. Both he saw as existing on a continuum. Yet for polemical purposes, he chose to deal with these almost dichotomously: the "traditional" approach at one end of the scale and a "person-centered" approach at the other. He wrote, "I think every educational effort, and every educator, can be located somewhere on this scale."

Traditional Education
On the traditional side, he listed: (a) the teacher as possessor of knowledge; the student, the expected recipient; (b) as the vehicle for evaluation, examinations; (c) the teacher as possessor of power, the student as one who obeys; (d) rule by authority is accepted policy in the classroom with (e) trust being at a minimum; (f) the belief that the students are best governed by being kept in an intermittent or constant state of fear; (g) democracy and its values are ignored and scorned in practice; and (h) there is no place for the whole person in the educational system, only for his/her intellect.

Person-Centered Education
At the person-centered end of the scale, Rogers established, first, a very important pre-condition: that the person who is perceived as an authority figure in the (educational) situation be sufficiently secure

within himself and his relationship to others that he experiences an essential trust in the capacity of others to think and learn for themselves. Then, presuming the first condition is met, that the facilitative person share with the others—students and possibly also parents or community members—the responsibility for the learning process. Third, that the facilitator provide learning resources—these from within himself and his own experience as well as from books or materials or community experiences. Fourth, that the student develop their own program of learning, alone or in cooperation with others. Fifth, that a facilitative learning climate be provided. Sixth, that the focus be not on the content of learning alone—which, while significant, falls into secondary place—but on fostering the continuing process of learning. Seventh, that the discipline necessary to reach the students' goals is self-discipline. Eighth, that evaluation of extent and significance of the student's learning be made primarily by the learner. Finally, ninth, Rogers asserted the judgment that in this growth-promoting climate, the learning tends to be deeper, proceeds at a more rapid rate, and is more pervasive in the life and behavior of the student than learning acquired in the traditional classroom.

Since Rogers' Talk: Conservative Reactions

If we begin with this last judgment and promise, in principle, there should be no contradiction between the objectives of the kind of educational politics proposed by Rogers in the classroom and the socio-political attitude in our nation, which judges its own current education to be in an acute state of crisis. Who would deny the desire to see "more depth in learning which takes place at an increased pace and which is more pervasive in the life and behavior of the student?" But that raises a troubling issue: If humanistic education could have delivered on this promise, even in small experimental settings, why has this orientation not been embraced rather than rebuffed to date?

Why the Failure to Date?

Even acknowledging that humanistic values have made "infrastructural" inroads into education via some now well-known writings of Rogers, Maslow, Combs, and other humanistic educators, to date, its impact on education as a whole has been marginal. I think this failure is partially due to the polarized identification of humanistic psychology and education uniquely with the affective and personal interests *versus* the cognitive and social interests normally attributed to "traditional" approaches, identification of the idea of "experiential" with techniques and approaches, as well as its "chaotic," "undisciplined" appearance. I would like, below, to look more closely at these apparent oppositions, identifications, and appearances, which Rogers himself helped to foster.

Is it a simple matter that humanistic education has not and cannot fulfill its promises? I would like to propose below that its promise has been fulfilled over and over again in what we have always recognized as the "best of education." That when we find that "best" in education, even in and through its current oppositions, we will find humanistic education at its heart.

Is humanistic education too radical for our times and culture? Below I would like to argue that there is nothing more American than this approach in the sense that it has the potential to restore, in new forms, the best of a quality education reserved in Europe, the East, and elsewhere for an elite within an American tradition which gave to the world the lived reality of a universal education. It is radical in the sense that it represents the next major, the next quality step forward, in that universalizing process.

In our current educational context, has the humanistic approach had a fair chance to deliver on the promises Rogers makes for it? I think a good case can be made that it has not had this fair chance, and this is due, partially, to a shifting and generally anti-humanistic socio-political climate. I would like to start by summarizing some of these socio-political oppositions and, later, attempt to show why real and significant differences do exist between humanistic education and constituencies that oppose it—and that in more ways than currently realized, these oppositions are more apparent than real.

Convergence of Socio-Political Forces

Let me start with a broad look at that socio-political climate as it pertains directly to education. There's little doubt that it has been anything but friendly to humanistic education. Ostensibly, the anti-humanistic *zeitgeist* of the late 1970s took root and was justified in the eyes of many educators and the public at large by: (a) a noted decline in standardized test scores (SAT), (b) a documented increase in illiteracy even among high school graduates, and (c) a perceived gap between what the student learns and what he/she needs to function in an increasingly complex and more technologically dependent society. At a minimum, humanistic education seemed inappropriate to cope with these perceived problems; at a maximum, this orientation was blamed for them.

The anti-humanistic trend emerged around a growing public consensus that the bases for these poor results and prospects were quite contrary to Rogers' assessment: abandonment of traditional education, which was equated with abandonment of "the basics"; lack of discipline, decline of authority; dissipation of a uniform sense of core knowledge; discontinuation of the inculcation of traditional (Christian and/or Western or American values); and disregard for the teaching of subject matter. In a word, students were viewed as being indulged in their "narcissistic" pursuits to the detriment of cognitive, technological, vocational, societal, and cultural interests. And this perceived indulgence as well as the tendency towards "narcissism" was, by a growing coalition of "conservative" forces within the nation, being associated with humanistic psychology and education and viewed as an offshoot of historical "liberalism."

More Specific Reactions: Religious Right

Students, and then teachers, were being seen as having been trusted too much—not, as Rogers had been insisting, too little. Humanistic education, quite unjustifiably, was often confused with secular humanism; was seen as a movement which replaced absolute (read, religious) with relative values; was explicitly or implicitly blamed for all these perceived educational failures by the Religious Right, a constituency whose views came to have heavy sway in the formation of the politics (in the broad and narrow senses) of the 1980s. The theoretical villains were designated as the likes of Freud, Dewey, Spock, and others in the "liberal," "wimpy," Rogerian lineage of thinking.

Economic Right

From another quarter which strongly influenced the politics of the times came the cry for increased competitiveness and public accountability in education to counter all the administrative and fiscal "looseness," a call which paralleled at the national level the new focusing on business and "supply side" economics. The "hard-nosed" business approach to education, it was seen, would also straighten out the "educational mess" via application of efficient management and accountability methods. This new economics-centered right also called for focus on vocationism over idealism and on the goal-directed instrumental learning over intrinsic learning. The promise of this shift was economic success and, consequently, for an increasingly large number of students, the business schools replaced the schools of education and arts and sciences as the "place to be."

Cultural Right

Still another wing of the new conservative politics affecting education, centered on cultural homogenization over cultural diversification—whether in the form of linguistically integrating immigrants or native minorities or in the form of Bloom's insistence that all education be centered on the classics of Western Civilization. This particular conservative trend was inconsistently supported by conservatives who, in other areas, notably economic, generally push for decentralization and diversity—and its centralized theme has culminated in the President's recent proposal for national educational standards, norms, and testing.

Humanistic Empowerment and Empowerment
of Education at its Heart

All these socio-political reactions which ostensibly militated against humanistic education in general and Roger's proposed "new educational politics" in particular could be easily chalked up to a simple shift from left to right in the nation's ideological and political attitudes. Such an attribution, while broadly accurate, is oversimplistic—and, if taken without further inquiry, could leave us with the false hope that an historically predictable shift in the other direction, from right to left, would reestablish a temporarily aborted humanistic movement and, thereby, resolve many of our educational problems.

This hope alone is, in my view, unjustified. First of all, both "liberal" and "conservative" are simple convenient rubrics which attempt to describe what are actually very different, shifting, and even alternating tendencies at any given period—and neither of these political rubrics, even in our times, is pure friend or foe. For instance, much of what is today called conservative embraces basic themes which are supported by humanistic psychology and education; that is, "self-help." Reciprocally, humanistic psychology and education have always contained dimensions which have been viewed, traditionally, in this country, as both "liberal" and "conservative"—e.g., stress on the individual or freedom. But beyond these bases, such a hope that success would be assured for humanistic education on the coattails of a resurging liberal *zeitgeist* is for a more basic reason unfounded and dangerous if we humanistic educators have learned nothing from our own failures to date.

In emphasizing the "person" and the "self," "approach" or "techniques" as well as the paradigm's own newness historically, humanistic psychologists and educators have not significantly, or loudly enough, addressed the unique value placed on education in all cultures and at all times. That which, like healing, made it an almost sacred call and mission for even faith-centered Christians as well as for rationalists of the Hellenic and Enlightenment periods. How does a humanistic paradigm speak to that call, which draws from a human source and then goes beyond and, when appropriate, resists ideological or political shifts in attitude and public power?

In this, the basic charge of education holds a status not dissimilar to art. Whatever was successful in the traditional educations of Europe persisted under church dominance, monarchies, revolutions of various kinds, and Fascist, Socialist, and Communist regimes which alternatively came into power. Out of the same educational systems came voices supporting and opposing each or all of these ideological or political positions. It is not intrinsically tied to any of these or to any economic system. Education has its own *source of power* and socio-cultural utility, and Rogers is right to speak to this *unique power* in and on its own terms when he distinguishes the politics of education from politics in general. Yet Rogers never really speaks directly and explicitly to that charge. On the contrary, he justifies person-centered education on social-utility grounds—i.e., "it works better."

One cannot doubt that Rogers personally knew what that unique intrinsic educational charge is. Yet at the end of his West Georgia talk, he left that view dangling ambiguously, almost apologetically, when he stated that better, faster, and more pervasive learning occurs in a "growth-promoting atmosphere." He put the cart before the horse. Here, he indulges a utilitarian—method or means—bias, implying the "growth-promoting atmosphere" as an instrumental technique, approach, method, or pedagogy. That is what sells these days.

He might better have summed up his proposal for a new educational politics on more radical grounds: that the power he speaks to as applied in education has the mutually enhancing capacity of making learning easier and better, and *reciprocally*, of more effectively fulfilling the charge of the educator *which at heart* is to foster, encourage, aid, and abet growth and understanding in the individual, society, culture—and these for greater human enlightenment and towards ultimate betterment of the human race. That, in my view, would have put the right (though not necessarily the most readily grasped) issue at center stage. For that charge is the special and unique source of educational power. It is also the source of personal empowerment and the power inherent in the unique charge of education, which needs deeper and further exploration if this humanistic paradigm is not to be just another fad.

That such a radical, foundational and bold defense of education's basic charge was not made more centrally and explicitly by a man as bold as Rogers says more, in my view, than anything else about where the real problems of education currently lie in America. Why do we educators, why does the American public during our period need such utilitarian rationalizations? Are we really afraid to look directly into the potential—scary and exhilarating as it is—of the personal power which Rogers alludes to? I do not believe that Rogers retreated from this more basic issue because of cowardice or even timidity. But, more discouraging, was the fact that Rogers was being Rogers and starting where he felt his audience was. And if, as I suspect, he was right in this assessment of his audience, this suggests that educators are, themselves—let us not talk about the public at large—very far from an understanding of that unique educational source of power.

Like Maslow—and in principle, all humanistic psychologists and educators—Rogers knows that the power he finds in the person is the same power which gives education its legitimate, unique, unconditional, universal basis and justification. Such a power, opened and fostered in the individual or in the educational setting, rapidly translates into questions about the society and times in the context of what it fully means to be human. That personal internal power opened raises questions of possibility: *What can I and we be and do?* It raises questions of value: *What is important?* It raises questions of proportion and perspective: *How can contradictory tendencies be integrated and optimized?* Above all, such a personal power opened and fostered brings about the recognition that others have this power. To speak to others, including the child, as an idiot, object, consumer, commodity, conditioned animal, helpless victim, innocent, genetic clone, or mere student or pupil is at best disingenuous and at worst is intentionally unauthentic, given that the conscious person knows better. I see a conflict (at least an ostensible one which cries out for debating) between the pedagogy of "starting with people as they are" and one which speaks forcefully, directly, and respectfully to the *best* in a person, which he or she may not yet have recognized.

"Traditional" Revisited

"Person-Centered"

In the early 1980s, I, a poet and an artist, undertook a research project. We came to call it "the Hidden Artist." Among other "handicapped" (what we called Special Populations) groups we engaged, we dealt with a group of acutely retarded individuals. Typically, these individuals were being treated at best paternalistically, at worst as if they were subjects in a conditioning experiment. By contrast, the artists I worked with treated these individuals as fellow artists, presuming abilities which neither they nor others could ever have imagined were theirs. They spoke directly and respectfully to the presumed hidden artist in these people, and the artist in these people responded. By the time the projects were completed, these life residents of the Georgia Retardation Center had produced very clever and humorous poetry, art, and a musical production—all of which was later featured on Atlanta television.

My own interest in the potentials of the retarded was not academic. Classified "retarded" myself, I had spent several years in special classes of our public schools. After years of menial jobs, such as factory work in Detroit, I began as a freshman in college at age 27. Although basically illiterate, I was prompted to go to college by music—classical music— which spoke to a part of me I had never before known. Then, at college, by great literature which spoke to another part of me I had never before known. Then by teachers, often authoritarian and via the lecture system, who spoke way above my head, background, and preparation but again, who spoke to a part of me I was only to discover and fully develop when this part of myself was taken as a given and was addressed directly and respectfully. In other words, much of what Rogers classes as "traditional" education was for me fully "person-centered" if we mean that it successfully spoke to the fuller person in me that I was yet to discover.

I mention these personal experiences not as a repudiation of Rogers or even as an argument against starting with people, students, clients, or anybody "where they are." And certainly, Rogers' ultimate objectives were no different from those I'd like to look at—opening of the fully empowered person. And the differences in approach, gradualism versus direct challenge, are more apparent than actual. I believe this direct challenge is implicit to Rogers' views but remains implicit to the degree that the oppositions he sets up in his talk remain unreconciled. I think these need to be reconciled if we as humanistic educators are to again gain credence and if we as educators are again to speak from the empowering center of our educational mission to the empowering center of the students.

Lecture-Examination
Rogers places what he calls the "traditional" approach to educational politics at one end, and his person-centered approach at the other end of a continuum. But to place the apparent absolutism of this opposition into question, let me ask, for example: Are the vehicle of "lecture" and the employment of "examinations" always the central elements of a traditional and, therefore, non-person-empowering education? We have all, I presume, attended lectures which have radically challenged us to new questions and ways of understanding and some have even transformed our lives. I once chanced to sit in on a lecture by Victor Frankl which had precisely this latter effect on me. During one examination in an English literature course, as I struggled with my first superficial—i.e., internally non-coherent—understanding of Keats' *Ode to a Grecian Urn*, the poem all of a sudden opened up and revealed both its and my own internal struggle with the matter of time and timelessness, or the philosophical issue of "the absolute and the relative." I use this poem frequently today in my psychology classes. Because I have become so intimate with it, that intimacy and the power that poem releases are transmitted with relative ease to many of my students and is often a transformative experience for them as it was for me. This is an example of how the "best in me," through a poem which comes from "the best in the poet," speaks to "the best in a student."

In fairness to Rogers, he does not absolutely deny the value of these experiences but specifically derides lectures and examinations when these and other verbal vehicles are a *major* means of conveying "knowledge." And there can be little doubt that many if not most lectures and examinations are as sterile as Rogers indicates. But it seems to me that this issue can be better looked at with a different emphasis. Regardless of the form—lecture, examination, or experiential exercise—the crucial factor seems to be, *where* is the person who lectures or who writes the examination *coming from*? And to *which* dimension of the personhood of the student is he or she *speaking*?

Knowledge

This brings up the question of "knowledge" which is, according to Rogers, presumably imparted in the traditional education from "giver" to "receiver." It was not knowledge I received from Frankl or knowledge I discovered in Keats. In both cases I discovered—better put, recognized—something highly significant to and about me and the world which I did not previously appreciate was even an issue. The consequence was a great sense of opening, of freedom, of possibility— even if, as with the darkness of human nature which Frankl imparted, what was conveyed as subject matter was grim and disillusioning. I might add that Frankl and, perhaps Keats, were highly "knowledgeable" about the subjects they treated. Those who know Frankl know he can come across as dogmatic in his certitudes. Yet, neither Keats nor Frankl spoke to me or their audiences from the mere perspective of their superior knowledge. There was something far more that was being spoken and heard which even the air of dogmatic certitude could not turn off.

Art

The "where" the lecturer or examiner is coming from and the "to which" dimension of the person he or she is speaking factors go hand-in-hand with another essential related to knowledge and the subject matter. This is the art of teaching. I might better say the art of speaking to the best in the other, whether or not that other initially recognizes that best in him or herself. Earlier, I likened education to art. But in some ways, at their best, these are identical. The artist goes beyond the "knowledge" he or she has to impart—beyond, even while through, the subject matter. Socrates realized it was not the specifics which he debated that were essential but, rather, the reaching through these with particular art to be a dimension of our shared humanness that glimpsed the whole and even and especially the whole-revealing process within ourselves. For Socrates and the schools which followed him, this inner capacity was the ability to "see" principles "behind" or "beyond"— better put, *in*—facts. Aristotle and most of his followers stressing experience recognized, nonetheless, that all was not said when an empirical fact had spoken. But they saw in sense experience, as the artist does, the potential opening through which what is seen in the eyes and heard with the ears cannot be fully defined or ever fully exhausted in language. In the classroom, we are not teaching "the battle of Marignano, which took place in 1515," or specifically "where Toledo, Ohio is located." We are trying to open in the student an internal "sense of" history, a "sense of" geography, a "sense of" relative meanings from which "sense of" comes the continued desire to learn and open the learning process that Rogers speaks of. The art of teaching, like any other art, is to use language or any other form in such a way as to open and reveal the unsayable. But the unsayable which the student comes to recognize in the best of him or herself: that space from which learning and questioning become intrinsic.

Given this analogy, nay identity, I draw between good teacher and artist, Rogers's (1969) pejorative attribution of the use of verbal instruction to the "traditional"—which he contrasted with the "person-centered"—seems to me misleading. Rather, the issue might better be put: *How effective, verbally or non-verbally centered, in touching non-verbalizable dimensions of experience, is any teaching approach?* That art continues to the next stage: *How can the student best articulate that ultimately inarticulable?* We are now speaking of the art of language or any other form of expression. Both Rogers and Maslow understood what the Gnostics of the second century knew, that evolving insight comes from an expressive process or intrinsic motivation rather than from a "coping process" or extrinsic motivation.

Power Relationship

All the above leads me to question Rogers' antinomy between a teacher who is the "possessor of power" and a student who "obeys." I think we all know from our daily teaching experiences what Rogers means by this. But this clear-cut opposition invites a more careful and subtle look, especially if there is agreement on the mission of education as one of empowering the student.

Let me put this in the most egalitarian (read, obnoxious) terms possible to help make the point. The trust issue which I will come to in a moment, works both ways. Hegel was neither the first nor last to recognize in what he characterized as the "master–slave" relationship not only the power opened but also the advantage gained by one who chooses to be a "slave" to the "master" he "obeys." A readiness to learn, to open up, requires a letting go, a receptivity, a trust in the other, both as a person who will not exploit his role as "master" and in the belief that the other holds a superiority in certain desirable areas such as understanding or wisdom. Both inequality and struggle are very much a part of this "master–slave" relationship. The initial power of the to-be "slave" is to recognize that superiority in the to-be "master," then to be sufficiently confident in him or herself to voluntarily let go of an abstract sense of "equality" which is belied by a concrete (realistic) recognition of "inequality." And then to trust oneself, as the creative individual does in Kris' sense of "regressing in the service of ego," and open a trusting, almost childlike relationship with the recognized "mentor," which leads through struggle—in the Socratic or psychoanalytic sense—to the ultimate equality of the former "master" and "slave" in mutually earned insight. I say "almost childlike" because this receptivity only "makes space" for an internal activity of reaching for something which is new, yet recognizable: meaningful.

Rogers, of course, recognizes the need for mutual reciprocal trust which he so obviously nurtures in his counseling relationships. He also realizes, as most therapists do, that gaining understanding in a meaningful and transformative way is not easy. What I feel he has not adequately emphasized as regards education is the recognition that some people do have much to offer in the way of knowledge, insight, and understanding which can better or at least sometimes be better offered by a temporary one-sided receptive attitude on the part of the person lacking these valued attributes.

I have watched the enormous amount of learning—the entire French language as one example, which my daughter gained from her French grandmother by allowing herself to open to a receptive state before her grandmother's recognized authority. Her grandmother had been a teacher in the traditional French public school system and her approach, at least on the surface, was anything but Rogerian. She taught in a single-minded, single-method manner and with a tone of stringent authority. But she taught from a love of what she taught and a love for the person she was teaching. Maybe, more accurately put, a love for the learning experience which she was helping to generate: that which I've called the unique and universal power of education. My daughter, at home a "know everything," recognized "where" her grandmother was coming from—no nonsense sternness, and all—and "let go" to her methods no matter how ostensibly authoritarian these were.

I say "ostensibly" authoritarian. I have come to appreciate that what appears to be authoritarian, the apparent claim of superiority which imposes itself on others as authoritative power, may actually be something else—i.e., the insistence that the other, the "receiver" of knowledge, not cop out on him or herself. I was always struck by the fact that my French wife treated my daughter, even as a baby, as if she was a fully-grown, cognizant, and responsible human being. She would literally debate with my daughter in the crib. With an air, all the facial looks and bodily gestures, of impatience, even anger, she would turn from her and say, "*C'est ton choix*" ("It's your choice")—just the same as she would often say this to me when I disagreed or didn't do something according to her desires.

I came to realize that in the French culture, and in fact in all the Latin cultures, there exists a lived concept of "*libre arbitre*" (free chooser), which is presumed present at birth in everyone. Something like this notion of a "responsible" being co-existing with innocence in the tot is proposed by the Adlerians, such as Dreikurs (1987), and was noted in many "primitive" cultures which D. Lee (1959) studied. It has a rough parallel in the theories of some post-Freudians, who see at birth if not in the womb an "ego" already coexisting with "id." To see things this way has enormous implications for American education and for its current concern with self-esteem.

As a graduate student in France, I noticed a significant difference between how my fellow French students treated their professors—and, reciprocally, how the professors treated them—and that relationship as I had observed it in the United States. On the one hand, the professor there was accorded much greater esteem and respect simply for the intellectual superiority his profession automatically implied. A student never called a professor by his first name, or the reverse, and always approached him or her—considered a good or popular teacher or not—with obvious respect. On the other hand, I sensed a kind of implicit equality—a mutual self-esteem—which guided the relationship between student and professor at the human level. As humans, we are all "*libre arbitres*."

This fundamental sense of human equality—this basic esteem of a self which is neither earned nor learned but which was implicitly recognized and grounded all relationships, I think—made it easier for the student to accept the "slave" role in the educational sphere. It was, for me, a strange combination to see a professor as both superior and, at the same time, see the student being treated by him as a colleague in a common search for knowledge, insight, and understanding. These two roles—one inferior, the other superior—come together at that level. Far from being incompatible, they serve the dual value of stretching out the student to the challenge of greater understanding while simultaneously respecting and fully valuing the mutual and equal humanness of both parties in the educational match. Put differently, the student is treated as a whole in the human sense (as my wife treated my daughter from birth) at the same time as he or she is treated as incomplete in the educational sense. So often among my students in this country, I see that to question ideas is for them the equivalent of questioning their very being. So, like anything "religious," the tendency is to stay away from them. This, I think, is due to a lack of capacity to separate one's self from the world of ideas. Because the self is nothing but the ideas "it holds," including the idea of itself.

Democracy and Freedom

This issue of authority raises another which Rogers speaks to as differentiating the "traditional" from the "person-centered" politics: the issue of democracy. Both Einstein and I had the right to one vote in our general elections. I cherish this sense of civic equality. I wouldn't have it any other way for local and national elections. However, I hope that the scientific community, particularly the community of physical scientists, does not give me equal voting rights with Einstein in deciding what is of current significance in the field. Having said that, I am delighted that physical scientists did not decide for me what curriculum I should follow in my undergraduate studies and, personally, I was and remain upset that I was *de facto* barred from taking an astronomy course as an undergraduate because the science faculty at my university had set up so many preclusive requirements and prerequisites. This tension between elitism and democracy needs to remain a tension and not be simplistically reconciled to the definitive advantage of one or the other side.

The issue of democracy raises the issue of freedom. No philosophical position over the past century has put as much stress on freedom as has humanistic psychology and education. The contemporary equivalent of "free will" was (against the numerous determinisms to which the human has been reduced by the rationalistic mindset) brought back into full force of awareness by the existentialists, who had so much influence on the development of this humanistic movement. Yet, to speak of existential "free choice" does not suggest that all choices are good or wise; nor, even more significantly, does this mean that there is an exact correlation between existential freedom and that accorded by the Rights of Man philosophies of the Age of Enlightenment. Both Read and Fromm have distinguished two types of freedom.

One of these forms of freedom, which Read would call "liberty," is better suited to the kind of "freedom" guaranteed in the so-called Four Freedoms—whereby no individual can be restrained from climbing a podium and speaking his or her piece, entering a church of his or her choice, disseminating in writing what he or she pleases, and associating with whom he or she wishes. But no government can guarantee, even if it wished to, that what is said on that podium will be insightful, what is experienced in that church will be inspiring, what is written will speak any—let alone the most profound—truths, or that the choice of associates will be wise or meaningful. There is a difference, in Fromm's (1941) terms, between "freedom from" (e.g., from lack of constraints, which a government can guarantee), which Read calls liberty, and "freedom for," which Read calls freedom, that speaks more to authenticity and inner opening or enlightenment.

We educators are dealing with both of these and must realize that while ideally these two can and ultimately need to be fully compatible, it is just as true that exercise of one (either one) may be in conflict with exercise of the other. Lack of constraint may not only lead to abuse of the rights of others, as our founding fathers realized, and to insistence on the "right" to be stupid, mediocre, or unauthentic—but partial insights and religious revelations gained internally may lead to elitism, intolerance, or ideological indoctrination of the sorts which history is all too familiar with and which psychologists and educators even of our day know all too well. I do not exclude here some such intrusions of one sort of freedom on the others that are attributable to "enlightened" humanistic and transpersonal psychologists and educators. The general point, which crosses over and is even blurred in Rogers' dichotomy between "traditional" and "person-centered" education, is that there exists a tension between two kinds of freedom and a tension which has particularly meaningful consequences in the world of education—at its *best*.

Wholeness versus Intellect

Finally, Rogers dichotomized what he implies is the humanistic vision "of the whole person" from "only his or her intellect," this latter which he attributed to the "traditional." This he did understandably in the historical context of the times in which humanistic education was associated with "affective" and the traditional with "cognitive" education. In fact, this same dichotomy, internally, preoccupied the Associations for Humanistic Psychology and Education for several years of their early development. Much depends here on what is meant by "intellect," and Rogers and humanistic educators were fully justified in pointing to the impoverishment of "intellect" as it was (and still is being) viewed in much of American education.

But let us recognize that intellect here refers to an impoverished, one dimensional view of "intellect." Seen thusly, *that kind* of "intellect" justifies, nay requires, the most serious criticism and overhaul. That overhaul begins by recognizing how "intellect" has come, in our society and times, to be viewed this way. This construal owes largely to a broad Western bias since the 17th century towards rationalism (vs. the "irrational") but, more specifically as regards the United States, "intelligence" has been narrowly defined by a utilitarian bias clearly expressed in I.Q. tests and their correlates (SAT, MAT, GRE and virtually any kind of standardized testing which correlates with or attempts to expediently assess what is taught) or the potential for learning in the classroom. Such standardized I.Q. tests follow the mass production mentality, the Henry Ford model of the individually and specially used measure of intelligence devised in France by Binet. Neither this nor other standardized correlates have been used in France, which nonetheless does have a highly centralized system of education.

One notable reaction to this skimpy view of intellect was expressed by the creativity research, so closely related to the humanistic movement, in the 1960s and 70s, and culminated in a vast broadening of our notion of "cognition." This research also opened for question a number of subjects regarding intelligence as it had been viewed in this country. I.Q. fit the expedience-learning, social adjustment model of the times. As Terman (1947) had boasted, "Our high I.Q. subjects were above all socially well adjusted." But some of the great creative thinkers of the past, as Lange-Eichbaum (1932/1962) retorted, were anything but "socially well adjusted." Of course, this opens the question which Maslow (1965) raised, "Well-adjusted to what? To a society that reduces intellect to a score on a standardized I.Q. test and then standardizes all subject matter in the classroom to suit this model?"

As nearly all the creative research showed or implied, unlike I.Q.-variety intelligence, creativity is already closely related to feelings and emotions, to past and future, to the "irrational" as well as (super)rational. Kris's notion of "regression in the service of ego," while heavily weighted down in psychoanalytic language, suggests what other creativity research suggests—i.e., that "secondary processes" are practically and instrumentally tied to "primary processes," or feelings and emotions. The "new and unique," which identifies a creative product, is linked to the "old": an insight given in the very term "originality," which has two vectors—one towards the new and unique; the other towards the "old" (the origins, the source).

The creative individual is more open to his/her experiences, memories—all of which provide a repertory, a palate, of possibilities which can be recombined in new ways of seeing things. From the perspective of a positivistic view of "intellect" (which is seen as progressive, utilitarian, goal directed, adjustment centered), feelings and emotions are conceived as the seat of the irrational—that which blocks, retards, or sets back progress in the "real world." This is because this positivistic vision has denied the cognitive power of these feelings (including passion and participation, imagination, intuition, insight, vision, and teleology) and counts only tangible, observable, logically consistent products as marks of intellect. Which great scientist, in his or her publication, gives credit for the final product to any of these "precognitive," "irrational," "feeling-dependent" contributions? That is, until they write their autobiographies which can then be—and typically are—dismissed by the scientific community as the ramblings of an old man who can't "get it up anymore."

Like creative solutions, which characteristically reconstruct previously seen incompatibilities into a newly seen compatibility, the creative individual and his or her process of creating are characterized by the full living-out of apparent incompatibilities. Barron (1963) described the creative genius (one very different from Terman's high-I.Q. "genius") thusly:

> The creative genius may be at once naive and knowledgeable, being at home equally to primitive symbolism and to rigorous logic. He is both more primitive and more cultured, more destructive and more constructive; occasionally crazier and yet adamantly saner than the average person.

The Next Step: America's Unique Potential Contribution

Project Free: Value Disclosing

Today, almost everybody believes American education is in crisis. When viewed in terms of national interest, this crisis is seen as a threat to this country's competitive status in the world. The image conveyed is of graduates unable to keep up with, let alone stay ahead of, the rapid technological changes. By this view, education is a subsidiary of progress, just as it has served other external forces in the past—e.g., in the service of God, in the service of morality or character building, in the service of democracy, in the service of social adjustment. Now it is in the service of business and technology.

Any of these "educational projects" that aims education at a particular value threatens to shift the emphasis from the intrinsic to the instrumental. And whether called this or not, shifts the operating principle from "education" towards that of "training." In fact, in their narrowly defined senses, there seems always to have been a confusion in American education between these two missions. This is partly due to an American propensity towards pragmatism—a pioneering reality (e.g., "one ax is worth a thousand philosophers") and partly due to our translation of ideas from the German school model that, before importation, clearly distinguished schools devoted to education from those devoted to trades. We often apply "training" approaches in what should be "educational" settings, which is one reason why behaviorism and multiple choice types of examinations so readily found their way into American schools—even the humanities (e.g., Iago is a) wise, b) foolish, c) rich, d) none of the above). This is a stress on all the things which Rogers rightfully criticizes.

The problem with this confusion between education and training is not simply that the two ventures are different—each having their valid *raisons d'etre*, calling for quite different approaches and attitudes—but that a fuller recognition of these differences would also reveal something essential that they, both at their best, have in common: an intrinsic, internally empowering relationship between learner and learning. I just watched part of an international table-tennis tournament taking place in Detroit. Little kids of 12 were playing, sometimes beating, older "kids" of 40. All these "kids" knew and loved their paddles, the ball, and the table's possibilities, which were in the continuing process of reciprocally revealing their and the "kids'" potential. These "kids" were at one with their game. Each had developed a very unique playing style, which was in the process of evolving as their game improved. Each kid's style was shifting to meet the differing styles of their opponents. Teachers of math, biology, computer science, and philosophy have much to learn from these kids.

Education differs from training, for one thing, in its unlimited, or open-ended, vision. But at its best, as Rogers insists, education's primary goal is to introduce the world of these open-ended possibilities directly and immediately to the student, who ultimately sees him or herself and, say, Keats or Shakespeare, in the same "space"—i.e., looking outwards and inwards for deeper understanding of the human condition which is increasingly recognized by the human learner. A space in our current world where business and technology are not only motivating and intriguing, even inspiring in their own right, but which reveal and simultaneously call out for inquiry and questioning of the larger human concerns, of our times and of all times.

But, again, this experience crosses over or underlies both education and training. Leontiev, a contemporary Vygotskian psychologist, speaks of an opening of memory—a revelatory recognition—of the entire history and culture of the farmer for a novice who comes to tune into a hand plow. The principle applies to all technology—as the pianist, at moments of "attunement" to his instrument, comes to "be" all pianists everywhere at all times. In the world of philosophy, likewise, Maslow constantly spoke of his ongoing dialogue with Plato, Spinoza, Jefferson, and Bergson. This was living dialogue going on beyond time and space—beyond the point where "fact" or "knowledge" can describe what is "learned" and beyond the alienations which give "fact" and "knowledge" their correct definitions. This is not goal-directed education or training but, rather, the opening of an ongoing process which links the human intimately and first-hand to the world in which they are an integral dimension: that Heideggerian sense of "Being in the World."

From Ford to Rolls Royce

Humanistic educators, without necessarily denying any of the specific goal-directed values referred to above, invert this "goal-directed" value priority. They see these other values as served—better served in the long run—as by-products of a centering on the intrinsics of education. In a sense, if we are to use the business technology model, humanistic educators are trying to do in education what Ford did in cars—i.e., make broadly available in public education what was reserved in the past for a small elite. Nothing could be more American. This already happened when America fostered the first great wave of popular education. But as regards humanistic education, the Ford model falls short. Humanistic education proposes the next step in this direction. Not just a basic car (education) for everybody, but a Rolls Royce education that reaches for quality even in and through the "mass production model." Nothing portends greater enhancement of personal, national, and global power. Nothing is more threatening to some than to release the fuller potential power of humanness.

Oppositions Revisited

This threat sensed, I believe more than anything else, is the prime basis for humanistic education's relative failure to date. One must have enormous trust in that creative power—in humans—to propose such a course. Nothing in my experience of two decades as a humanistic educator suggests that trust is unwarranted or that trust would be put to values other than those most Americans can agree upon. In this light, let us reconsider the values of the opposition on the so-called Conservative Right relative to the values of most humanistic educators. There may be much more in common than differences between humanistic values and those above. But the differences are significant and are grounded in a basic trust of each person's full humanness.

Fundamentalist Right

Fundamentalist Christians charge that our education is "value free" or "surface value." Many humanistic educators agree. Humanistic educators reject a value-free education just as they reject a value-free science. But they, as do many Christians, also reject the implication that Christian values should be the only ones certified for everybody and also reject the belief that values of any sort are something to be externally imposed as indoctrinations by educators.

This rejection of imposed and unexamined values, native to Socrates, formed the basis for Simon's Values Clarification, an approach simply aimed at the student's understanding of the values he or she lives by. The basis for the Fundamentalist Right's rejection of this approach seemed to be a fear of this questioning. Another charge often heard from this group of conservatives was that the Values Clarification approach fostered "relativistic values." Again, this complaint seems based on an assumption that universal or "eternal" values cannot be intrinsically gleaned through an understanding and extended questioning of relative ones or an assumption that the deepest spiritual insights cannot be gained through human experiences intrinsically lived and reflectively questioned. Humanistic educators loudly proclaim that the trusted student in the right stimulating and challenging atmosphere is the most likely to discover the "Christ within"—and/or Buddha or Moses or Mohammed.

Economic Right

Many humanistic educators agree with economic conservatives on freedom when this is meant as liberty from undue constraints. But they go beyond this and insist also on existential freedom of Read's sort, which has no guarantees but which can be fostered by the right kind of education. Humanistic educators agree with the economic right on individualism and the notion of "self-help" (which they borrowed from humanistic psychology as the military borrowed "Be all that you can be... in the Army"). But they understand this as extended beyond the business world and, as Maslow put it, to "the farthest reaches of human nature." They certainly agree on social responsibility. But not restricted to the marketplace and also with a sense of intrinsic responsibility for all of humanness and the human environment. They agree with the conservatives on opportunity—but extended to educational opportunity for self-exploration and discovery. They agree on diversity of values and freedom of choices—but, again, not reduced to a business model of education that swings "with the market," "centers on competition," buys "appropriate learning" with tokens, or counts everything and everybody in terms of numbers, profitability, and "products."

Cultural Right
Many humanistic educators can agree with the cultural conservatives, like Bloom, that culture is collective human memory and that dialogue with it gives both cultural identity and the potential basis for understanding others and oneself more profoundly. This latter is one reason some humanistic educators reject cultural homogenization of immigrants, who are recognized as needing their own roots and collective memories. But also, many humanistic educators, especially those who were there themselves, understand those American youth of the 1960s whom Bloom (1987) attacks—who rejected the socio-cultural indoctrination and who in a desperate effort to know themselves reached across centuries and continents to speak with Gibran or Lao Tze or, lacking a philosophy which spoke to them in the classroom, went to the local concert to hear this from the Beatles.

Still, in agreement with Bloom, a narcissistic "now" is not a "now" devoid of past and future and other. In this, the cultural conservatives are right. But the enlightened "now" of the humanistic educator is also not the "now" of the positivists, whose educational model of the sciences rendered everything not currently useful in the past or present "obsolescent." Or the model of those who value "culture" for the purpose of instilling nationalistic sentiments alone. Or who ignore the gender, ethnic, and racial biases built into the heritage. Or who valued and thus taught this heritage simply as useful facts or for social one-upmanship purposes of appearing "cultured." Much "classical" education has been taught, rather than explored. Much has been centered, means and ends, on utilitarian principles alone. One need only look at the cultural sections of standardized tests, the beat to which nearly all American education currently dances to, to recognize this.

Having lost its *raison d'etre*, the humanities in America have been undergoing a near-death experience. Bloom, most humanistic educators couldn't agree more, is right in trying to resurrect them. But the power of these works can only come alive if they are encountered where the best of the works joins the best of the person through the best of education. Otherwise, these humanities, old or revived, are but a pretentiously propped up set of dry bones.

How did this value-free, "dry bones" education in America come about?

Cross-Cultural Insights

Those who claim that cross-cultural comparisons of student achievement scores—on which our American students tend to show poorly in the so-called "basics"—are of little value, have their point. American education is broader based. The populations are different as are the global objectives and underlying values. These and other factors render educational cross-cultural comparisons of this sort questionable if taken too literally and especially questionable if such comparisons are used to coerce copying. But the very cultural differences which set American education apart from that in other countries can be instructive if we gain deeper insight into some of the cultural–historical bases for these differences, as seen in light of what humanistic education has to offer.

All of Western education owes much to the Church, which in Europe established the first formal systems of education. And while it is obvious that this early education was centered around Christian values, objectives, and especially *answers*, much of what we now call secular education also owes enlightened Church educators such as Cardinal Newman and the Oxford school, who recognized the value of this secular education even in the practical interest of Christian values. More intrinsic, the Christian Church historically is our living vehicle for the rationalistic values we derive from our pre-Christian, Hellenic, Western tradition. Plato comes to us through the Augustinians, Aristotle through the Thomists.

During the Age of Enlightenment, the "Age of Rationalism"— especially with the advent of science and the call for more democratic or, at least, more populist governments—the trend was towards a Church–State split, which affected education differently according to country or culture. A Protestant-dominated country and one born of Enlightenment philosophy, such as the United States, tended to make that split very clear and etch the line drawn between the two into the constitutional framework of national law. As a consequence, public education, at least in principle, dealt with secular values and issues; religious values and issues were left to the church and Sunday school.

The French, for instance, by contrast, dealt with this historical Church–secular split differently. In secularizing its education, it held on to many of the questions raised historically in the Church-dominated schools but treated these secularly—that is, without terminating in the Church's answers. Thus, within the education itself, there existed an ongoing debate between Christian and secular answers to long-standing spiritual and philosophical questions. For those going on to the universities in France, the last year of "high school" is called *l'année philosophique* (year of philosophy), where all the "Who am I?" and "What is Man and Humanity?" type questions are fully raised and flushed out. Evidently, the years of education leading to this final one in "high school" are heavily devoted to such "spiritual–philosophical" issues.

Since much of the Church-centered education was grounded in the normative—i.e., morals and values and spiritual (not necessarily religious) ends—and had incorporated many of these questions from pre-Christian Hellenics, even secular education in France and much of Southern Europe was "value ridden" and "spiritually" infused. As an example, in Southern Europe, the social sciences, including psychology and pedagogy, remained very late into this century as sub-areas of philosophy, along with morality and ethics. Furthermore, much of the rationalistic philosophical thinking of the Enlightenment period, which grounded this philosophical discourse, was centered around Kant rather than, as in England and the United States, the empiricists. American education was strongly funded on a *tabula rasa* notion of empiricists such as Locke and Hume, which Kant opposed. Kant, like Plato, had presumed disposition for morality as well as reason to be largely innate, or *a priori*, rather than by-products of environmental influences etched on a child seen at birth as a *tabula rasa*.

Justifications for discipline in a Kantian-centered religion are much closer to those of the Eastern disciplines than those of many "discipline"-oriented American educators. Kantian discipline is related to the belief that the senses need quieting so that child (disciple) can open up to and speak from his or her "inner self"—not merely to maintain order in the classroom so that teachers can impart their knowledge.

Likewise, if as proposed in the Kantian education, there is an "inner self," an inner wisdom waiting to be tapped, that becomes the first and ultimate source of value. From that "inner self," then, other proposed sources of value can be weighed and judged, prioritized and proportioned. This makes it less likely that any proposed "external" source of value can become *the* source. For instance, one can recognize the truth and value of functionalism which issues from Darwinian insights into nature without allowing one's self and the society to be engulfed in, reduced to, merely conditioned by that value determinism alone. One can be enamored of the progress of science and technology (methods and techniques) without making these the ultimate hopes of mankind. On the contrary, the creative origins of science, the art of teaching—the teachings, the objects and subjects of education which open the student, rather than their products—are retained in highest value.

Excesses of European Stress on Nativism: American Correctives

Evidently, this stress on the "nativistic" taken to its absolutist extremes—which has often been the case in the history of the West and particularly in Europe—can lead to, and has led to, horrible consequences. These include a notion of "homunculus," which predisposed the treating of little children as small adults and justified exploitative practices so well documented during the early industrial age by Dickens. It has led to fixed socio-economic classes, to the "Divine Authority of Kings," to elitism, to rejection of experiences as guide to wisdom and knowledge, to dogma and doctrine, to wild claims of paranormal powers, to Fascism and all the horrors associated with it.

Much that is best about American education has countered many of these excesses. But much that is deficient in American education—many of the problems we now lump under the term educational crisis—may be attributed to a rejection or unrooted application of educational foundations specially valued elsewhere. The pioneering notion of "one ax is worth a thousand philosophers" freed America for its pragmatic future but also left it with a disposition which wildly oscillates from one going "truth" to another—e.g., from functionalism to fundamentalism—and deals with these "truths" either atomistically or superficially.

Disconnections from elitist education made this nation truly an "opportunity society," but one overly dependent on material success for satisfaction. America, through the likes of Horace Mann, borrowed the externals only of a formal European education from Germany, where it was centered in a Kantian philosophy—and here, lacking its grounding *raison d'etre* of the "inner self," has reacted periodically against the predictable negative offshoots of this dry formal skeleton. Yet when it longs for traditional education, the American public, as now, thinks in terms of these formalities—e.g., "We have to go 'back to' basics and discipline."

Spanning from Best to Best

I feel that the emergence of humanistic psychology and education in the United States provides, within the American context, the potential of a corrective to many of the excesses and weaknesses that ground our own system while retaining and greatly enhancing the values which set this system apart and in advance of others. In reacting against the behaviorists' environmental determinism, Maslow (1968) did not speak of *a prioris*, instincts, genetics, or nativism in reporting on his hierarchy of human values and motives. Rather, he carefully selected the term *instinctoid* to describe human tendencies towards self-realization and self-actualization. He did not deny the Darwinian functionalistic determinisms—or any rationally conceived determinisms which would tie the human to natural or even Divine law. Rather, following the existentialists, he found a freedom in the sense that Read uses and which is inherent to the human spirit. The determinisms are the *givens*, whether these be social or biological. But there is something more—more basic, an often-frail tendency that, when encouraged, can affirm itself through or against these *givens* towards an assertion of full selfhood and full humanness.

Human Potentials

How full are these potentials for selfhood and humanness? Maslow indicated some of this potential in describing his self-actualizing subjects. The transpersonal psychologists which Maslow brought to the door of Eastern philosophies have opened up to read and explore nearly endless maps of "inner" potential hardly imaginable by our greatest Western philosophers. And, totally beyond the scope of behaviorists, in particular, to begin to fathom.

The need to know, for Maslow, is *instinctoid*. There is, of course, the knowing of skills or the knowing of philosophies. But beyond and through any of these is the need to *know* self (the *unlearned, unearned,* but opened to recognition by respect, self)—not simply as I am seen as a social being or an individual, but the most extended *self* which opens me to and towards my fuller humanness and at one stage of recognition opens *the recognition of that self in others* and therefore the need to know and share what is human with others.

Neither Maslow nor Rogers were anti-technology or anti-progress and certainly not anti-business. Maslow's writings (e.g., *Eupsychian Management*; Maslow, 1965) had their first and most complete hearings and applied usages in the world of business. Maslow had been influenced by competency theories, and he appreciated that kind of knowing which helps reveal self as it expands self, even in ostensibly limited and menial areas. Such learning as a mechanical skill (e.g., table tennis) is experiential in this sense, as are the insights gained into the most difficult philosophical works. But these are experiential in the sense that my daughter and her French grandmother shared the experience of learning basic French.

This raises the notion so completely related to humanistic education these days of "experiential." Such inner "expanding, transformative, experiences" *are* what is experiential. Not as some humanistic educators have interpreted this term to mean—i.e., experiential exercises versus, say, lectures, cognition, or subject matter. Any technique or approach, like those "kids" playing table tennis, is experiential if it advances the basic and unique charge of education— that experience which opens and deepens and transforms. Poetry and philosophy (as subject matter; lectures or drilling as approaches) could qualify as experiential if they touch and open the person that way. Entering into the world of other cultures through language, native rituals, mythology, etc. is experiential if it is intrinsic—i.e., it becomes the opening, freeing, and revelatory experience of the student.

By this humanistic formulation, and totally consistent with phenomenology (which has been a methodological support to this orientation), there is no incompatibility between subject and object; student and subject matter. Experience is experience of *something*, and through that experience, both the something (an auto in repair, a fellow human encountered, or a philosophy disclosing its meaning) and the experiencer—values and paths, personal and collective—are opened and more fully revealed. It is that intimate, yet humanly shareable, moment and process of mutual revelation which forms the heart of the educational experience, and this experience is at the heart of education's unique mission.

A more profound revelation and reflective understanding of this moment and process and their greater potential significance for humankind is what the humanistic orientation has to offer to American education and its educators. It is an orientation that speaks not only of "mass distribution" (historical step #1 in the American contribution to education) but also to *quality* (the next great contribution). Nobody was more at the center of this vision—which can reempower the student, the teacher, and the fuller unique mission of education–than Carl Rogers. While I understand his need to speak to educators "where they are," I wish, during that talk at West Georgia, he had spoken less oppositionally and also more directly to the *best* in those educators and the *best* in their chosen, unique, and humanly sacred mission.

Part 4:

Hermeneutic Excursions

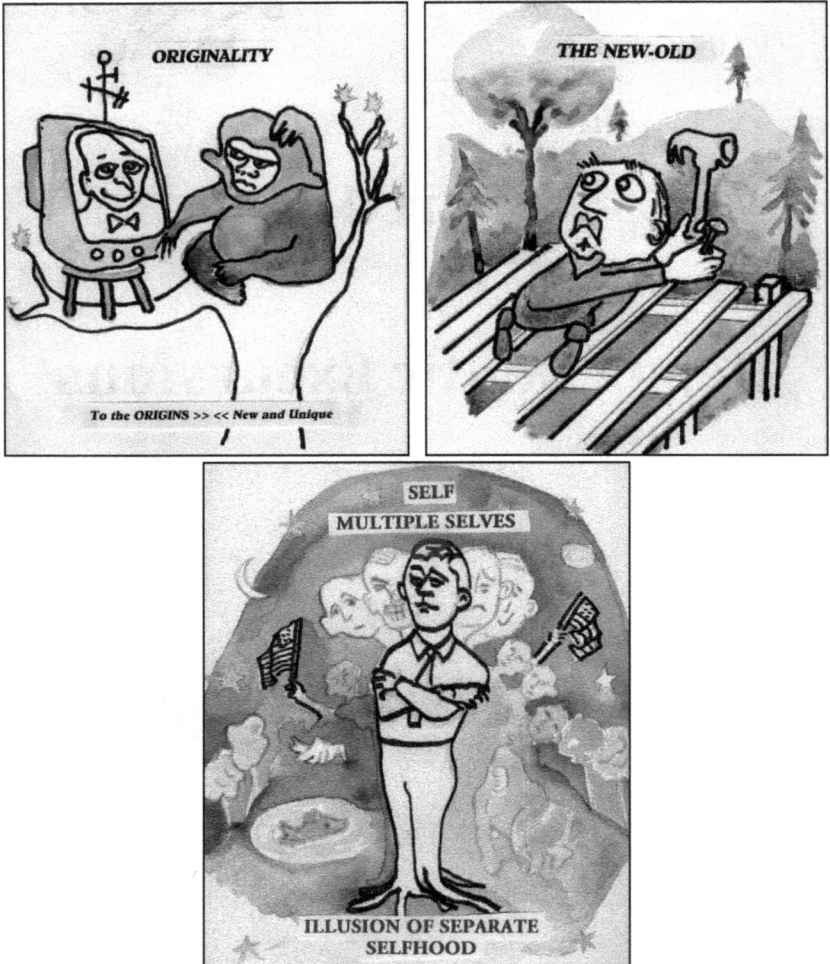

A selection of drawings that Mike developed to illustrate talking points in his unfinished book on the upright body posture, circa 2004. From left to right: (a) originality has two vectors—one toward the origins (that which is already there from our evolutionary history) and the other toward beginnings (the new and unique); (b) Mike's (1999c) "platform experience" while building a deck behind his home (discussed at the beginning of Part 2, see p. 28); and (c) Mike's (1999d) reconciliation of humanistic, constructivist/postmodern, and transpersonal views of self (discussed in Chapter 13).

Perhaps Mike's greatest gift was his ability to creatively forge connections between seemingly incompatible worldviews, be they political (as noted in Sandrine's preface and as witnessed in Chapter 11) or philosophical, as observed in these last two papers. As mentioned in the introduction, Mike described his delivery style as an "excursion" (Bland, 2002, p. 1), in which he drew from his background in Ricoeurian hermeneutics to guide readers and audiences on a journey that spiraled around and then into the core of a given topic.

In Chapter 12, Mike examines the relationship of reason with instinct and intuition in the interest of "de-alienating a number of polarities we've been living as consequences of our centuries-old war between faith and reason" in the interest of opening "the path for a more spiritual and vital rationalism." In Chapter 13, Mike compares/contrasts perspectives on self though the lenses of humanistic, constructivist/postmodern, and transpersonal psychologies. After reviewing critiques of each orientation, he concludes by emphasizing "the compatibility, even necessity of a compatibility, of differences" between the three viewpoints.

In doing so, he brings this volume full circle by revising a point he made in Chapter 1: despite their nuances, when their respective contributions are taken together as a whole, the perspectives that have characterized the unfolding of the greater humanistic psychology movement are capable of addressing the social, ethical, and spiritual problems of the 21st century.

Chapter 12

Instinct, Intuition, and the Supraconscious:
De-Alienating Reflections
(1993)[1]

"Intuition is when you know something. But where did it come from?"
~ Goldberg, *The Intuitive Edge*

Introduction: De-Alienating Dialogue

APA's Division of Humanistic Psychology recently took concrete organizational steps in the interest of healing a breach between *third* (humanistic) and *fourth* (transpersonal) force psychologies. Beyond these organizational initiatives, there was evidence on both the Division and the Transpersonal Interest Group boards of a determination that differences (apparent and actual) should be dialogued and that continuities, or kinships, between these areas be elucidated. The most obvious mark of kinship is that *fourth force* psychology shares many historical roots with *third force*, and the tap root they most share—and in this, differentiate themselves from most of our field—is that they have an intrinsic, holistic model of the psychologically healthy human.

Some transpersonal psychologists, however, feel the humanistic model does not go far enough into the spiritual. Some humanistic psychologists feel religion is what these transpersonal psychologists

[1] Arons, M. (1993). Instinct, intuition, and supraconscious: De-alienating reflections. *The Humanistic Psychologist, 21*, 158–179. doi:10.1080/08873267.1993.9976915 | Copyright © 1993 by the American Psychological Association. Adapted with permission from the American Psychological Association.

are getting into; others are concerned that these spiritual preoccupations become escapes from personal and historical realities. The one concern I have is the separation, as distinct from individuation, of the two orientations, which I have viewed as endogenously related, both historically and organically. I see these orientations, and others questioning the modernistic paradigm, as needing to constantly recontextualize themselves historically and internally.

Another danger I see with this transpersonal stress on the "spiritual"—just as occurred in the early movement of humanistic psychology relative to the "experiential," and both in a climate which is post-rational—is a tendency towards anti-intellectualism. Let me acknowledge the limits of the intellectual, particularly as regarding the subject undertaken here, but insist that it also has its important place. Reflection helps to remind us where we are together, where we are relative to our times. I agree with May that we, individually and as an orientation to psychology, have a responsibility to history and humanity to leave something tangible of our own experiences and the sense we make of these. I think our experiences and struggles with them represent an historical moment of transformation. Current suspicion of the intellectual and of language (shared by many humanistic and transpersonal psychologists and deconstruction postmodernists) is a significant mark of this transformation. We have reached, and are now reaching out beyond, the limits of rationalism as this has been construed. Existential-humanistic-transpersonal psycho-logies and postmodernists are major contributors to this reaching out beyond. I personally feel, however, that all of these experiences and claims for potential human experience call not for a replacement of rationalism—the current limits of which are becoming obvious—but for a vastly expanded, vital, and spiritually enlivened version of it. This version is not an escape from opposition and tension replaced with another form of duality and alienation; rather, it is replaced by a de-alienation process which recognizes in dialogue one pole inherent in the others while retaining and honoring the space, the distinctness, and uniqueness of all claims to human reality.

Between the Blind and the Dumb

In fact, the rationalism we are now outgrowing is, historically, much defined by the pole it came to oppose, "blind faith." It is a reactively skeptical rationalism which tends to "play dumb" to any experience it cannot observe or measure. Consequently, we as a culture have been living between the authorities of the blind and the dumb. Who voluntarily would elect such leadership? Intuition is one of those common human experiences which has been a casualty—sort of left ambiguously dangling—in this struggle between "other"-worldly "revelation" and "this"-worldly fact and function. The humanistic model restores credence to intuition as a vital and essential dimension of human everyday experience and as instrumental to self-knowledge both in the sciences and in personal quests. The transpersonal model gives intuition in all its forms and manifestations a coherence. That coherence, called the *supraconscious*, has the dual disadvantage of seeming "other"-worldly to skeptics, and to others, too intimately real to lend itself to intellectual dialogue. I respect both these positions. However, my purpose here is to de-center the debate about intuition from one of seeking proof for the validity of intuition or the supraconscious to one of de-alienating a number of polarities we've been living as consequences of our centuries-old war between faith and reason. This, by looking at some of these polarities in the light of a radically different view of intuition. And this in the interest of expanding the assumptions underlying current rationalism.

There is no pole more distant to current rationalism and to those humanistic psychologists with a highly secular bent than a notion such as the supraconscious. In the following, I would like to take on this reality, be a forceful advocate for its ultimately significant status of reality—in fact, its claim is that of ultimate reality—and undertake this advocacy with a de-alienating intention. The paradoxical oppositions begin with recognition that the supraconscious cannot be grasped with words or reason. Furthermore, the supraconscious—long familiar to much of the world by one or another name—is an almost completely alien notion to the West, alien to all but a few persons' experience, alien to all "personal" experience, yet very well-known under the name intuition.

The Supraconscious is Intuition

The current interest in intuition is being born of an emerging historical antinomy. It emerges with postmodernism, which, in the broadest terms, can be seen as both reaction against or completion of the Age of Enlightenment understood as "rationalism." During this "modernist" period, certainly its recent stages, the epistemological status of intuition was diminished, rendered suspect, or denied entirely. The current reaction is now reclaiming for intuition a legitimate epistemological place in a broadened rational discourse. Many transpersonal psychologists (e.g., Harman & Rheingold, 1984) even claim for it a special and greatly expanded power beyond reason and one central to the most comprehensive vision of full humanness.

The fragile epistemological status of intuition during the "modern" period is now being confronted in transpersonal psychology by a notion of the supraconscious. By this view, intuition is not merely, at best, a mysterious, unreliable aid to reason, or a voice heard from a theologically understood God. Epistemologically speaking, those supposing the supraconscious make the most intriguing and far reaching claim for it: *the supraconscious is intuition.*

Such a claim as this and its implications are clearly foreign to the Western rational mindset. This claim is also foreign to some humanistic psychologists who want to ground the human in natural experience or experience of the lifeworld and who see any moves in the direction of the mystical or transcendental as regressive and dangerous. Such claims divide many *third* and *fourth force* psychologists and yet unite many of these in reaction to what they see as the "far out, airy-fairy" ends of New Age thinking.

The broader purpose of this reflection is to help reduce the alienations which are developing around the resurging interest in intuition. This purpose will be accomplished in three steps: first, by taking seriously the notion of the supraconscious; second, by attempting to "ground" this notion of the supraconscious—i.e., contextualizing it to make it less alien to Western thought in either its naturalistic or phenomenological forms; and third, to view the supraconscious as a radical re-centering which may heuristically shed light on a curious and contradictory place to which intuition has been assigned throughout much of Western history: a simultaneous kinship to both the gods and the instincts.

History and Antinomy

Intuition is linked today by some visions of transpersonal psychology with myth. By extrapolating this view to history, we might conclude with those who see Homer at the origins, that intuition itself is at the source of our Western intellectual tradition. The most renowned early battle between myth and rationalism in the West is the Platonic attack on the poets of the Homeric tradition. Yet, even as Socrates demoted the myth makers to the sixth basement of reality (a demotion he later rescinded), he referred most gratefully to his own invisible personal spirit-source of inspiration which he called Daemon, intermediary between the gods and himself.

At the dawning of the Christian Era, the Gnostics tended to retain this Platonic individualized intuitive source, which through personal creating of fictions led to deeper insights and to development of "spiritual maturity" (Pagels, 1943). The fact that Gnostics, like Plato, placed the intuitive source of knowledge in the human sphere is supported by their central term "recognition"—which, not completely unlike "reminiscence" for Plato, presumed this search for knowledge to be an opening of oneself to what *is* (already there): an innate, given power of understanding. Intuition gave glimmerings of, and provided guidance to, this pre-knowledge. By the fifth century, the personal intuitive source was rendered suspect. Socrates' inspirational Daemon—teasing, furtive, mischievous, as May (1969) points out— becomes Demon: untrustworthy, misleading, evil. A clear split was made by Saint Augustine between the Divine source of the intuitive word and the human receiver. Augustine drew a clear distinction between the secular, reasoned truth "Scientia" and the Divinely inspired which led to wisdom that he termed "Sapientia." God was the source and revealer of this Divine word. The Divine word, revealed, was called "revelation" and the means to accessing this Divine word was an act of faith, a distinctly different path from the human reasoning capacity.

After the fifth century, revelation, and the condition of faith that supported it, came to mark the extreme pole in the Western tradition against which later incarnations of rationalism came to pit themselves. Theologians such as Saint Thomas Aquinas attempted to reconcile the kind of knowing given by reason with that revealed through an act of faith. This philosophically primordial battle between reason and faith-engendered knowing left intuition (that nonetheless persisted in a wide variety of forms) mangled in an overlapping complex of antinomies to which, it is possible, some of our own current confusion may be traced. Today, for example, we may see in modern psychology a secular analogy to the good–bad (*Daemon—-demon*) controversy of old when we ask, "Is it intuition or projection?"

The list of antinomies in which intuition is currently entangled in the West includes the following:

1. If it is logic, it cannot be intuitive.
2. If it is intuitive, it must be individual and esoteric rather than collective and scientific.
3. The intuitive is archaic (old-brain, preconscious, and childlike)—from perspectives of evolutionary biology, microgenesis, and developmental psychology—relative and in contrast to the evolutionary "state of the art" frontal lobes, reality consciousness, and maturity.
4. Both quasi-nativist Kant and arch-empiricist Hume acknowledged intuition, leaving indecision as to whether it comes innately "packaged" with the human "hardware" or can be discerned uniquely in the "software" of human experience.
5. Bergson, under the term "elan vital," argued for (most modern biology against) intuition as teleology.
6. Intuition is seen as direct versus indirect (mediated) knowing.

7. Its source is attributed either to the secular human or Divine; and finally, as noted above, intuition is a lower or higher power—that is, it is associated with the instincts or the Divine.

Instinct and Intuition: Ambiguities

Let us begin and end with this latter antinomy: One thing Christian and rationalist share is a nearly unquestioned belief in the superiority of the human mind relative to the "mere" instincts more associated with animals. This is a belief not without its own internal complications. While the human mind is held superior to the animal instincts, there remains a recognition—even admiration for—the apparent grace and clocklike perfection observed in much animal, but rarely in human, behavior. Near-universal belief in the superiority of the human mind rests on the human's ability to translate, by reflective understanding, the instinctual (biological needs) into the conscious. Therein, for both Christian and rationalist lies the evidenced basis for assuming will, choice, and freedom—*as well as flaw, lack.*

While mind in the West is historically clearly distinguished from (in fact most often opposed to) instinct, intuition (unlike mind) is often mistaken for instinct—as when we say, almost interchangeably, "feminine instinct" or "women's intuition." Yet a moment of reflection reveals not only a difference, but an apparent opposition between, instinct and intuition. Instincts are seen as species-wide—regularly appearing, readily identified with certain activities, repeatable and predictable and associated with body and energetics. By difference and even contrast, the capacity for intuition is identified more with some humans than other humans. Even here its appearance is most often furtive, unpredictable, not easily associated with any single activity. It is a capacity to which we give sparse reliability, in which we recognize its power only in certain specifics (e.g., some particular moments, events, or ideas of creative activity) which are typically identified with the fresh and new (originality) and which we normally associate with mind and meaning. Despite these significant differences between instinct and intuition, let us see if we can better understand why they are often identified with one another.

The Supraconscious

On a flight returning from San Francisco with my daughter (she was in her mid-teens and we had just spent a weekend with an artist and poet), she said, "Dad, there are two selves—a little one and a big one. The little one is like a marionette, but one who thinks it is acting on its own. But all the strings are connected to the big self. That big self is you and me and everybody." After that she began writing poetry, to me and about everything, which she said just came to her without thought or preparation. Through this poetry, my relationship with my daughter has blossomed.

The notion of the supraconscious (Harman & Rheingold, 1984) in the West is ostensibly new and radical—new in that it is largely a Western rendition of that taken from Eastern traditions; radical in that it is not merely a source of intuition or informed by intuition but *is* intuition. This supraconscious is variously and tentatively known by such other terms as "transpersonal mind," "unitary consciousness," or "universal" or "cosmic" energy. It is mistakenly described in any normative terms. It is what is "attained," or "opened" in states of enlightenment variously named in its original traditions. It is transpersonal in that it is the source of consciousness not only of individuals or even humans but of all. It is "in" all. It is supraconscious in the sense that all other forms and levels of consciousness are but manifestations of it. It is unitary consciousness in the sense that it is fundamental energy which operates through mind and body in various ways to produce cognitive phenomena, and it is the media between the various psychic phenomena we encounter or experience (Chobe, 1993).

Mediations: Creativity

What the West struggles to grasp in the relationship of intuition to the creative processes, the notion of the supraconscious takes for granted. From the perspective of the supraconscious, all the antinomies relative to intuition viewed by the West might be likened to wrinkles in a balloon not yet fully blown. The following is an attempt to "blow out" some of the wrinkles from a more familiar Western perspective. The sphere in which intuition is most fully recognized in the West is creativity. Central to this sphere is the notion of *originality*. Originality has two vectors of meaning reference—one back, temporally, micro-genetically, or developmentally to the *origins*; the other to the *new and unique*. What is original is, by definition, not predictable. This "regressive–progressive" unity emerges throughout the creativity literature. The creative process, according to Kris (1953) is at points dependent on "regression in the service of ego." Or that the ego becomes "permeable." For Kris, a psychoanalyst, this meant a regression from secondary to primary processes. The creativity literature is resplendent with variants on this "regress–progress," "progress–regress" paradoxical unity. To see the "old" as "new" is a letting go of what is currently in "grasp"—fixed perceptions, established thoughts or thinking patterns, or emotionally or volitionally preestablished traces. But more, it is the transformation of the old, fixed, static, and sedimented into inspirational resources which give the new meaning. Postmodern architecture, finding its freshness in the recombining and whimsical play on past forms, is no less an example of this than was the use by Spanish colonists of cornerstones from Aztec temples as foundations for their cathedrals—perhaps, also, equally as mocking. The well-known creative incongruity is a divergent play on static (predictable) meanings: "Are you free tonight? No, but I'm reasonable." This incongruity required a de-centering from expected focal meaning. This de-centering allows, so to speak, fresh air into the old "set-up." This "airing" process, like the aeration of water, transforms the stagnant to the fresh. De-centering is a letting go of what was, the allowing of what was to be seen in new, potentially meaningful ways. A Buddhist rendition of this theme in the interest of fresh consciousness is the emptying of the cup of old tea to make room for the new (in the Buddhist sense, the ultimate letting go of individual consciousness itself). In this case, the opening to nothing—or what amounts to the same thing—opening to all the "resources" of supraconscious.

While the creative process, West or East, stresses a "letting go," in the light of personal processes, this moment of "letting go" does not generally occur without provocation; nor is the impetus which results in this "letting go" undirected. It hinges on personal or collective volition based often on sensed defect or limit. There is the creative project, or "enlightenment" project—valued by a sense of limit or of "other" or "more possible." One is impelled out and drawn towards. Thus, the paradox of the Buddhists that one must desire to succeed, where "success" requires the loss of desire.

Static (Reflected) to Fresh, Fresh (Innocence) to Static: Deepening Insight and Engendering Intuition

The "progress–regress," "regress–progress" movement characteristic of creative activity may be viewed in cognitive terms as an interplay between innocence (in phenomenology, "naivete") and reflection. Or, inversely, it can be viewed from the reflected to the freshly inspired innocent: from the fresh towards the static; from the static towards the fresh. The incongruity example cited above is movement from the static to the fresh—old words, all of them with revitalized meaning. Read Heidegger on this first passage from innocence to reflection. The poet's vehicle is language, all right, but: "The poet speaks the essential word. This implies that poetry is not ready-made language. It is that particular type speech which for the first time springs open all that which we then discuss and deal with in everyday language" (as cited in Read, 1957). Fresh insights are brought by the poet to everyday discourse.

Implicit to phenomenology is its movements in both directions, from the taken-for-granted of the "natural attitude" to an intuitive grasp of the "essential structures." But, inversely, this achievement of insight results in a "deuxieme naivete," in which the now "known" is intuited as extending to unknown—previously unrealized—horizons of potential meaning. Thus, Husserl (as cited in Spiegelberg, 1960) was led to characterize the phenomenological task as "inexhaustible."

Broadly speaking, two manifestations of intuition seem to play significant roles in this passage from innocence (naive) to reflected, reflected to innocence: one dealt with at length by Gestaltists under the term "insight"; the other an intuition which helps (along with more formalized reasoning processes) lead from fixed to new prospective meaning. Are these really different, "insight" and "intuition"? Or two different types of intuition? Or are the distinctions we typically draw in English more related to the operations and vectors of the cognitive activity we observe—one which might broadly be viewed as "discovery," the other "creativity"? The term "insight" in French is *prise de conscience*, or the *taking of consciousness*. We judge students on their ability to achieve such insights. The consciousness "taken," arrived at—starting with some apparently unrelated facts, observations, or events—is a unifying truth or principle. That which we typically call intuition seems to be the *tapping of consciousness*, a "cognitive" aid from some pre-cognitive gratuitous source. That source of consciousness which deepens our understanding and that source of consciousness which opens us to new possibilities are not reducible (as the Gestaltists and most intuition theorists agree) to other cognitive processes—e.g., logical thinking, learning, memory, etc. Although there is no evidence, at least in Western intellectual and creative experience, that this unaccounted-for source operates independently of these other processes. In fact, we propose below that both the experiential and logical, in their way, are intuitive doorways. They are also informed by—rendering them informative vehicles of—the supraconscious.

Projects: West and East

If what is termed "insight" and what is known as prescient intuition may be distinguishable in terms of the vector of cognitive activity we witness, we need to consider the possibility that what is recognized in the West as intuition (such as that related to creative activity) may be the same as, or tap, the same source as that indicated in the East—but distinguished by *cultural values* and the *project*. That, in fact, this intuition (or source) may not be different—only manifest itself differently—is indicated by the artist John Ferren (1953):

Both artist and mystic at the time of insight, experience a deep sense of personal fulfillment. But the mystic works gratuitously for revelation alone. The creative worker is predatory; he grabs the insight for a filled purpose, he is far less than divine, and the Promethean fire symbol seems very apt.

What is the intuitive source which can be put to such different purposes as tangible creative activity and "mystical" revelation? And how is this related to the sense of "personal fulfillment" which Ferren uses to describe the experience at moments of insight (taking of consciousness?) of both creative artist and "mystic"? In fact, something akin to that described as a "mystical" experience is anything but alien to the creative experience. The literature is resplendent with descriptions which place the completion of the creative task "outside" the artist or scientist—exemplified by such descriptions as, "At some point, the painting seemed to complete itself" or "It is as if God had taken over my hand and completed the work with such ease and with such a sense of rightness that I cannot even claim the work belongs to me." These are the sorts of descriptions that Maslow (1964, 1966, 1968, 1971) used to describe the "peak" experiences of his self-actualizing subjects.

Far from these creative "magical moments" being internal experiences (like a headache or anger), they are rather characterized by a sense of loss of or expansion of self as the choice of wording ("... as if God took my hand") would indicate even and, especially, when spoken by otherwise not very religious individuals. Or "the painting painted itself"—as if the artist were just there for the ride. However, the term "outside" is misleading. There is only a shift in focus experienced, from that of *author* to that of *vehicle*. The experience is subject-/object-less, or both, as occurs often in states of intimacy. One has the sense of being infinitely expanded and/or infinitely permeated, just as the "he" or "she" is diminished (less opaque, a sense of being "spaced out"). It is a sense of completeness and a sense of self-evident certitude, yet nothing one can grab onto. A previous alienation between self and other is now recognized in the very disappearance of this alienation, and yet otherness and oneness stand out even more vividly. Time stands still (eternal or, put differently, as if one has achieved a consciousness not dictated by clock time or even Kant's time–space *a prioris*). Or, put experientially, one is in tune with the "is-ness," or "suchness" quality, as Eastern philosophers call this (Laski, 1962)—or simply *quality*, as Pirsig (1991) calls it.

Typically, we are alienated from this quality. Even, if not especially, alienated are the persons with a project—tangible or life. One is separated not so much by the "idea" of the project (its "urging") but, rather, by the gap between this sensed project's worth and validity—its necessity, its ultimate reality—and the current "reality" he or she thinks and lives. Or separated by the previous judgments of which pathways to take to move the project along. It is the "letting go" at certain key moments, the surrender (in French, *se rendre*, rendering or opening of oneself) of the attitude which identifies with these prejudgment fixations that the alienation is "transcended." Achieved in this transcendence is not yet the realization of the project. It is the state of "mind" which clears the minefield of obstacles, impossible contradictions—and by opening their other features to perceptions reveals them in their now-obvious inherent relationship. Everyone and everything is de-alienated.

I am fully aware that "magical" creative experience (such as the moment just described) and "mystical experiences" are not identical with or required for intuition to occur. Intuition may well occur in quite different states, in virtually every aspect of life, although these do often—in the form of inspirations, new perceptual construal, and ideas—reveal themselves in spontaneous or "letting go" moments. But, rather, it is the source—the "is-ness" and "attunement" (Marx, 1992) or "being with" or simply "being" quality achieved in such creative or "mystical" states—that gives experiential evidence for the plausibility of the supraconscious. Too often we laud the genius for the creative product we value while discounting that "genius's" story of the experiences he or she had in the creative process. Einstein received no prize for his intuition, yet he said, "The really valuable thing is intuition" (Goldberg, 1983). When we speak of the supraconscious, we are speaking of a certain immediacy—as with insight (all of a sudden) and intuition (where no source, logic, or causal account can be given), which gives a strong qualitative sense of "rightness."

Everyday Faith

Of the "letting go" experience, are we not speaking here of a "micro-faith"—and perhaps even a "macro-faith"—one not alien to phenomenology? Beyond Husserl's methodological bracketing of the predispositions of the "natural attitude," Merleau-Ponty (1962) likened phenomenology to positivism, with a difference—the difference related to alienation and attitude. First, he de-alienated the apparent opposition between positivistic science (objectivity) and phenomenology. If it is a fact, it is not alien to that which phenomenologists explore. Then he indicated a difference in attitude between positivist and phenomenologist, distinguishing a kind of skepticism from a kind of faith: The positivist walks cautiously, expecting the ground under his next step to be deceptive, unsolid, and to collapse; the phenomenologist walks confidently and spontaneously as if always on solid ground and occasionally falls into a hole (Merleau-Ponty, 1951). Or, one might even consider a more foundational or "maxi-faith" upon which the whole method is based. Husserl spoke of a foundational "believing in the world"—that which is prior to any willful "letting go" and which, in fact, makes phenomenology and its creative (the "true constituting") aspect possible (Dufrenne, 1966).

Oscillating De-Alienation Movement: History of Western Ideas

In the philosophical dialogue of ideas, the West, like a temporal accordion, has been moving closer, then further, closer, then further to a rational recognition of the power of the intimacy described in certain individual creative experiences. Plato himself began to recognize the primordial heuristic power of the poet but ended up with an idealism grounded in the forms—a valuing of metaphysics or the (actually) separating "master–slave" relationship between internally grasped principle (ideal) relative to externally perceived event (fact). Aristotle attempted to reduce the alienation by grounding principle in experience. Descartes, of course, not only split mind from body—giving unto God what is God's (idealism); unto science what is science's (materialism)—but in his search for certitude found this only in the "I think," thus increasing the separation between "mind" and "matter." Bishop Berkeley carried idealism to an ultimately alienating solipsism (each subjective worldview unconnected from others and unreliable relative to the "world" perceived); only God knew the connections. This solipsism (untrustworthy subjectivity) in the evolution of modern science led to a "need" for externally validating (objective) attitudes and methods. Kant reduced the alienation somewhat by opening a reliable communication between humans about things which could be known (their knowable or graspable "sides") by grounding reason and morality in *a priori* (innate) categories (Dufrenne, 1966). This still left the idea the "chief authority" and experience subservient to it. Much of modern experimental science reversed the idealistic priorities, in the case of behaviorists, denying the inherent validity of experience and non-conditioned cognition altogether.

For those of our humanistic number who worry that transpersonal psychology is taking us to "otherworldliness" in this entire Western debate (which I will summarize below), with the exception of an "outside" God, no thinker, no thought has been outside of human experience or nature. And Jesus himself claimed God to be an "inside job"—i.e., "Seek the Kingdom within." None of this dialogue has been outside of nature—only, at points, alienated from it. I am suggesting that consideration of the supraconscious, also, does not take us into some domain which transcends human experience and even nature viewed in a broadened way.

Descartes split the eternal from the perishable in the subject—the former which he joined through "soul" to God, the latter to the object world. Mind, sometimes in drag as brain, worked both sides of the street. Most idealists before and after him (e.g., Plato and Kant—ironic in that idealism generally is viewed as setting man apart from animal) placed the mind (the predisposing basis for logic and reasoning) at the level of the animal—much as instincts, given and built-in (a point we return to later). That everyday experience is untrustworthy relative to some "ideal reality" was presumed the fault of limited sense experience.

Empiricists tended to ground the consistencies found in human experience—as did Freud and most behaviorists—in instincts (e.g., thirst, hunger, sex drives, etc.). That everyday experience is untrustworthy relative to some presumed "outside natural or divine reality" was attributed to the distortions engendered by these drives.

Maslow (1968), by the "mind" route but based on experience (his own and that reported by others), attempted to encompass all the positions in the previous historical debate via a hierarchy leading from the most basic instinctual needs through that which he also considered a somewhat "innate" human drive ("instinctoid") towards *self-actualization*. Here he joined Bergson (1992). Maslow saw this path towards full human blossoming as a de-alienating one. In the sense that the distortions separating truth and experience diminish on the way "up." Wilber (1983) follows a similar path but takes it into what are now seen as transpersonal domains. The "up" (*Up from Eden*), however, as we noted in the "progress–regress" paradox of creativity, is also down: "down" from "self," "down" from "ideas," "down" to what "is," down to the human condition in its finitude–infinitude. The former is stressed by existentialists such as Sartre and Camus—and Buddha (whose writings at points parallel those of the existentialists, which value lucidity, authenticity, freedom, and responsibility)—all based on recognition of the finitude of the human condition. The latter is stressed by Buddha, who (at least linguistically, is not all that different) values full consciousness, being in tune, liberation, and compassion. This latter is born of a recognition, a reminiscence, an insight—an illumination into the reality that one *is* other.

One Recent Path of De-Alienation

Over the past century in the Western tradition, the phenomenological movement has, within itself, been step by step reducing the alienations identified with idealism and materialism, between experienced and experiencer. Husserl plied a new soft path between alienating idealism, where the idea is authority of order, and materialism, equally alienating, in its complete surrender to chaos. His was a path oscillating between experience and reflection. Heidegger established a more intimate link, a fundamental "being in the world," which implies at the start "belongingness." Merleau-Ponty rendered this epistemological– ontological relationship even more ambiguously intimate by discerning it in the lived body. All the phenomenologists by one variant or another found an endogenous teleology and volition—a human path and impetus for the search—in *intentionality*, "the remarkable property of conscious to be conscious of" (Ricoeur, 1967), a "property" which is humanly given and which comes the closest in this position to being "instinctive." All phenomenologists recognize the inherent (not link of strangers) link between experiencer and experience: "Consciousness is consciousness *of* something." They also recognize, at least methodologically, the pattern of "progress–regress" inherent in the creative process—e.g., bracketing and the passage from "premiere" to "deuxieme naivete." They certainly recognize the diversity of lived realities that nonetheless are, as human experiences (far different from the solipsism of Bishop Berkeley, which predisposed both "introspectionism" and "objectivistic" psychologies) potentially understandable to other humans. They certainly recognize the role of intuition, which plays a significant part throughout the methodological process.

Methodological Phenomenology Lacks the Lacks:
Nothingness, the Vital Quality, the Radical Innocence

As close to intimacy as phenomenology gets in its foundational thought and by its method (and Moustakas' [1990] *Heuristic Research* comes very close as method to the space of the poet), it cannot on its own seem to shake a certain Apollonian complacency which, were this Mount Olympus, would smell of raw meat to Dionysius. The missing ingredient is *lack*, as experienced individually: the nothingness which has no essential structures; the implicit vitality which lights up life and a poem; and the indescribably more radical source of the innocence which, for each, uniquely engenders that sense of lack and energizes the dynamics for overcoming it.

Existentialists from Sartre to May have found the universal human sense of lack in the finitude of the human condition as experienced—and that experience aerated by the experience of nothingness. But the psychoanalytic schools have particularized, and in the case of original psychoanalysis energized, that sense of lack and its generative possibilities. Why does this, and not that, human individual sharing the human condition reach from personal tragedy to, say, Adler's triumphant creative self? After all, not everybody sharing the human condition suffers the "long dark night," or fights the evil demons to achieve Christ or Buddha consciousness or even the inspirational friendship of Socrates' Daemon.

De-Alienating Intuition–Instinct and Energy–Consciousness

To locate the radical innocence which generates by its own lack an energetic path to self-understanding, Paul Ricoeur (1970) leans on the father of psychoanalysis himself. He gives full acknowledgment to the primacy of Freud's instincts—the energy furnace—or the clamorous Life Instincts, and the most silent, the Death Instincts. By the path described above of moving regressively–progressively from reflection to innocence, "telos" to "arche" through Freud's own de-sacralizing hermeneutics, which terminates with the unsurpassability of the instincts, Ricoeur discerns in these very instincts—asserting their desires in a world of "no"s—a hermeneutics of the sacred. Sublimation, in Ricoeur's view, is the path not only of accommodation to prohibition, but through its creative expression the path of self-knowledge. It is a path moving from the timeless archaic (the repetitious, unchanging cry) of instinct out through its expression in symbols (characterized by multiple and changing meanings) born of its struggles, which consequently "progressively" light up new meanings and potential for consciousness that grow directly out of this dynamic. The instincts—energy, at virtually every level—are intimately involved in the emerging meaning and self-understanding. It is *their* meaning. Telos is the meaning of and for the archaic. In a like vein, Read (1957) sees intuition as an expression in consciousness of the instincts, an expression which through language or other symbol-creating vehicles attunes us to the source, itself, of the instincts.

These positions of Ricoeur and Read at least bring us into the ballpark of understanding how ever-present, repetitive instinct—associated with body and energetics—may be both close to yet manifestly different from the furtive yet originality-engendering intuition typically associated with mind or consciousness. But, also, how the term supraconscious might have another, apparently opposite name—that is, universal or cosmic *energy*.

From recent transpersonal literature where the relationship between Eastern and Native American spirituality is being explored, Gallegos (1990) has been looking at the relationship of body, image, and consciousness by relating Native American animal spirits to the Hindu Tantric Yogic tradition and its Chakra system. "In" each of us are a series of animal spirits which, when recognized and spoken to, become our guides from lower to higher consciousness. We are guided by their characteristic instinctual patterns. In this system, instinctual behaviors are linked by levels of consciousness—or, put inversely, an energetic pattern is broken open, via imagery, by new insights. For instance, the insight of recognition that "one *is* other" parallels the opening of the "heart Chakra." Both openings, body and consciousness, are accompanied by a profound sense of compassion.

Experience, Intuition, and Instinct

Many parapsychologists class the various manifestations of psychical phenomena under the broader category of intuition. Roll (personal communication), who has been studying psychic phenomena for over a quarter century, particularly in relationship to the philosophical mind–body problem, not only conceives of these phenomena in natural terms but concludes that they manifest themselves much more frequently and completely in intimate relational settings. While differentiated in sig-nificant ways from what are typically called "transpersonal" experiences, psychical phenomena seem to have in common with one another a specific, tangible, concrete (temporally and spatially limited) side, along another "side" that seems to defy normal time–space dimensions. In other words, psychic phenomena (the remarkable part) seem not to take place out of experience but through the intimacy of experience and relationships.

Leontiev (1984), a student of Vygotsky, in a sphere of inquiry quite distant from that of the paranormal, speaks specifically of how the concrete (technology) and the relationship one has to it opens up historical (archetypical?) memories for an individual. As an example, over the centuries, the plow has evolved as an instrument to meet the soil perfectly at one end (the blade) and at the other end (handle) to suit perfectly the plower. Evolved over centuries of experience, the plow "speaks" best how it is to be optimally used by its "voice" of producing gracefully. As the novice plower, through experience, moves in closer and closer to the plowing skill, attunement to the plow, there begins to open up for him a sense of the farmer, an experience memory of all farmers at all time. Again, the concrete experience is the vehicle for this passage beyond the concrete and ordinary time–space dimensions. Put differently, this "opening" is a consequence of an achieved intimacy with the instrument, which by design and evolution intimately links farmer and soil. To recount a like personal experience, my greatest childhood desire was to be a graceful, dancing, ice skater. I was embarrassed when my young daughter asked to learn how to skate, and I realized that my "skill" had in all these years not moved beyond that of a clumsy novice. Soon, she was skating the dream I always had for myself. One day, in discouragement, I simply let myself fall dejectedly back to where the whole (the rear) of the blade touched the ice. I realized I had always been in a position slightly forward, as if to run. At the moment the whole blade touched the ground, I realized "I had hit it," the secret of others. I felt I could do, and within days was doing, everything I had ever dreamed of on skates. I sensed myself in a state of "grace." I was the skater and understood all that meant.

There is also what we might call a maturational or developmental preparation for what is experienced. *Gulliver's Travels* is a well-known classic. The way the language of Swift—words, sentences, paragraphs—is configured, it is a story distinct from any other classic which may, in fact, use the same language. Yet this story, typically, speaks differently to the child and adult. The child sees "little" and "big" people. The undergraduate student picking up the same book he or she read as a child, now (at least by the professor's expectations) sees much more in the story. Any student may see more or different in the story than another, but no student can see more than it is humanly possible to see—that is, as a coherence. But what we know from literature, this passage in words takes us through archetypical experiences to the eternal. What else is a classic but that which speaks to all times and places?

For children, this beyond-time–space is given in the "Once upon a time" and "forever after." Is this not also an unreflected sensing in the present moment of that "consciousness" beyond time–space—what Merleau-Ponty called the world of "ultra choses"? Like fantasy, play and imaging bring us adults closer to the "primary processes" of imagination, and closer to the source of creativity; such play consciousness, as Piaget pointed out, is not confused by the child with that of everyday "reality" experience. Piaget tells the story of the little girl playing with her "sick doll," offering it an aspirin. Gramps comes up and trying to join her asks if "we should take the doll to the hospital"; the child looks at him and retorts, "Don't you know this is just make-believe?" I am not suggesting that fantasy or imagination is supraconscious or even intuitive. But rather, this is a spontaneous state of consciousness more attuned to the "realities" which speak from a beyond-time–space dimension.

Postmodern Diversity: Self, Diverse Selves, Selfless

A striking observation made of creative children, versus those "more reality-bound" (Getzels & Jackson, 1962), is that while both groups tend to live out contradictory vocational fantasies (I want to be a doctor; no, a lawyer; no, a dancer; no, a . . .) up to a certain age, the testably more creative children maintain this pluralistic "tolerance for ambiguity" space considerably longer than those who settle for and begin working towards a realistic goal. Much postmodern thinking (e.g., Gergen, 1991) tends to see this pluralistic identity as the reality into which our times are moving. One lives multiple selves more attuned to the postmodern reality that there is nothing but "relative truth." It is also via the necessities of modern technology, according to Gergen, that we arrive at this recognition of multiple selves. This multiple-selves conception (distinct from the romantic sense of "inner self") may be closer to the selflessness which Eastern and transpersonal philosophers speak to in the passage towards the supraconscious. At least the illusion of a solid (integrity-valuing) self which needs transcending to succeed on this illumination path is no longer an obstacle. Thus, the movement would be from self to multiple selves to selfless. The path towards illumination in the Eastern sense is one (being discovered now in the Western postmodern experience) which recognizes the apparent contradictions lived out by a single self. In a world now void of truth, this multiple self-essence ("things in themselves") needs a new, empathetic, non-dualistic language. So postmodern man, unlike rational man, communicates largely through intuitive, inherently paradoxical, non-linear, language—e.g., metaphor. H. Smith (1972), in the context of Tibetan Buddhism, puts the typical contradictory nature of experience this way: To the drowning man water is a bane; to the swimmer a boon. This partly accounts for much of the internal contradiction we often (disturbingly) recognize in ourselves—e.g., I love my wife (under these circumstances but...). It is on the path to illumination that we recognize this relativism of everyday reality.

Intuition and Variations on a Life Theme

One does not have to accept at full value Gergen's contentions that plural selves are the reality of the future. And, beyond this, imagine a Zelig or Protean human more attuned to "cosmic" reality to recognize that that value so associated with creativity, "tolerance for ambiguity," may be an experiential way of tuning in more fully to the power of intuition. Paradoxical and metaphorical (intuitive poetic) language is also the mark of creative individuals and of those who by other thinkers' visions are able to integrate (Maslow), individuate (Jung), or "turn the diverse and apparently discordant variations of 'self experience' into a life theme, discovered and created in process" (Bergson, 1940).

Bergson's teleological metaphysics implies two other historical notions: *vocatus* = call and *missus* = mission, associated with intuition both by Western classical philosophers and Christians, which they class with deepest insights and revelation relative to personal attunement— e.g., the call to the "greater self," for Maslow, or "Being all that you can be." This "attunement" that one finds in the project, creative or those identified with Eastern practice, is typically identified with a moment of "effortlessness"—e.g., the painting *painting* itself, or the farmer through the plow attuned to the soil, or, as I described, the skating experience as one of "grace," that quality we often jealously ascribe to animals who operate by instinct.

Reason, Intuition, and Instinct

When coming to God, we are told by Christians to "come small." In the Western mind, nothing is smaller than the instincts. And no mindset more humble than that of innocence (the *beginner's mind*). We are also told to listen to that "still small voice." In the Western modern world, nothing is more fragile or furtive than intuition. The human, of course, is an animal, in the Western mind most clearly distinguished from others by the power of reason. That reasoning mind, not surprisingly in support of what it does best, has put down both intuition and the instincts. Or put differently, that mind is reduced to such parochialism left unguided by these that it cannot recognize its own kinship to them. More likely the problem is the dualistic split we've lived between mind and body, spirit and soul. It is the de-alienating of these splits, not an opposition to intellect, that should mark the onset of the postmodern epoch.

So, the question opens: Is reason (even logic in its hard-core form) an opposite to instinct and intuition? Plato's mature answer, of course, was no. Reason could build on itself and detect certain flaws, in the way the poets couldn't, and Daemon was mischievously unreliable. Yet both were more immediately attuned to a source of inspiration than reason was. Looked at differently, for all the mischief and tricks it could play on the mind, intuition had a very solid source of validation—that is, reason and experience themselves. Remindful of the Haines underwear ad, there is no intuition until reason and experience have said so. Still, from the perspective of supraconscious, intuition knows—and, as the supraconscious, is—the bigger path. As history tells us about creative projects rejected in their time, the validation might not be immediate. In the greater view, the kinship between reason and intuition may be far more intimate. In both the Platonic (the innate forms) and Kantian (*a priori*) sense, the basic structures of reason come with the human hardware. As such, they hold the status at least akin to that of human instincts. Sensing a logical contradiction has much in common with the "I smell a rat" intuition. And as the internal lawfulness of mathematics and metaphysics indicate, and the intriguing way they have so much in common, one might even propose the hypothesis that logic and intuition—so sharply separated in the modern period—are kissing cousins, two openings to the same source. And, like these, are prone to family squabble.

Chapter 13

Self, Multiple Selves, and the Illusion
of Separate Selfhood
(1999)[1]

Editors' note: This was Mike's invited address upon receiving the first
Abraham Maslow Heritage Award *presented by the Society for*
Humanistic Psychology at the annual meeting of the American
Psychological Association in Boston, Massachusetts, 1999.

Part 1: Historical Split

The "Who Am I?" Question

Just when it seemed that the self had been safely and comfortably
brought back into psychology, mainly as the centerpiece of a humanistic
psychology, we in the field—and especially humanistic psychologists—
find ourselves again asking the "Who am I?" question. Either "I" am an
intrinsically core responsible self, as humanistic psychologists would
have it. Or, from some postmodern perspectives, the term "I" speaks for
a multitude of "selves" playing themselves out reconstructively in their
embedded cultural, historical contingency. Or "I" speak from an
enlightened recognition that "I" am *other*, my greater identity is with
the whole of Being, having dropped the illusion of my separate selfhood.

We encounter this schism nearly forty years after Abraham
Maslow published his *Toward a Psychology of Being* (Maslow, 1968),
and as currently the "*self*" he spoke of finds itself challenged more from

[1] Arons, M. (1999). Self, multiple selves, and the illusion of separate selfhood. *The Humanistic Psychologist, 27*, 187–211. doi:10.1080/08873267.1999.9986904 | Copyright © 1999 by the American Psychological Association. Adapted with permission from the American Psychological Association.

its *zeitgeist* allies, postmodern and transpersonal psychologists than from its *positivist, behaviorist,* or *classical psychoanalytic* opponents of yesteryear, all of whom had thought themselves able to explain the self away.

Long-Term Competitors, Recent Allies

The tension expressed in the current three views of self has a long history in Western philosophy, going back to the pre-Socratics under the rubric "Flux and Essence" and implicated in the debate between Plato and the Sophists. It was argued through six centuries of post-Aristotelian debate about the eudaimonic or fulfillment, then to some degree variously under such problematics as the "Absolute and the Relative," "One and the Many," "Sacred and Profane," "Nominalism and Realism," and in psychology as "Elementism" vs. the "Molar," "Gestalt," or, recently, "Holism." And it is a constant issue in what Huxley called the "Perennial Philosophy."

And yet humanistic, postmodern, and transpersonal psychologies share a current history as post-positivist. Indeed, the three emerged at mid-century as a shared critique of the limits of the natural science model as applied to human beings. And as consequence of this allied reaction at the methodological level, they all share a leaning towards qualitative or human science research methods.

That which the three viewpoints share should encourage us not to conclude off the bat that we are dealing with hopelessly contradictory visions. Moreover, the length of the tensional history they share and the fact that no historical conclusion has yet been drawn definitively favoring one over the other views suggests that all three claims deserve to be held in due respect. This means neither being reduced or subordinated to the others, nor left in a state of tolerant eclecticism, nor left as the famous postmodern "pastiche" (like the current expression "Whatever"). Those easy outs give us political peace but leave us out of touch with the problematics' inherent profundity, that which empowers and lights up the search for a more integrated understanding, the first steps towards which take us to a paradox.

Paradox of the Universality of the Relative, No Stranger to Any of the Contending Views

The fact of this ongoing historical dialogue paradoxically *universalizes* the changing and the relative. That is, each claim is recognized universally valid. But only as relative to the validity of the others which contest it. And only as this contest emerges and reemerges, culturally and historically ventilated in changing contexts via an ongoing hermeneutic. At first blush, given the ongoing tensional ambiguity, this is a status which would seem more supportive of a postmodern view. However, I suggest it is a status inherent to all three positions on self.

If the historical debate amongst the three views has no definitive victors, that doesn't mean it gets nowhere. These three positions (each with its own reality claim and unique historical place and cultural mission, to be sure), seen developmentally and microgenetically, are mutually referential and revealing. Each is redefined and made clearer as history rolls on, in a way as the wheels, pedals, and handlebars refer distinctly to the integrity of a bike—an integrity recognized in the riding. Moreover, I contend, these three infrastructural dimensions, even as they seem to oppose themselves as alternatives to it, actually support the integrity of a humanistic psychology vision as this vision evolved in Maslow's day. In other words, humanistic psychology is comprised of and requires all three notions of "self" and should, and I feel does and always has, felt at home in each and all.

This lived comfort with the postmodern and transpersonal shows up consistently in the architecture of current humanistic psychology, where postmodern views are part of the orientations' woodwork (such as those expressed in the social constructivism of Anderson and Warmot or in the attempts to blend these views by Kvale, O'Hara, and Gergen). In addition, transpersonal presentations comprise a large share of the programming of Division 32 and AHP. More basically, it is no accident that the founders of transpersonal psychology—such as Maslow, Vich, and Sutich—were also founders of humanistic psychology and humanistic and transpersonal journals and organizations.

Even May's celebrated and controversial concerns with the

transpersonal, as it tried to establish itself as a division in the APA, were not a denial of that viewpoint but a warning by him about precipitously jumping into these realms without full existential and cultural grounding. Nor, as I will try to show below, would this compatibility of humanistic, transpersonal, and postmodern be surprising to Abraham Maslow or many of the founders of humanistic psychology. This is because they found within the humanistic self what some postmoderns and some transpersonal psychologists find missing from it.

Thus, the issue and the contest of selves is with us. And I raise this issue from a current humanistic psychology position not, as some have suggested, because humanistic psychology needs postmodernism to save it or needs transpersonal psychology to provide its spiritual dimension. I believe and hope to show that the self of humanistic psychology opens to both of these naturally—simply by being what it is.

Rejoining the Ancient Problematic
in the Contemporary Psychology Context

Here, at the turn of the millennium, it is report time in our history. History requires a parting of the ways and return. It is time for these three ways, all sharing a long tensional history in the West and allied in the recent post-positivist *zeitgeist*, to report back on their journeys and to make sense of their stories together. First, we must recognize that each of the three versions of self comes from a different place in that *zeitgeist.*

Humanistic place in the *zeitgeist.* Humanistic psychology, as its name indicates, grows out of and remains one outgrowth of the discipline of psychology. It is a reaction against a psychology expressing the greater model of modernism, which is defined as study of the individual—but where the individual self had been dealt out of that psychology or reduced to scientifically quantifiable causes or other sources of determinism.

Postmodern place in the *zeitgeist.* The postmodern emerged largely from and has prospered in the other social sciences and the humanities. Its historical role in the West was as necessary arbitrator between dichotomous hegemonies, claimants to ultimate authority and power from a greater source beyond—the one of religion and its divine source, its mode of knowing, blind faith; the other a positivistic science, its source natural lawfulness, which skeptically plays dumb to everything it can't measure. Both hegemonies of faith and science and the broader modern link to metaphysics have been undergoing a series of deconstructions along with the historical worldviews which had empowered them. The notion of a core or "source" self is one, and the autonomous power attributed to it is another of these hegemonies under deconstruction.

Transpersonal place in the *zeitgeist*. Transpersonal psychology emerged as reaction to the de-sacralization of everyday life in modern Western technological society and to de-spiritualized religion.

Metaphorically speaking, in the West at least, these three have battled on different fronts, but of the same war, prompted by the same classical question, *"Who am I?"*—all recognizing that the "unexamined life is not worth living."

Part 2: Critiques of the Humanistic Psychology Self

The humanistic psychology self, for both postmoderns and trans-personal psychologists, is seen as too narrow and overly assuming to itself core status, agency, credit, choice, and power.

Postmodern Critique

For postmoderns, the humanistic psychology self is a relic of modernism, specifically romanticism, but of a general enlightenment philosophy going back to Descartes. It's a fiction of centralized identity and authority and power of the individual will, and the Cartesian source for all knowing, reposing on "I am, therefore I exist." It places the individual over the culture. Thus, it leaves one's sense of self-determinism blind to one's infrastructural embeddedness in language and the cultural history of that language and, therefore, leaves one bereft of full awareness of contextual currents which are the ground of one's path of understanding and activity—like the water the fish doesn't know because it is so intrinsically a part of it. Yet, this portrayal of self in humanistic psychology by postmodern critiques appears strangely fixed, with little recognition of itself in it. It is repeated as if an incontrovertible, unified, truth, a postmodern "mantra," a strange position to be in for an orientation which questions all totalisms. Moreover, Maslow seems to give more credit to the reality of culture in the making of the person than most postmoderns give to the reality of Maslow's self, largely because most postmoderns start with a sophistic dismissal of reality, per se. I propose a quite different interpretation of the humanistic psychology "self"—one which both supports the postmodern position to a point and, yet, one which avoids some pitfalls of that position, especially its own acknowledged proneness to nihilism and its apparent inadequacies as ethical guide.

Transpersonal Critique
For transpersonal psychologists, "the illusion of separate selfhood" is recognized as a limitation of consciousness, the cloud of ignorance that obscures the fuller realization of self (which joins by reciprocal opening of consciousness to compassion); the paradox is that by being one's self "fully" consciously, "one is other." Many transpersonalists see this humanistic psychology self too tied to this illusion of separateness. Many see it too bogged down at the level of personal feelings and id–ego demands. Viewed from the transpersonal vantage, the self often implied in humanistic psychology activities can appear narcissistic, locked in ignorant pursuits (including certain ideas of "self-actualization") which are illusory in the belief that they will bring fulfillment. Reciprocally, many humanistic psychologists liken the transpersonal to religion and, sharing a view of religion with Freud, find the illusion reversed. That is, they see transpersonal psychology trying to skirt the responsibility which goes with existential freedom identified with the humanistic self and, looking beyond this—or too precipitously arriving at this state of consciousness—leaping to the equivalent of a "father figure": a greater authority or power which would fill a more banal need (rather than a higher state claimed by transpersonalists) for a sense of consolation, security, and assuring union. Through these differences sometimes expressed, it should be

recalled that humanistic psychology was one significant opening in mid-century to Eastern (and transpersonal) views. And this opening occurred as the more "transpersonal" qualities of the "self-actualizing" subjects emerged to recognition.

Understandable Critiques of the Self of Humanistic Psychology

If both postmodern and transpersonal understandings do not do the *self* of the humanistic psychologists full justice (as I contend here), I think nonetheless that these critical views of it do not emerge without grounds. There are understandable, if not fully justifiable, bases which ground these views of the inadequacy of the humanistic psychology *self*. Let me touch on some of these. But let me also point out, without getting into the same detail, that both the postmodern and transpersonal orientations are also subject to distortions of their own—and often for the same reasons. Indeed, at the stereotype level, we can view the humanistic as "touchy feely," the transpersonal as "airy fairy," and the postmodern as "wordy nerdy."

All historical reactions. One of the reasons all three lend themselves to stereotype is that they are all reactions and point to something "missing" or seriously "amiss" in the *zeitgeist* they shared. Some of that noted "missing" was unique to the reactive movement; much of it was shared across the three movements. That reactivity itself is a source of distortion and limit. All three views are prone to this critique of limitation and distortion to the degree that they are forces of historical reaction, each taking up its (unique) charge against (what they shared) the modern from different angles.

American humanistic psychology emerges specifically as reaction to a period characterized by social conformism within the greater socio-historical context of depersonalization and inauthenticity largely associated with scientism and modernism. Any reassertion of self in any form, in that *zeitgeist*, needed to ring bells of positive recognition of that which was missing. It is not surprising, then, that the self which would emerge from the humanistic psychology revolution would be in large degree formed by the "recognizable" from a cultural past. The early auto looked like the carriage.

Another obvious basis for the limits noted of the humanistic psychology self resides in the sphere it grew out of. It was a psychology which, by its historical disciplinary charge under the traditional paradigm, dealt with individuals. It was a field at mid-20th century which had forgotten or forsaken its name of "psyche," whereas the humanities, out of which the postmodern grew, deals with individuals in context and the social sciences in specific disciplinary contexts.

Another possible source of the critique of the humanistic self, its limits, and distortions derives from its philosophical parentage. Humanistic psychology borrowed much of its notion of self from the existential exploration of authenticity, which for many gained a reputation as a philosophy of despair. And, for one example, a misunderstood view of Sartre's "Hell is others" left the popular impression of each person being condemned to inescapable isolation and burdened by choice and responsibility from a meaning vacuum. Such stereotypes of existentialism, which Maslow (1968) himself criticized, certainly reinforced a kind of "ideal-less lone ranger" image of the "self" re-emerging in the humanistic psychology literature.

Still another understandable basis for the limits and distortions perceived in the humanistic "self" lies in its mission. Humanistic psychology speaks of the elite but to the popular; it is an aristocratic vision distributed to the masses. And this was done quite consciously, intentionally, and proudly by the founders of this psychology. Such popularization is not without serious dangers.

The popularization of the traditionally esoteric problem: Down and upsides. This condition of elitism requires a moment's reflection. Especially in the form Maslow rendered it, humanistic psychology—the self which could fully actualize its potentials to the point of "self-realization" and "self-sufficiency," even to the point of touching the divinity within—previously belonged exclusively to those who had already the means to fulfill their basic needs. Seen retrospectively, it is not a coincidence that this view of self took hold in classless, melting pot, homogenizing America at the time of great general prosperity. But also, such dissemination of what had been esoterically cloistered was endogenous to the modern worldview. It is the basis of political democracy and science. In his own words, Maslow was both a patriotic American and great believer in science. And humanistic psychology has a distinctly "American," "democratic," and even "scientific"—if we mean proving its validity in the field of scientific psychology–flavor to it (Maslow, 1966).

The task of "popularizing" the traditionally esoteric was risky. There is a danger in vulgarization, noted in the Biblical "don't feed pearls to swine." Just as the story of Gulliver will be understood differently by the child and literature professor—though through maturation, learning, and insight, one could (and by the humanistic self-actualizing model needs to) pass from one to other states of consciousness and meanings—so also are the presentments of humanistic psychology with its fuller notion of self; but, and even more so, poststructural and transpersonal views are also subject to the same interpretive vulnerability/strengths.

The upside of this popularization is to offer wide access to profound insight. The downside of popularization can mean reduction of that profundity to simplistic literalisms and mass-produced and reproducible "profoundities," one of which is the stereotyped humanistic psychology self criticized by postmoderns and transpersonalists.

But let us also note in passing that Maslow and other founders of humanistic psychology disseminated their views of self popularly because they believed these views to be universal and cross-cultural. They also believed that these views of a self fulfilling its potentials—this being a good and valued end—was also good for the culture and times people lived. But this wasn't only a view of an autonomous individual isolated from culture, as is currently suggested by many postmoderns. Maslow (1968) wrote:

> The authentic or healthy person may be defined not in his own light, not in his autonomy ... not as different from the environment, independent of it or opposed to it, but rather in environmental terms, e.g., the ability to master the environment, to be capable, adequate, effective, competent in

relation to it. (p. 179)

Return to other critiques of the humanistic psychology "*self.*"
But let's get back to the sources which justify the criticisms of the
humanistic self. Beyond the normal process of popularization was the
tendency among early humanistic psychologists—one which persists—
to accept, even encourage, pluralistic versions of this psychology and
human science approaches which stress the relative and interpretive.
This openness is based on the belief that different people are at
different stages of their own development and come from their own
spaces to those spaces and activities which best serve them.

Here again we have a two-edged sword. On the one hand, this
openness to everything left humanistic psychology and its "self"
vulnerable to being seen and rubricized as anything. On the other hand,
this openness defies the criticism by both postmoderns and transpersonalists that it is a closed, narcissistic, lonely, and deluded self.
Instead, the self of humanistic psychology is *where it needs to be*. And
that being where it needs to be could be, variously, coming from the
resources of language and culture, split into many selves, or in state of
disillusionment with its separate self.

The humanistic self was more like *Gulliver's Travels*, interpretable
at all levels of where one is in one's life and meaningfully open to all
other levels and dimensions at appropriate times and passages. By
being open to nearly every interpretation, I mean that there was no
attempt to establish a single cult-like true view of self or a standard by
which to know it. This led to the criticism of humanistic psychology as
a kind of circus. All interpretations and exercises and practices which
were "self"-developing were accepted, like so many gods in the Roman
garden. But these self-developing manifestations could also be seen as
self-indulgences; and in some cases, they were either or both. That is
what that wonderful ongoing celebration of the Association for
Humanistic Psychology much resembled, and all the growth centers
and practices which spoke to self at all levels of its awareness. Like the
1960s itself, its temporal home turf, what was so wonderful about it is
also what lends itself to such criticism.

This openness which characterized humanistic psychology not only in theory—not only in intention to popularize the esoteric but carried throughout in application—clearly established that psychology's vulnerability: engendering and sustaining stereotypes. But (let's recognize this relative to our theme) on the other side, this consistent openness to diversity is also a *de facto* rejection of the critiques leveled by both postmodern and transpersonalists of a "closed," "isolated," "narcissistic," or "touchy-feely" self. Consistently in the development of humanistic psychology, many of the activities were fully open to culture, many fully open to transpersonal dimensions. The historical openness of humanistic psychology to diversity—its historical coinciding with popular counterculture movements and the drug culture of the 1960s, at the same time—explains some relatively valid bases for the critiques generated by the postmoderns and transpersonalists and yet, by the same token, imply their ultimate invalidity. Because even these excursions into excess were also excursions into the home bases of the postmodern and transpersonal.

The humanistic self at its most populist and criticizable was openly exploring itself from outside-in, from top to bottom—from its source in body through intrigue with Reich, Merleau-Ponty, or yoga to its reopened search for cultural roots as in Black-White encounter, women's groups, or ,more broadly, in the cultural revolution. And its search for a ground of being via encounter groups, meditation, diet, or in the music, art, and drugs of the period. The humanistic *self* played itself out fully in postmodern and transpersonal territory because that which preoccupied "it" was recognized as "home turf."

Considering the Philosophical Differences Together

At this point, let's play some hard ball to try to seek reconciliation amongst the three views of self without reducing one's to the other's, without resorting to a pleasant and peace-engendering eclecticism and mere tolerance, but instead by going to the integrity which intrinsically joins all three in their very tensions. Let's pass from history to core philosophy, and here go after the most serious differences we find between the three positions.

Here are a few fast balls. I extrapolate and stretch to take them to their clearest and most extreme affirmation. At points, for reasons that become clearer below, I have added to the three views a fourth, that of our Hellenic ancestors as they pondered the question of human fulfillment.

A: Nature of self. For postmoderns, there is no essential self. There may be multiple oft-competing dispositions, or selves. For Maslow, there is a *core* self that in the process of awareness and realization comes to see the coherence of its multiple, often contradictory, pulls. Each person has a nature, biologically based—part species, part individual. For transpersonal psychologists, there is an individual self which, by profound realization, in deep compassion-opening recognition, comes to a greater identity. A realization is brought to consciousness through this self and linguistic culture context, but is not limited to it, exhausted by it, or understandable solely in its terms. It, like the individual self, is known in transcendence.

B: Self and culture. For postmoderns, all is subject to context. For Maslow, this self is species-wide, universal, and its characteristics go across culture and times. For transpersonal psychologists, there are states of awareness which are non-culture bound, but these reveal culture and self in ways not given directly by the normal culture, language, or contextual interpretations. These states are not limited to, or exhausted by, interpretation.

C: Self-consciousness. For postmoderns, we are born into language and culture and are historically embedded, all of which predispose meanings which precede us and inescapably guide and limit our individual meanings and values. For Maslow, the self-actualizer is recognized as transcending culture as acculturation. Maslow shares this insight with the Hellenists who saw the first steps towards self-knowledge as the questioning of one's enculturation (Annas, 1993). Transpersonal psychologists speak of states which transcend Maslow's self-actualizers.

D: Self—Construction, discovery, or realization? For postmoderns, the self is a construction. For Maslow, the self is discovered. Again, like the Hellenists—or the basis for entering therapy—one begins the search for self because of dissatisfaction, and one seeks, as an end, self-sufficiency. For transpersonal psychologists, one is brought to the search for self by the wheel of desire/dissatisfaction, which suffering is not transcended until the illusion of separate selfhood is realized.

E: Ethics. For postmoderns, there is no inherent universal ground for ethics; whereas for Maslow, the self being itself fully is that ground. The development of self is movement towards the intrinsic; one comes to recognize the source of ethics less from rules without, more from realizations within. As with the Hellenists, the person seeking fully him/herself discovers that others have that same self-interest and, thus, ironically, the search for self gives credibility to the polis, or community (Annas, 1993). For transpersonal psychologists, the ground of ethics is identified in the very consciousness which comes with compassionate realization that one *is* other. It is no longer *do unto others as you would have them do unto you*, but to do unto others is to do unto you. All is you in the broadest identification.

F: Ways of knowing. For postmoderns, knowledge is grounded in dialogue and interpretation, through a language already preformed by history. For Maslow, there is such a thing as *direct* knowing, manifesting more frequently and becoming more accurate with the advances of self-actualization—i.e., "being cognition," which is less distorted by "deficiency needs." The Hellenists understood that one came to self-understanding through a tandem of intuition and logic, both operating in their cultural contexts (Annas, 1993). For transpersonal psychologists, there are both indirect and direct routes to states of enlightenment.

G: Growth and identity. For postmoderns, there are discontinuities—imposed by a number of factors, including event/context requirements and multidimensionality itself—which defy all efforts at a rational coherence and ultimate predictability. For Maslow, these discontinuities are the creative resources of deeper understanding and are unity and grainy sources for personal growth and stability of identity. For transpersonal psychologists, expanding states of consciousness are both platforms of discontinuity and steps to insightful unity.

Seeking a Unity Thanks to Diversity:
Coherence Thanks to Contradiction

Even discounting the necessary oversimplifications in this list of comparisons, are we really speaking of three different, partially or fully incompatible selves? I think not. One can go pretty far with the postmoderns and their stress on the primacy of language, culture, and history without necessarily discounting even the most radical views of the core self. Indeed, Thesis One can actually support and provide the necessary resources for Thesis Two. And one can admit the core self, even in the strong sense that Maslow gave it: biologically grounded and universal, across time, culture, and history.

Distinction: Self and identity. First, we need to make the crucial distinction Maslow makes, often unnoted, between "self" and "identity." Maslow's self is biologically grounded. That is, self is part of human nature across culture, language, history. He notes, "Identity has various real, sensible, and useful meanings to self." Maslow (1968) puts it this way in assessing the peak experience: "My feeling is that people in peak experiences are most their identities, closest to their real selves, most idiosyncratic" (p. 103).

Next, identity, that which the nature of self needs and seeks in its own interest and actualization, is relative in a number of ways. First, there are the various meanings one gives to identity, as in different cultures and times and as expressed in different languages. The picture Maslow gives is that identity is to the self like the food the body needs. That is, identities serve along the route to self-actualization—developmentally, culturally, vocationally, and open in transpersonal transcendence. There are identities speaking to the "real" (I am a boy, born to this family, in this nation, etc.); to the talents, skills, and circumstances (e.g., I am an artist, carpenter, etc.); and those identities which change with consciousness. One identifies with the "whole." There was, after all, a male Jesus born in Nazareth, an historical individual, carpenter by trade, a messiah by "vocation" (calling, *vocatus*), and fully identified with God.

And this notion of identity as "self food" is analogous to a fetus's need for a mother's womb, in the interest of outgrowing that womb, just as the creative individual needs a strong ego to allow it to regress in the interest of greater insight than the current reality lived. As transpersonal psychologists argue, a culturally well-fed self (fed on the identities it needs) can develop self to such a degree that it can let its own individual and cultural identity go—not so much as marks of identity but as the *all of him or her*, in the realization of a greater identity with the ground of being. By analogy, in the creativity literature Kris, using psychoanalytic language, spoke of "regression in the service of ego." Only a strong and secure ego, supported by identities, could "afford" to let go of its attachments and hold on reality in its own greater creative interest.

Self's "multi-identity." Let's expand this important point. The fact that self is not its identities *per se* is implied in the transpersonal idea of the *illusion of separate selfhood*. The word *separate* is key. Separate implies only one identification, which implies it is none "other"; hence, the *separate* self. That implication taken as last word is the illusion. In fact, as mentioned, *one* has a number of identifications—member of a family, town, culture, vocation, interest group, etc.—or the identity one has as a separate individual. The illusion is not that these are false or need to be *traded in* on a big transpersonal identity with the whole, but that these were multiple and limited in that greater identification was not yet realized. The new identification with the whole, the compassionate recognition that one *is* other, alters everything in its insight and yet, in another sense, it changes nothing of these other identifications.

More whole, more idiosyncratic, more fully the diversity of identities. Maslow indicates that in "peak experiences" people are most their identities—closest to their real selves and, he adds, "most idiosyncratic." This is a paradox of *self-culture* where, as people become more themselves, they are less bound by the cultural forms which nonetheless remain part of their identities. Yet they are more capable of joining these directly, more intimately, from "where they are." They become more the culture as they become less enculturated and more "themselves ideographically" in the way a lover senses him or herself more fully and uniquely and yet more intimately apart or "at one with" their lover. Or the way the creative individual more profoundly enters into his/her problem precisely as he or she is freed via creative breakthrough from its formal guides and limits. As Maslow (1968) said, "The more they feel themselves, the more they are able to fuse with the world, others" (p. 103).

Self and Life

Just as we needed to distinguish identity from self in order to see how each implicates the other, we need to distinguish these from "life." When Socrates says, "*The unexamined life is not worth living*," he doesn't say the unexamined *self* or *identity*, even though one has the full sense that something of what we understand by these are implied. Certainly, life in the "generic" sense is implied but not alone. Also, any person's life is what is at issue in the Socratic inquiry. All life may not be worth living if not examined, but the individual is doing more than an examination of life in the abstract. To get to this—even to the judgment of whether or not it is worth "living"—requires going through one's individual life. The inquiry itself may bring the answer, spark the life, bring the self to life, break the old identities, offer itself as reason to get up in the morning—i.e., go sit and inquire with Socrates. Or it may give meaning and worth to living by the insights of meaning gleaned in the inquiry. That is, if before I saw no reason to love my neighbor or myself, now I do. Or have good reason not to. And I may find in my inquiry the meanings of "life" in general, or none.

Just as with the identity of parenthood or culture, I am "stuck" with my life. But because of this very inescapability (even if I commit suicide, that marks *my* life) and idiosyncratic nature of life (my life is lived from wherever and whoever I am), I am linked through and by my life to the lives of others and to life itself—i.e., implied in the general question, "Is life worth living?" So, in questioning my life, I am questioning life—and in the process, the very differences and uniqueness of my life approach me to all other lives, to human life, to life. Here again, like identity, the very things which separate me (inside)—define me as distinct from others—are also the doors which can swing open to that which was, and in a sense still is, "outside." The "door-opening" inquiry doesn't reduce all life to my life or reduce my life to some general principle of life, or put me in the shoes of my neighbor across the street, or he or she in my bed. These distinctions remain and are all the more fully appreciated even as the isolation of lives, the estrangement of a life from others and all life, recedes in process. The work patterns of ants, the migratory patterns of birds—their lives which seemed before not to touch significantly my own—are now seen as one precisely recognized by the variations.

Fate as the Tools of Destiny

Playing a crucial role in *identity*, *life*, *self* are culture, history, language, and the contingencies of context. On the one hand, these are, as postmoderns contend, the primal juice into which one is born, and by which one is nourished and receives life meanings and values of identity. But at advancing levels of self-development and opening of consciousness (what the Gnostics called "spiritual maturity"), new relationships are established—with others, with the culture, with language, and with the changing context—just as the more an infant becomes him/herself, the relationship with the parents and family changes but remains also immutable. One doesn't change fathers or mothers or place and date of birth. Or what would be the value of a genealogical chart?

At the very minimum, as Sartre would see these, language, culture, history, they are the *givens*. As the Ancients would see these, they are our *fate*. But as Vygotsky (1978) points out, the givens become our tools to make tools, including the language into which we are born. The creative writer isn't simply limited and guided by the grammar and meanings in words, but uses these as resources and even, to the degree that he or she is idiosyncratically creative, enters this language in a loving intimacy and comes out of the process with new meanings and new tools for greater insight.

That which is given—which is our limits, our fate—is also that which provides the leverage for discovering and fulfilling our destinies; for fulfilling, in Maslow's sense, our "ideographic, or true, self." In creativity, the term *originality* has two vectors—one towards that which is, what we have, where we came from (i.e., the *origins*); the other towards the *new and the unique* (Arons, 1996). All this creativity and idiosyncratic quality, the adventures of the *self*, also enter into the culture, into the language, into the acts and meanings of history. There are implicated in all of these our courageous heroes, our pathetic cowards, bringing human experience from triumph to failure into the cultural pool. And language, culture, and history all become the repositories which nourish us at various levels of our search for selfhood. Like the story of Oedipus, which speaks at various levels to our relationship between fate and destiny, or *Gulliver's Travels*, read at one stage as little and big people, at another as social satire.

When postmoderns point to the primacy of language, culture, and history as distinct from an "autonomous" self of humanistic psychology, they often miss the point that language is an attempt to express human experience; that human experiences (like that of "self") cross culture and times, while the particular meanings (identities) vary with the cultural–temporal idiom.

Values and Ethics

Regarding values and ethics, this is a sphere of recognized weakness in the position by many postmoderns because the infinite regress of deconstructions makes it hard to escape a state of nihilism. Maslow did not have postmoderns in mind when he kept distinguishing the "nay-sayers" from the "yea-sayers." By the former, he meant those who would reduce the human to a rat or mechanization or to the impersonal. But he did warn of nihilism which he found as one of the dangers European existentialism could fall into. Whereas, by contrast to the "nay-sayer" view, the self, in its realization, is the highest human value, as noted in Socrates' admonition that "the unexamined life is not worth living." The Hellenists realized that there would always remain dissatisfaction until *self*—the path to fulfillment, the sense of self-sufficiency—had been achieved. Transpersonal psychologists speak of the wheel of suffering, which one gets off of only with the deepest realizations of the illusion of separate selfhood.

Eudaimonia, Ethics, and the "Good Life" of the Hellenists

Maslow had leaned heavily on the Western history of ideas, with a particular emphasis on Aristotle, which, through his own research into self-actualization, brought him out on the other side to the Eastern traditions. No accident. This post-Aristotelian, Hellenic line of inquiry focused on the question of "What is the good life?" Here was a turn towards pragmatism and humanism. Truth in some "abstract" or "cosmological" sense was not enough; there were truths especially relevant to humans because of human values. According to this human-centered, or humanistic, stress, some things (facts, truths) are more important to humans than others. Happiness, or fulfillment, or what came to be variously understood under the term *eudaimonia* (what Maslow will call *self-actualization*), had a special and unique value.

And this special and unique value became evident to logical test. We do money, longevity, relationships, power, etc., for happiness; we do not do happiness for anything else. Happiness (however it is construed) is the valued end. All other values are means relative to that end. Even the schools of "skepticism" and "cynicism," as well, ultimately, as Christianity, developed within that eudaimonic value framework. Annas (1993) points out that this eudaimonic path of inquiry exhibited across the differences of schools a common structure.

This includes an inquiry path that starts with the experience of dissatisfaction, which leads to a questioning (*deconstruction*) of one's *enculturation* by dual means of *reason* and *intuition*. The search for one's self interest—just the significance of the search itself—opens to the realization that others share this interest and value. This recognition of shared value for the Hellenists was the intrinsic ground of ethics. From within this intrinsic realization, the *polis* (or community) becomes a means towards the common good life. The eudaimonic path continues to a stage of "self-sufficiency."

Here, as with Maslow and transpersonal insights borrowed from the East, the search for human fulfillment becomes also the ethical path. For the Hellenists, it's recognition that "others'" interests are "my" interest; in Christianity, *"There but for the grace go I"*; for Maslow, the *self-actualizer* (i.e., Albert Schweitzer, Eleanor Roosevelt) is also the moral model—i.e., opening to self finds the deepest relationship to other; and for certain Eastern traditions, ethics is grounded in the fuller human realization—the opening of compassionate consciousness— that *"one is other."*

The point is not that these Hellenic, Christian, Maslowian, or transpersonal insights are exactly equivalent. They are not identical. For instance, the Hellenic "My interest is other's interest" is not the same as "I am other." Rather, the point is that there is in all a link between the value realization and fulfillment and ethical insight paths. These are the deepest insights, typically achieved by a small number of persons. And they cannot be understood in their fully intrinsic sense except by those who have followed the "self" searching, or examined "life" in and through their own contexts and contingencies, which search puts all "identities" into question (i.e., to forms of *deconstruction*). But clearly these insights enter the culture as ideals—e.g., "right to life, liberty, and the pursuit of happiness."

Ethics gleaned intrinsically through the Western eudaimonic or Eastern enlightenment inquiries enter into and are reflected in the culture and language and serve there as guides and bases for rules, laws, and forms (as we saw Hellenic insights transformed into Roman law) but which, though born into by babes, reflect the intrinsic adventure of self and its realizations in process of actualization. That babe, born into culture and language, uses the laws and cultural forms extrinsically at what Maslow calls the *deficiency* levels and takes his/her first step towards self-knowledge in a state of dissatisfaction that would lead to transpersonal insights or attunement with the "perennial philosophy"—those insights which are expressed in all cultures but which cross cultures and times.

Even though these experiences identified with this transpersonal stage of realization (that in some Eastern traditions take consciousness even beyond itself) is consigned to a sphere of the unspeakable, language, culture, and history bring those ready to "see" it to the very brink of that realization. These transformations are embedded in the language and cultural forms, such as myths. When we speak of classics, we refer to the expressions of humanness which are recognized across the contexts of time and culture. But also, these classics are those which can guide us from the most evident levels of identity and concern to the brink of the most supreme and furtive. There is nothing incompatible (only apparently inconsistent and contradictory) between this cycle of a self realizing a value telos and the community he or she comes to first question and then, with insight, support in the process. There is no incompatibility—indeed, only full compatibility—between the deconstruction and actualizing of self. Or between the fact that we are born into culture, language, and history, and the humanistic–transpersonal proposal that self insights provide the architecture of culture, and culture provides the tool or vehicle—the path from *safety* to *being* needs and values, for fullest self-realization.

The Postmodern Critique

One of the most persuasive arguments made by postmoderns for the primacy of language, culture, and history is that these are our "ever-presents" from birth to death which, like water for a fish, are taken for granted. The argument goes, we are born into a language whose history and structure we speak even as we think we speak our "selves." Indeed, *our selves* are of that substrata of language, culture, and history.

While that is true, it is also true that language speaks us—our history and culture, our values. "Our" means not the horse or that of the Martian but, as Merleau-Ponty said, that of interest and value to humans. And if these values, such as the realization of "self," are embodied in language and cultural forms, then even as we speak language, that language we speak speaks us.

Moreover, it speaks us from top to bottom. Campbell makes an interesting point about mythology. While we are born into myth as the very bottom of our experience, that mythology already speaks our telos. The telos of human value and interest, the top of our wisdom, enters at the bottom in the language we breathe from birth.

That telos of self, the hero's adventure of obstacles and frustrations, is implicated in the language. For Maslow, the calling to self is *instinctoid*—easily blocked and frustrated in poor choices, as our bodies pay the price of poor nutrition—but is persistently present as a biological pull. That towards which the biology pulls, one must imagine (like the merchant who wisely displays that which is ultimately of most value to clients) is prominently embedded in the language and culture. So that while the learning of language may be primary, what is learned already has implicated in it the great values including, if not especially, those of *self*. Even and especially when the "self search" opens to a transcendent identity with other, culture, species, and life.

Art and classic literature are good examples of how language and culture have to stretch themselves to be these guides to the development of self, which ultimately (as transpersonal psychologists point out) go beyond the speakable. So, language and culture do their best. As postmoderns point out, language lies to tell the truth, hides to reveal, deceives to be loyal. This is why a hermeneutics of the sort they propose for human research is such a significant cultural form in the interest of self-understanding.

Part 3: Multiple, Core, Transpersonal Self

Finally, I'd like to return to the issue of multiple vs. core and transpersonal self, inspired by an example that philosopher Bergson (1940) shared of his own life. Implicated in this single example are a number of other tensions we've alluded to, including that of the diverse and unified, the discontinuous and the continuous, self as discovery or self as created, cultural forms and self, and separate and transpersonal self, as well as value and ethical issues.

Bergson noted that as a child he was pulled by different, often conflicting, identities without (like son, brother, peer, boy—my examples) and conflicting pulls within, like the proverbial little girl who is one day very, very good and another day horrid. The young Bergson was torn by these internal, often contradictory pulls and claims to his temperaments, identities, and character. One day, it occurred to him that all this diversity tearing him apart was like the variations of themes in music. Indeed, the theme is often recognized only in its variations, as diverse and contradictory as these may appear—e.g., bass–treble, point–counterpoint, consonant–dissonant, etc.

So, Bergson began to listen, to take awareness of the diverse variations of his life to seek how they made up the theme of his life. As he tuned in to these, he found himself, like the composer, writing down these notes that came to him. Listening to discover his real self, he found himself creating his own symphony—and in the creation of the symphony, he found himself. And when in advanced years he had completed it, he wrote, "Now I can see that the last note was in the first note I wrote, the first note in the last note I've just written."

There was something transpersonal embedded from start to end in Bergson's own search of personal self—a greater identity which drew him. The path of discovery, as Maslow indicated, is one of both discovery and creativity. The multiplicity of identities were, like variations, all paths to the self theme. And the theme lit up the specialness and significance of the variations, each related with resonating relevance to the others.

Moreover, relevant to the postmodern claim that we are merely subject to our cultural forms, the cultural art form of music provided the language and metaphor for both Bergson's search for and his deepening understanding of self. And, now embedded in his writings, such universal cultural forms as music serve as the tool of choice—i.e., as the best means possible to convey that experience to the rest of us. This recognition of the cultural form of music and Bergson's creative choice to use it as an analogy of the diversity–unity of his life, speaking as it does to others, joins his life experience to that of the human experience—his life to that of fellow humans—in the way that Maslow saw his self-actualizers becoming more fully human, more fully a member of the species, even as they become more fully themselves uniquely.

Yet, all metaphors—like the language out of which they are constituted, heuristic as these are to serve in art, science, and life inquiry—are also limited. While these refer to realities and unities beyond their capacity to exhaust, they are limited to serving this interest like the finite instrument of our pointing finger. They are culturally incarnated resources: means and embedded intimations of a *more* suggested by transpersonal psychologists, a *more* only fully realized existentially in what Maslow called "peak," "unitary," or "self-transcendent" experiences. An example of such profound unifying realizations is Bergson's recognition of the unity of the first and last note of his life symphony.

Bergson, in the contextual conditions of his life, experiences an evolving realization of the unity of that life—a personal dialectic joining maturation, experience, reflection, and a gleaning consciousness. This dynamic reveals unities of his multiple and transforming identities. He sees and expresses the unity–distinctness of his own life, and this relative to the lives of others, through a universally shared art form which makes his metaphor humanly recognizable and palatable. And he artistically links this expression of personal insight to a unity with the whole. His creative skill is in evoking the power of a specific cultural art form's aesthetic—an aesthetic which, while distinctly cultural (in this case, a symphony), also crosses cultural forms; an aesthetic we recognize across individuals and cultures in the fluctuating asymmetrical symmetry of nature, one current expression of which we call ecological consciousness. Moreover, these insights are simultaneously a realization of the full value, the telos, of that life, related to others and Other and the ethic that all this implies—an ethical realization which intrinsically joins his own interests and destiny to those of others and the whole of being. And he shares these insights with us when, in our own personal and communal development, we are ready to grasp them, via his own existential contingency. In his case, under the legitimate agency-authorship of Henri Bergson—born: in France, 1858; profession: philosopher; religion: Catholic; died: 1941.

Bergson was one of Maslow's many sources of inspiration. He became this inspiration at the point when Maslow's own stage of reflections, under quite different contingencies, were ready to intuit a unity with his. In our own reflections, we recognize how even the uniquely different contingencies of these two thinkers were united, and with our own.

Concluding Remarks

by Andrew M. Bland

Psychology has transformed in the half-century since Mike Arons arrived at West Georgia in 1968, partially by way of the presence and influence of humanistic psychologists including himself. His genius was to simultaneously introduce lived experience to the field and provide impetus for psychology to live out its greater intellectual heritage and potential as a non-exclusive science in the tradition of William James (see Taylor, 1991). Mike frequently pointed out that *originality* has two vectors: one pointing toward *origins* (that which is already there) and the other pointing in the direction of *beginnings* (the new and unique). He genuinely embodied this dialectic of *new–old* in the same way that folklorist Izzy Young described Bob Dylan (another major figure from the cultural *zeitgeist* out of which humanistic psychology flourished) as writing songs in the 1960s that "sounded current and ... 200 years ... old at the same time" (in Scorsese, 2005).

Today, Mike's non-dualistic insights on epistemology/ methodology and his emphases on interdependence, on transcendence *and* inclusion, on differentiation *and* integration of self-in-lifeworld, and on creatively making best use of our human and ecological potentials and resources provide essential guidance for our current era. They not only provide a cautionary tale against polarization and anti-intellectualism but also demonstrate both the necessity and possibility of reconciling the paradoxes that underlie our personal and societal problems.

Radical as they may have appeared in their time, Mike's commentaries and proposals astutely anticipated comparable observations made by contemporary psychologists. Just a few examples are: (a) the sociocultural conditions that set the stage for post-truth society and proposals for its constructive resolution (Wilber, 2017); (b) the perils of psychological polarization (Schneider, 2013); (c) the need for mindful use of technology and cautiousness (but not alarmism) about its problematic effects (Schneider, 2019); (d) psychological flexibility in optimal health and development (Wilson, Bordieri, & Whiteman, 2012); (e) existential and phenomenological approaches to learning ("something about a person's life circumstances [is] changed such that he or she cannot go on as before," DeRobertis, 2017, p. 43); (f) Sternberg's (2018) triarchic model of creativity (defying the crowd, oneself, and the *zeitgeist*) and his proposal for employing assessments of creative abilities in lieu of standardized tests for college admissions (Sternberg, 2013); (g) reconciliations of the humanistic and cognitive revolutions in psychology via phenomenology (Gallagher & Zahavi, 2012); (h) Cardeña's (2018) meta-analysis recently published in *American Psychologist* that supports the validity of psi phenomena; (i) Walsh's (2015) synthesis of emerging psychological literature on wisdom in *Review of General Psychology*; (j) the questioning of statistical normality (Rose, 2015) and the legitimization of qualitative, statistical modeling, and mixed-methods research as alternatives to the natural science model in psychology (Howard, 2019); and (k) revitalized and contemporized psychological theorizing on self (L. Hoffman, Stewart, Warren, & Meek, 2015; Polkinghorne, 2015).

Furthermore, Mike's predictions about the future of science and his calls for non-dichotomous relationships between science and the humanities in psychology, education, and society bear striking resemblance to recommendations made by today's economists about 21st century careers. These include the need for creative thinking, flexibility, tolerance of ambiguity, empathy and emotional intelligence, appreciation for and adequate background in the humanities beyond science, technology, engineering, and math (STEM) disciplines, sense of fulfillment in leisure, etc. (Pinsker, 2016). Mike's work also anticipated Ito and Howe's (2016) advice for individuals and organizations in the current era to strategically embrace risks instead of mitigate them; to draw inspiration and ideas from existing networks; and to focus on compasses over maps, practice over theory, systems over objects, diversity over ability, and resilience over strength.

Although Mike Arons has been deceased over 10 years, his spirit shines on. As I wrote when he died:

> Mike's are powerful shoulders to stand on. He was a passionate and compassionate presence who invited and inspired us to celebrate our uniqueness and our humanness as inextricable. Mike lived for the extraordinary in the ordinary. He discovered possibilities where others may only have found realities, and realities where others may only have found possibilities. He dared to articulate the unsayable, to illustrate the unexplainable, to cut through the boundaries of convention, revealing genuine traditions which bind and sustain us. Mike stood up for what is worth living for. A torch has been passed. Thank you, Mike. (Bland, 2008, p. 9)

Mike at his home in Carrollton, GA, 2004.
(Photographer: Christiane Arons. Contributed by Andrew Bland.)

Appendix

Annotated Bibliography of Mike Arons' Complete Writings

Prepared by Andrew M. Bland

Mike Arons contributed exhaustively to humanistic psychology, and he presented extensively during his career. However, on the whole he published relatively little—and sometimes in publications of limited circulation. Whereas this edited volume by necessity has included only the most essential material, here my intent is to present as complete a collection of Arons' works as possible. To convey the essence of and maintain fidelity to the nuanced quality of his original writings, I have liberally incorporated direct quotations, especially for entries that are not easily located. Arons' works are presented in seven sections: (a) his inspiration and influences; (b) history and evolution of humanistic psychology; (c) humanistic education; (d) creativity; (e) research (experimental studies, the hermeneutic method, intuition, psi phenomena, and human science research in psychology); (f) humanistic ethics; and (g) Arons' final musings. Within each section, the papers have been arranged thematically (rather than alphabetically or chronologically) and ordered so that the content of each paper sets the stage for those that follow. Entries included in this volume are preceded with an asterisk (*).

Unfortunately, a handful of writings included in Arons' (2000b) vita is excluded because they could not be located in spite of extensive searching of the internet and multiple libraries and archives. These include: (a) a study Arons conducted and delivered to the Canadian Senate in 1967 on the effects of legislation on LSD research (also referenced in Arons' [1967] letter to Maslow); (b) "Nailing Down the

Windstorm" (in *Aum*, 1968); (c) "Research and Humanistic Psychology" (in *The Humanistic Psychologist*, 1980); and (d) "Paradox of Psychoanalysis and Psi" (in *Parapsychology Review*, 1980).

Arons' Inspiration and Influences

This section includes three autobiographical accounts. First, Arons (1994b) offers reflections on how he was drawn to humanistic psychology via a sense of resonance. Then Arons (1992c, 2004) describes his formative encounters with influential teachers.

* **"Recognizable Paths of Humanistic Psychology" (Arons, 1994b)**
Sketches Arons' journey from childhood to chairing the West Georgia program. Arons emphasizes that although humanistic psychology is considered by some to be a "relative vision" that is "socio-temporally bound" (p. 371) to post-World War II America, for him its emphasis on full humanness by "rejoining [psychology] with the humanities at the essential value level" (p. 372) gives it a universal, eternal quality that renders it capable of addressing the social, ethical, and spiritual problems of the 21st century.

* **"Two Suns of My Student Years" (Arons, 1992c)**
Arons reminisces about his encounters with two professors who "spoke to a part of [him that he] was yet to discover" (p. 46): Roberto Giammanco at Wayne State and Paul Ricoeur at Sorbonne.

* **"My Passage Through Maslow" (Arons, 2004)**
Traces the series of events—sometimes synchronous, sometimes serendipitous, often both—that constituted Arons' excursion out of existential frustration in Detroit in the 1950s into a classroom with Maslow in the 1960s.

History and Evolution of Humanistic Psychology

Arons' writings provide a fly-on-the-wall perspective of the lived history of humanistic psychology and its impact both on psychology and on American society/culture. Arons entered the movement just as its institutionalization as the *third force* in American psychology was rapidly blossoming (see Aanstoos, Serlin, & Greening, 2000; DeCarvalho, 1991) and was an active participant in each wave of its developmental trajectory to date (i.e., *third force*, existential, transpersonal, constructivist/postmodern, integration with conventional psychology; see Bland & DeRobertis, 2019). He was ever loyal to the movement, despite whatever tensions emerged vis-à-vis what he described as "all the storms" (Arons, as cited in Smith, Moerman, & Wertz, 1986, p. 53) of its unfolding. To illustrate, at an executive meeting of the Association for Humanistic Education, some board members suggested that the organization change its name to make it more palatable to the mainstream. Arons countered, "If the Jews had followed this line of thinking they would have stopped identifying themselves as Jews years ago! He felt the term 'humanistic' had a noble and strong tradition and ought to be preserved" (Allender & Richards, 1986, p. 137).

This section begins during the early 1970s, with Arons' descriptions of humanistic psychology for the public (Arons, Harari, & O'Donovan, 1972/1973) and for students (Arons, 1970). Next, Arons overviews Maslow's theorizing (Arons, 1999a) and recounts the early history of humanistic psychology (Arons & Harari, 1992/1994). Thereafter, Arons addresses humanistic psychologists in his role as president of the newly established Society for Humanistic Psychology (SHP) during the mid-1970s (Arons, 1976a, 1976b; Arons & Graham, 1976). Then Arons reflects on the next steps for the humanistic movement as it negotiated its relationship with the human potentials movement in the late 1970s (Arons, 1977c), as it matured in the 1980s (Arons, 1985b, 1988a), and as it reconciled its theoretical assumptions on self in the 1990s (Arons, 1999d), having expanded to include transpersonal and postmodern perspectives.

"What's It All About?" (Arons, Harari, & O'Donovan, 1972; republished as "Humanistic Psychology: An Overview," Arons, Harari, & O'Donovan, 1973)

Provides a brief, lay-friendly position statement of humanistic psychology's emphases on (a) people "in all [their] complexity," including the dimensions of "love, creativeness, will, choice, belief, purpose, meanings, and values," and (b) the importance of a "process-centered" approach and of psychologists' own personal growth as integral to the pursuit of studying individuals "as [they] live in [their] engagement in the world" (pp. 1–2). Outlines humanistic psychologists' accomplishments as of the early 1970s, including the development of educational programs, research methods, community applications, therapeutic approaches, and professional organizations and seminal texts.

"Foreword" to Stewart and Thomas's *Introductory Experiential Psychology* (Arons, 1970)

With no other textbook available at the time to guide the newly developed experientially oriented courses at West Georgia (designed to "open [students] to a more sensitive understanding of [themselves], others, and psychology," p. x), Arons encouraged the faculty to develop their own. In his introductory remarks, Arons addresses the problems of psychology's inheritance of Western philosophical bifurcations of mind and body, spirit and matter, and emotions and intellect. He also suggests that "opening [oneself] perceptually, emotionally, *and* intellectually ... expands [one's] capacity for discovering relevance" (p. viii, emphasis added).

"Abraham Maslow: Yesterday, Tomorrow, and Yesteryear" (Arons, 1999a)

Originally presented as part of a symposium on humanistic icons at the 1996 APA convention in Toronto. Reviews Maslow's contributions to psychology in their biographical and cultural–historical context. Suggests that despite his influence in decades past Maslow's greatest inspiration has yet to take place. Specifically, "Maslow had much explicitly to say about values, and this value orientation implies much about ethics," which constitute "a central problem of our times" that is "related to a chaotic historical stage of passage from a modern to a postmodern epoch" (p. 341). Accordingly, "if chaos is pregnant with order, as much of the creativity literature leads us to believe, there will likely be much of Maslow in whatever new ethical order emerges" (p. 341). Arons justifies this claim by critiquing the critiques of Maslow by transpersonalists ("ethical elitism [that] does not fully respond to the range of concerns for a population as a whole") and by postmodernists ("deconstructive processes [that] are regressive and nihilistic"). He continues, "Maslow's model, on the other hand, speaks to the whole range of human need and value states and does so from vantage points that include the biophysiological, sociological, anthropological, and ... psychological as well as spiritual" (p. 343).

"Recollections and Reflections: Snippets from an Oral History of Humanistic Psychology" (Arons & Harari, 1992; republished as Arons & Harari, 1994)
Arons was designated Oral History Archivist by the Executive Board of the SHP. In 1991–1992, he facilitated three group interviews in New York and San Francisco "to let 'longtimers' recount their memories of humanistic psychology" (p. 200). This article summarizes participants' reminiscing about (a) the first humanistic psychology program at Sonoma State and early Association for Humanistic Psychology (AHP) conferences in the 1960s; (b) the human potential movement and the establishment of Division 32 and the Association for Humanistic Education during the 1970s; and (c) humanistic luminaries such as Perls, Rogers, May, Maslow, Klee, Bühler, Angyal, Murphy, and Sutich. Arons' own input includes comments about the isolation of humanistic psychologists in academe and a critique of the historical cultural homogeneity of humanistic psychology.

* **"Presidential Address (1976): Transformations of Science and Religion Through Humanistic Psychology" (Arons, 1976b)**
Arons suggests that humanistic psychology's focus on consciousness has helped or can help "to transcend the historical opposition between science and religion" and therefore "to restore a basis of authenticity to both" (p. 1). He cites numerous examples of how the values associated with humanistic psychology (e.g., orientation to process, potentials, meaning, fulfillment) offer the alternatives of (a) "direct salvation" to scientists who "play dumb" to subjective experience in their "bit-by-bit elimination of darkness and irrationality" and (b) "enlightenment" to fundamentalist religion that "offers significance only to the extent that one [buys] a hopeful future on blind faith" (pp. 1–2).

"President's Column" (Arons & Graham, 1976)
At first, the development of Division 32 was controversial among humanistic psychologists. Arons later recalled that many humanistic psychologists were ambivalent about joining the organization out of concern that doing so would "dilute the movement" (in Aanstoos et al., 2000, p. 10) and/or "would be competitive and harmful to AHP" (Arons & Harari, 1992/1994, p. 195). Arons was among the first presidents of Division 32. As the result of a tie vote, he shared his presidential year with clinical psychologist Stanley Graham. In this column, Arons and Graham exchange views on the priorities of the fledgling division.

"The Changing Winds" (Arons, 1976a)
Arons expresses concern that as humanistic psychology was gaining ground in academe, "some ill-advised measures [were] being instituted, mostly out of fear and pressure by university systems, which would put the focus back on standardization and quantification" (p. 5). While "the numbers game is highly appealing to those whose game is numbers, [it] is a catastrophe for those of us whose reality is people" (p. 5). Accordingly, he recommends that humanistic psychologists advocate for "quality" (p. 5).

"Humanistic Psychology versus Human Potentials Movement" (Arons, 1977c)

This column was written in response to Gilbert's (1977) warning about humanistic psychologists' affiliation with the one-sidedness of the human potential movement. Arons reviews the American cultural context within which both humanistic psychology and the human potential movement arose and acknowledges the excesses of the latter. On the other hand, he also suggests that with time the extravagances will work themselves out, and he cautions against humanistic psychology becoming watered down in an effort to cater to the mainstream. "When one goes to purchase an automobile, the standard model is the mediocre one, the one where every part is the most standardized and interchangeable. The more deluxe, the more unique" (para. 4).

"A Quarter Century of Humanistic Psychologies" (Arons, 1985b)

In this conference report, Arons compares/contrasts the atmosphere of the Quarter Century Conference in 1985 with meetings of previous years. While "intellectually provocative, ... it was not rebellious. There were no beads or bandanas around the head, few jeans, none torn" (p. 55). Humanistic psychology had grown up. On one hand, the mind–body exhibits "were commercialized" and "required little active participation" (p. 55); on the other hand, the information booths for humanistic graduate programs and the book tables were in abundance. Humanistic psychology was no longer "alien to the wider society" (p. 55). Arons reflects that the presentations clearly implied that "the experimentation with experience [was] now ready to evolve a more serious scientific and social dimension in the broader humanistic sense that Maslow, May, Jourard, and others had envisaged" (p. 60). Accordingly, citing Will Harmon, Arons identifies "three agenda items" for humanistic psychologists in the coming years: (a) to not "reject ... the idea of objectivity" but rather to replace "the old flawed one" (positivism) with "a different sense of seeing reality as it is, the non-attachment of Buddhist philosophy"; (b) to participate in the "respiritualization of our institutions" (i.e., "economics cannot be the value center of our society"); and (c) to promote focus beyond national security ("either we have global security or no security") via further developing "new and positive images" of humanity ("we've had ample negative images … to bring on the power of human destruction") (p. 60).

"The Legacy of Maslow and Rogers" (Arons, 1988a)
Surveys the contradictions of humanistic psychology during the late 1980s. On one hand, it had "brought the East and West together" (p. 4) by bridging the present-centered temporality of existentialism and the eternal now of transpersonal psychology. On the other hand, despite its "progressive process to transcend polarities and become more holistic," by having assumed the American visions of ongoing progress and the split between science and spirituality, it also had managed to become "caught up in newer polarities" (e.g., bifurcating cognitive–affective and intellectual–experiential and "[embracing] humanistic techniques while reacting against technology") (p. 3). As an antidote, Arons proposes that humanistic psychologists lead a "resurgence of the humanities" (p. 4). He suggests practical applications thereof in education, organizational development, and therapy and also proposes that humanistic psychology could contribute to constructive dialogue with cognitive psychology.

* "Self, Multiple Selves, and the Illusion of Separate Selfhood" (Arons, 1999d)
Arons' address to Division 32 upon receiving the first Abraham Maslow Heritage Award in 1999. Compares/contrasts perspectives on self though the lenses of humanistic ("an intrinsically core responsible self"), constructivist/postmodern ("a multitude of 'selves' playing themselves out reconstructively in their embedded cultural, historical contingency"), and transpersonal ("'I' am *other,* my greater identity is with the whole of Being, having dropped the illusion of my separate selfhood") psychologies (p. 188). After reviewing critiques of each orientation, Arons concludes by emphasizing "the compatibility, even necessity of a compatibility, of differences" between the three viewpoints (p. 187).

Humanistic Education

This section commences with Arons' portrayals of humanistic approaches to education for university administration (Arons, 1978a), for incoming students (Arons, 1972c), and for other psychologists (Arons, 1969). Then Arons (1977a) reflects on the social conditions that established the need for humanistic education. Thereafter, he offers practical suggestions for humanistic approaches to exams (Arons, 1977b), to teacher selection (Arons, 1977d), and to training/credentialing of psychotherapists (Arons, 1988b, 1999b). Finally, Arons discusses the role of intuition in learning (Arons, 1978b, 1990a) and of values in education (Arons, 1991b).

"The Humanistic Orientation" (Arons, 1978a)

A mission statement of humanistic psychology for university administration. Contextualizes humanistic psychology's role in the history of American psychology (transcending the limitations of psychoanalysis and behaviorism while subsuming their contributions in the interest of "discovering means of greater personal and social realization," p. 1). Emphasizes its contributions to scientific methodology ("a rigorous approach which takes human experience of phenomena as its primary source of data," p. 1) and education ("reaffirmation of personal uniqueness, of choice, of individual responsibility," p. 2).

"Humanistic Psychology: West Georgia College" (Arons, 1972c)

A welcome statement from the chair to new students. Emphasizes humanistic psychology's focus on growth, paradox, and epistemological and methodological heterogeneity ("What is growth inducing for one, at one time, may not be for another at another time," p. 2). Arons concludes, "The most encouraging part of the program is that not everybody—student or faculty—leaves as they came" (p. 3). Arons included this statement on a poster display that he carried to conferences. Today it is exhibited prominently in the lobby of Melson Hall, home of West Georgia's psychology department.

"Humanistic Psychology and the Academic Curriculum" (Arons, 1969)

Contextualizes the appeal of humanistic psychology to late 1960s youth, "a generation which has the leisure to transcend the self-preservative values of the rat race, to transcend—in Maslow's words—the *deficiency* needs and values for the *being* needs and values. And providing this affluence, I believe, is the real success of their parents" (p. 3). Addresses the contradiction within psychology at the time to "tell the students that our psychology is young, ... then we act like old men and oblige them to do the same thing" (p. 4). As an alternative to the "assumptions and prejudices" of experimentalism (p. 11), Arons outlines a humanistic curriculum that "makes a better scientific psychologist" by (a) "starting with a richer view of [humans]" (p. 9) and then (b) employing a rigorous human science approach in the traditions of Husserlian phenomenology and James' radical empiricism.

"The Future of Humanistic Education at the Heart of Crisis" (Arons, 1977a)

Emphasizes the value of and need for humanistic education as a "starting point for all questions related to self-knowledge" (p. 3). This provides an alternative to (a) the ethical void wrought by American society's dichotomization of church and state and (b) the cultural assumption that "the 'higher self' is that which is infinitely adaptable to the changes [brought by] technology" (p. 5). Arons identifies the connections between these problems and American education's centering around the three Rs (reading, writing, arithmetic) in the interest of "social conformity, psychological adjustment, and corporate goals" (p. 6).

"The Group Oral: An Exam Which is Not Inhuman" (Arons, 1977b)

Arons' group oral exams, which he imported from Europe and hermeneutic tradition, are legendary among his students (see Richards & Whitehouse, 2008). He delivered presentations on the utility of this method several times, including to Division 2 of APA (Teaching of Psychology) (Arons, 2000b). Arons describes, "It is a natural vehicle for synergistic learning and, above all, for the encouragement of the experience of major insights from the diverse material covered in the course" (p. 3). In addition to addressing practical considerations, Arons reflects that an indication that the exam is going well is "when ... students who looked rather dumbfounded at the beginning or who were waiting to go last or who were about to give rather superficial answers to their isolated question, now show excitement and want to go next" (p. 3). He attributes this to the discussion having "opened up all sorts of things—ideas, possible new relationships, heuristic tangents—which the student was unlikely to have seen in his/her question alone, in isolation" (p. 3). Rather, "each question and each discussion over it adds new dimensions, perspectives, and ways of seeing the other questions" (p. 3).

"O. J. and Teacher Selection" (Arons, 1977d)

Addresses the limitations of employing standardized, quantifiable performance-based criteria as the basis for assessing quality of educators. Although such is a step in the right direction beyond teachers appealing to emotion in their "[insistence] on raises based on the fact that *we are professionals*" (p. 58), it does not adequately account for "our most qualitative means—human discernment" (p. 66). Arons proposes the development of educational talent scouts who "would look, as we do with athletes and, above all, artists, for talent at the earliest ages" (p. 65). Then, "when signs of it are discerned, ... establish the conditions for developing this talent" by honing competencies in an individualized manner (p. 65).

"A Proposal for Credentialing Humanistic Practice" (Arons, 1988b)

Ever flexible by virtue of his ability to "[be] fully where [he] was" (Arons, 1990a, p. 125), as the credentialing movement for clinicians had "gone too far" by the 1980s, Arons advocates for the development of accrediting bodies within humanistic psychology to "say that our students have been educationally prepared to practice as 'growth therapists'" (p. 382) in order to "give [them] a more even playing field in the therapy marketplace" (p. 383).

"New Vocation for an Age-Old Market" (Arons, 1999b)
Provides a middle-way, holistic perspective on the development of humanistic psychotherapy training. Cautions against "totally [extricating] from the medical or natural science models" (p. 4) but rather, "while decentering from the medical model, recognize where the two models (medical and humanistic) overlap—e.g., symptom of traditional pathology which may speak to frustrated realization" (p. 5). Accordingly, "a new humanistic vocation needs to find its own authentic center and cross all other areas from that center—e.g., pathology seen from the medical model perspective may also, or more fruitfully, be seen from a 'creativity,' 'existential,' or 'transpersonal' perspective" (p. 4).

* "The Value of the Arts for Special Populations" (Arons, 1978b)
Reviews the role of intuitive experience in the learning process, of seeing "well beyond the tangible details to the hidden obvious" (p. 5). Challenges the notion of linearity and convergent thinking as "the best or only way of conceiving of human progress" (p. 3). Explores how "art expands our awareness without one form superseding or rendering obsolete the previous ones" but rather by "[deepening] and [preparing us] for insights at another level" (p. 4).

* "The Growing Chasm between Mission and Job" (Arons, 1990a)
Arons' presidential address to the Association for Humanistic Education in 1989. Provides an autobiographical account of Arons' journey from public school to college and how his ability to apply intuitive and empathetic processes enabled him to be successful:

> My reading pace was no more than two pages an hour. ... [But] I stayed with the page, with the word, until I felt myself at the inside of [the books I was assigned] and, finally, on the inside of the authors. I came to share the human space they were coming

from and then knew what they were saying because I could see what they were seeing. (p. 125)

Proposes that burnout in teachers is the outcome of "powerlessness before the social forces" (e.g., preoccupation with testing, mechanical productivity) that result in "experienced conflict" between their values (sense of calling) and their "job description or task orientation" (p. 127).

* "The Politics of Education, A Critical Tribute: From the Heart of Rogers to the Heart of Education" (Arons, 1991b)
Carl Rogers visited West Georgia in 1975. Fifteen years later, Arons reflects on the contributions and the limitations of Rogers' talk on humanistic education during a more conservative era. Arons critiques Rogers' dichotomization of traditional and person-centered approaches, suggesting that doing so ultimately backfired and begat a "generally anti-humanistic socio-political climate" (p. 7). Arons attributes this in part to Rogers' underestimating the "unique educational source of power" (p. 9) and the "best in [educators'] humanly sacred mission" (p. 17). Arons proposes a middle-way approach for education to get back on track and outlines its numerous dimensions: that is, promoting "the opening, freeing, and revelatory experience of the student" by focusing on universal values and transformation (p. 16).

Creativity

Questlove (2018) describes creativity as "a mix of unfocusing your eyes in the right way, while still remaining focused on the picture" (p. 30). Based on this description, if forced to choose one subject area that encapsulated the essence of Mike Arons—as a person, psychologist, educator, and writer—it would be creativity. The entries in this section are highly interrelated. Arons (1965, 1972a, 1985a, 1987/1991a, 1992a/1994a, 1996, 2000a; Arons & Richards, 2015; Krippner & Arons, 1973a/1973b) explores the implications of the concurrent infusions of creativity research and of humanistic psychology in American psychology, science, culture, and values during the mid-20th century. Then he (Arons, 2007) presents his musings on the upright body posture as a platform for creative outlooks in human consciousness.

"Le Problème de la Creativité: Discussion Méthodologique, Reactions dans la Psychologie Américaine (The Problem of Creativity: Methodological Discussion, Reactions in American Psychology)" (Arons, 1965)

As noted earlier, Arons' dissertation on the contradictions in mid-20th century American psychology's general dismissal of creativity was supervised by Ricoeur. For it to be accepted, Ricoeur, who served on *L'Académie française*, aided in having the word *créativité* added to the French language (Richards & Whitehouse, 2008). See Arons (1992c; Chapter 2 herein) for further recollections of Ricoeur's enthusiasm for the project. "How could I, an average student who had never produced any recognized creative work, be writing a dissertation on creativity?" Arons (2000a) later reflected (p. 1). Having encountered psychology as an undergraduate:

> [With] its claims to detachment and objectivity ... as its central themes, psychology revealed itself to [me] as a story of particular intrigue: an ironic ongoing story that erases its fuller historical, cultural, and existential meanings with the very 'positivistic pen' it uses to itemize its achievements. (in Aanstoos, 1991, p. 170)

For the remainder of his life, Arons frequently referred back to a factoid from his dissertation: whereas prior to 1950 there were only 186 psychological studies on creativity, following Guilford's APA address that year (see Arons, 1972a, 1987/1991a, 1992a/1994a; Arons & Richards, 2015), the literature blossomed to 800 studies in a decade.

* "At the Juncture: Creativity, Humanistic, and Transpersonal Psychologies" (Arons, 2000a)

Traces the intellectual history that culminated (a) in the reductionistic, monistic, homeostatic, value-free science model adopted during the early history of psychology and (b) in the challenges posed thereto by the concurrent advent of creativity literature and humanistic and transpersonal psychologies. In the latter's emphasis on eudaimonia, the issue of happiness is taken up "not in the simple terms of 'Does prosperity and the products of science and technology make us happy?'" but rather by addressing "how these benefits and products are experienced and lived in terms of fulfillment values, creativity [itself] being a central value" to well-being (p. 11). This also "raises [questions] for those who seek happiness in products alone" (p. 11).

"Two Noble Insurgencies: Creativity and Humanistic Psychology" (Arons & Richards, 2015)

Suggests an operational definition of creativity as entailing both originality and meaningfulness. Explores the historical impact on psychology of Guilford's "bemoaning the paucity of research on creativity" in his 1950 APA presidential address (p. 163) and of Maslow's self-actualization psychology. Outlines myriad "modern outcomes of the humanistic psychology–creativity insurgency" (p. 168), including the development of nonlinear dynamical systems (chaos theory) approaches to science; awareness of self in interdependent relation with culture and environment; integration of mind, body, and spirit in medicine and psychotherapy; destigmatization and reconceptualization of psychopathology; ecopsychology; positive psychology; qualitative research methods and interdisciplinary inquiry; socially engaged spirituality; etc. Proposes that today, "everyday creativity is anything but a frill or an extra [but rather] it helps us adapt to changing conditions, may keep us alive, and shows us just what we are living for" (p. 168).

* "Creativity: Person, Product, or Process?" (Krippner & Arons, 1973a; republished as "Creativity East, Creativity West," Krippner & Arons, 1973b)
Examines the role of mystery in creativity and its purpose of "bringing new order out of non-order" (p. 116). Compares/contrasts Western and Eastern approaches to creativity through the lens of their respective relationships with nature (conquering for the former, harmonizing for the latter): "It is difficult for [most Westerners] to accept helping things to be what they are because we have been too successful in changing the nature of things ... to serve human needs" (pp. 120–121). Calls for research to explore the interface of creative people and products (Western) and creative process (Eastern). Discusses implications for parenting and child development.

* "Creativity, Humanistic Psychology, and the American Zeitgeist" (Arons, 1992a; republished as Arons, 1994a)
Reviews the "intrinsic relationship between" the study of creativity and the emergence and development of humanistic–transpersonal psychology as "expressive reactions" to the "limitations of psychology and the social climate of the times" (p. 158). Surveys the contradictions of America's linear conceptualization of progress and the relationships between creativity and intelligence and between mistrust of divergent thinking and social conformity. Celebrates humanistic psychology's accomplishments of contributing to the legitimization of consciousness, experience, and "inner development and personal understanding" (p. 169) in psychology via its focus on personal growth as creative process (as distinct from talent-centered productivity). Laments the devolution of the "meaningless" social character of the mid-20th century into "meanness" by the end of the century as "our stewarded earth in pain bites its master [and] the ghost of McLuhan taunts that of Gutenberg" (p. 172). But concludes hopefully that "some of our humanistic-transpersonal psychologists, who yanked psychology from the old physics, are feeling right at home in this new [chaos theory], recognizing in it familiar and exhilarating messages from the creative heart, viz., chaos is pregnant with order" (p. 173).

"Creativity, Humanistic Psychology, and the Emerging American Consciousness" (Arons, 1972a)

An earlier paper that eventually culminated in Arons' writings cited herein as 1992a/1994a. Examines the relationship between creativity and intelligence in more detail. Also reviews formative humanistic psychologists' interdisciplinary contributions to an image of the person as an alternative to the reductionistic, deterministic one posed by behaviorism; the contributions of phenomenology and Eastern philosophy/psychology as alternatives to the "fixation on technique at which Americans have always been consistently good" (p. 12); and the emerging emphases on subject–object unity, responsibility of care, and multidimensionality in "a more feminine era" as alternatives to the "adolescent attitude of omnipotence" in American society (p. 15).

"Humanistic Zeitgeist, Science, and Religion: A Meta-Historical Account" (Arons, 1985a)

Another earlier paper from which Arons (1992a/1994a) was drawn. Offers further exploration of humanistic psychology's contributions to philosophy of science as a creative endeavor and its foci on (a) spirituality as "the most concrete experience of knowing firsthand what it means to be more human" (p. 19); (b) recognition (i.e., resonance) as "holistic, integrative, profound, and sacred" (p. 19); (c) temporality ("one feels to be in the infinite or eternal but also extraordinarily finite—miniscule in relation to all there is," p. 20); (d) vulnerability as leading "to natural, right action—an inner valuing criteria" (p. 21); and (e) creative experience as "a revived respect or sense of awe before ... profound truths and horizons" (p. 22).

"Frank Barron and the Creativity Revolution" (Arons, 1996)

Arons further outlines the role of standardized intelligence tests in upholding values of conformity in American society and their failure to measure originality and bona fide *genius*. He then identifies and celebrates Barron's creativity research as exemplary of the dialectics in creative genius: "imaginative yet grounded, forceful though sensitive, spiritual but still tangible, scientific but humanistic, ... [and]

simultaneously existential and rational, psychological and philosophical, clinical and theoretical" (p. 67).

"Creativity and the Methodological Debate: A Mytho-Historical Reflection" (Arons, 1987; republished as Arons, 1991a)

Note: Page numbers here refer to Arons (1991a). Arons' presentation at the *Second International Symposium on Qualitative Research in Psychology*, Netherlands, 1985. Further explores humanistic psychology's qualitative methodological contributions as a creative alternative to conventional American psychology's "early and total autonomy from philosophy" in which "hedonism largely provided the energetics and functionalism the telos," and therefore "the scientist played dumb to the man, to his feelings, to his own personal experience" (p. 16) as well as "to the claims of an invisible spiritual world proclaimed by those of blind faith" (p. 17). "There is no doubt plenty of room for misunderstanding and mischief when a society stands between the authorities of the dumb and the blind" (p. 17). In addition, Arons identifies parallels between Maslow's portrayals of psychologically healthy people and descriptions of creative individuals from the early creativity literature (e.g., "[dealing] with the world intrinsically rather than instrumentally and ... prone to take psychological, creative, and spiritual risks," pp. 23-24).

Furthermore, overviews the connections between phenomenology/hermeneutics and creativity/humanistic psychology: for example, mending the subject–object split via detached-engagement; "revitalization of the sedimented symbols and meanings of the past, historically and personally" (p. 29); and "inherent validation—necessity, intuitive coherence, and heuristically suggestive of next paths to follow" but via "a well-thought-out method which has the essential quality of reversibility" (p. 30). Arons advises that while psychology has been "altered radically" by the presence of humanistic psychology and the study of creativity, it "has yet to take full stock of the directions and meanings suggested by these changes" (p. 25).

* **"Standing Up for Humanity: Upright Body, Creative Instability, and Spiritual Balance" (Arons, 2007)**

Arons dedicated his post-retirement years to exploring and delivering presentations and preparing a book on the relationship between "human creative capacity, values, and aspirations" and "tensions inherent in the lived ... biped upright body posture" (p. 175) that is unique to humans. Unfortunately, he did not complete the project before he died. However, during his final year, a succinct synthesis of this work was published in an APA Press volume on everyday creativity edited by Ruth Richards, who recalls that "the chapter became a favorite of the volume's APA development editor, who even shared it prepublication with his minister" (Richards & Whitehouse, 2008, p. 267). Evaluates the relationships between humans' vertical platform, our evolutionary history (and its contradictions with our inverted pyramidic geometry), our consciousness and spirit, our longing for balance and harmony, our use of language, and our notions of progress and originality. Suggests that the upright body posture serves as a metaphor for negotiating dialectics (e.g., adult–child, detached–engagement, survival–potential) in the creative process. Arons concludes, "Just as the wonder of upright posture may be taken for granted, perhaps we are not adequately recognizing potential for creativity and spiritual growth that are embedded in the activities of everyday life" (p. 190).

Research

Although Arons generally devoted his career to promoting human science (qualitative) research in psychology, he was ever a proponent of methodological integration: "I have been a consistent advocate of blending qualitative and quantitative methods, where appropriate and heuristically promising. Some subjects and dimensions of these lend themselves better to one or another" (Arons, as cited in Richards & Whitehouse, 2008, p. 267). This section begins with Arons' experimental studies early in his career on time perception (Arons & London, 1969). Then, he presents the hermeneutic method (Barrell,

Aanstoos, Richards, & Arons, 1987), overviews Ricoeur's (1970) application of it in dialogue with Freud (Arons, 1982, 1998b), and then demonstrates it himself as applied to (a) the topic of intuition (Arons, 1990b, 1993a) and (b) understanding the circumstances under which psi phenomena have been eschewed by science and fundamentalist religion (Arons, 1986, 1990c) and how they may entail more than ghost-hunting (Arons, 1992b) but rather non-pathological embodied intuitive/meditative space or spiritual energy (e.g., *qi* in Eastern philosophy and medicine; see J. Lee, [2009]). Finally, Arons (Aanstoos & Arons, 1985; Franco, Friedman, & Arons, 2008) discusses the general place and purpose of human science research in psychology.

Experimental Studies

"Correcting for compensation in studies of time estimation" **(Arons & London, 1969).** The experimental research Arons conducted early in his career involved perception of time. First, in France, Arons and his wife served on a research team with Michel Siffre, a speleologist. Arons (2004) recalled that "Michel spent two months in an Alps cave without access to time, reporting his subjective time estimations to clock–calendar time monitors above, and as these related to his sleep-wake cycles, dreams, routines, and feelings and moods" (p. 4). They discovered that Michel's internal body clock, in isolation and without access to a watch or sun, operated on a 24.5-hour cycle. (For more information, see J. Foer & Siffre, 2008; Siffre, 1963.) Later, at Brandeis, Arons conducted another study on time estimation. For this study, participants were asked to estimate the amount of time they spent on a marble sorting task. Some participants were led to believe that the task indicated their level of creative potential and other participants that they were engaging in a routine mundane activity. Results indicated that: (a) the participants estimated time as passing faster when they were invested in the task and (b) the presence of a question that stimulated participants' beliefs that their estimation could have been inaccurate enabled researchers to correct for participants' time compensation.

The Hermeneutic Method

"Human science research methods" (Barrell, Aanstoos, Richards, & Arons, 1987). This article presents four qualitative research methodologies—experiential (Barrell), hermeneutic (Arons), perceptual (Richards), and phenomenological (Aanstoos)—and applies each to exploring the topic of anxiety. Surveys the formulation of the research question, purpose of the research, and methods for data collection and analysis. Arons surveys the Ricoeurian hermeneutic method, which "emphasizes interpretations from one to another apparently different and even seemingly opposing meaning systems" to arrive at "many overlapping meanings" in a "single word or symbol" to achieve "contextual awareness" and "a larger perspective that allows [one] to see [a topic] from many different angles (vantage points)" (pp. 433–434). Overviews the steps of the method: (a) determining *multidimensional significance* from various texts; (b) *differentiation* (describing experiences that represent oppositions and similarities); (c) *dialectic process* (e.g., contrasting related phenomena); and (d) *intuitive understanding* ("discovering the many sides of something rather than what it is") (pp. 435–436). One then returns to the original starting point from a "new and larger perspective"; although one can retrace the steps back (*reversibility*), it is "never in the same way because one now carries a different perspective" (p. 436) that "can aid the process of specifying particular questions for formal research" (p. 437) and thus a "continuation of the process" (p. 436).

"Hermeneutic of a complementarity between energy and meaning in Freud" (Arons, 1982). Applies Ricoeur's (1970) *Freud and Philosophy* to explore "the power of hermeneutics to find fuller meaning across irreconcilables—the ability to communicate over distance" (p. 5). Arons suggests that Ricoeurian hermeneutics both (a) introduces "movement from estrangement towards intimacy" in psychology (p. 2) and (b) poses a challenge to phenomenology in its "basis for grounding reality" (p. 5). With regard to the latter, because phenomenology "begins and ends with the objects of consciousness," it does not account for "a reality more fundamental than consciousness," which "Ricoeur concedes to Freud" is the "unsurpassable reality of the instincts" and "liberation by demystification" via "progressive ... movement of the instincts ... out toward the world, [not only] as desire for gratification but [also] to transcend ... desire and death" in creative activity (p. 5). Arons concludes that the multi-determined symbols in creative works "are like [hermeneutic] texts which gain autonomy beyond their author's intentions through [participation] in the deeper human reality, a mixed discourse ... of energy and meaning [that] is not exhausted in explanation or in understanding alone" (p. 5).

"Sacred and symbol: From Ricoeur's *Freud and philosophy*" (Arons, 1998b). Arons further explores the hermeneutic path of interpretation which renders "what was previously presumed known—concrete—the less or least known" insofar as "every ending of a cycle is the fresh beginning of—a new call for interpretation by—the next" (p. 1). Employs Ricoeur's (1970) *Freud and Philosophy* as a platform for "[starting] along the path of resacrilization" by leading "us to a fresh view of what might be sacred both beyond the idols and a reality shorn of idols" (p. 6) via "the passage of interpretations of that which ... the *other* of symbol ... presents to consciousness" (p. 9). That is, symbols' "enigmatic language" (p. 11) pulls us toward inter-being, a "fuller consciousness and intimacy with [that which] we cannot know directly" (p. 10).

Intuition

"Intuition and the intimacy of instinct and consciousness" (Arons, 1990b). Applies the hermeneutic method to identify and explore four kinds of intuition and their points of convergence with and/or divergence from creation myths, psi phenomena, and superconsciousness. First, *dawning/creative intuition* involves "forward movement from innocence toward reflection" (e.g., Heidegger's interpretation of poetry) (p. 4). Second, *recovery intuition* "starts with reflection and returns toward innocence" (e.g., phenomenology revealing the essential structures of an experience) (p. 4). Third, *spontaneous intuition 1* entails "pure consciousness" that "embodies itself (creates everything) and expresses itself through its embodiments" and that "engenders all mediated intuitions" (p. 7). Fourth, *spontaneous intuition 2* is represented by a "gut feeling," that is, "unmediated ... awareness of the flow of action ... [via focusing on a] specific activity and [using] the body itself as a subtle vehicle for ... [recognizing and discerning] that [which is] valid in some immediate, essential way" (p. 7).

* **"Instinct, intuition, and the supraconscious: De-alienating reflections" (Arons, 1993a).** An extension of Arons (1990b). Applies the hermeneutic method to trace the intellectual history of Western thought that has "discounted or dismissed" intuition via "a skeptical rationalism which is a reactive pole to blind faith" (p. 158). Reexamines the relationship of reason with instinct and intuition in light of transpersonal psychology's "claim that supraconsciousness is intuition" (p. 158) to demonstrate that the "kinship between reason and intuition may be far more intimate" (p. 178) than is espoused in "the assumptions underlying current rationalism" (p. 160). By "[de-centering] the debate about intuition from one of seeking proof for the validity of intuition or supraconsciousness to one of de-alienating a number of polarities we've been living as consequences of our centuries-old war between faith and reason" (p. 160), Arons "seeks to open the path for a more spiritual and vital rationalism" (p. 158).

Psi Phenomena

"A new look at the enemies of parapsychology" (Arons, 1990c). Abridgement of a talk given at the Gathering of Explorers, Consciousness, Wisdom, and Energy conference in Atlanta, 1989. Proposes "the possibly revolutionary idea" that parapsychology "represents, *though in no way encompasses* [emphasis added], the middle ground" between "Christianity and science," which are "inherently related by their apparent opposition to each other" (p. 24). Explores the basis for which parapsychology is "the enemy common to both" insofar as they each "represent a monopoly of extremes" in their "division of a single territory of reality into two kingdoms of mind and matter" (p. 24). Suggests that the humanities "have been historically less antagonistic to psi phenomena" because they "stayed closer to the middle and not the extremes extrapolated out from the Platonic-Aristotelian debate" (p. 26). Therefore, they serve as "our culture's ultimate friends" in that they acknowledge how "the spiritual [can] be implicitly disclosed through the tangibles of nature" and facilitate the realization of "potentials of the middle ground within ourselves" (p. 26).

"Letters: An open mind" (Arons, 1992b). One of several letters to the editor expressing concerns about McCarthy's (1991) article, "Belief in Paranormal Isn't OK, It's Harmful." Arons challenges the hubris of "psychologists who set out to use 'science' as a way to debunk anything that doesn't fit into current science's, their own, or their culture's construed systems"—especially when such endeavors are "based on easily refuted popular excesses" and not on serious "open inquiry" of a "persistent cross-cultural, cross-temporal claim for a class of human experiences" (p. 4). Arons continues that during his lifetime psychology has "rejected many phenomena that later became quite legitimate or returned to a stage of legitimate interest and focus," and concludes, "Psychology cannot at one time claim both to be a young science and to know everything" (p. 4). As justification for Arons' sentiment, Cardeña's (2018) meta-analysis recently published in *American Psychologist* "provides cumulative support for the reality of psi, which cannot be readily explained away by the quality of the studies, fraud, selective reporting, experimental or analytical incompetence, or other frequent criticisms" (p. 663).

"Memory of things: Convergence toward a plausible psi context" (Arons, 1986). Evocation of Merleau-Ponty's theory of the body to present memory not only as "a package of recall" but also as "[engagement with] the world in a variety of intentions, each coextensive with the world it engages" (p. 2). Then, drawing "from diverse sources—Soviet psychology, phenomenology, classical philosophy, sensory and perceptual psychology, and creativity," Arons suggests that these all "share commonalities beyond a stress on memory and things"; that is, "they all involve activity and a unitizing experience which makes memory coextensive with the world experienced" (p. 5). Accordingly, "that unity of subject–object is often made through" the body that also encompasses "the subject lived in a certain way" (p. 5). Arons concludes, "The step further is to see the object, the thing, as having qualities of the subject, i.e., memory" (p. 5).

Human Science Research in Psychology

"Report on the 1984 Human Science Research Conference" (Aanstoos & Arons, 1985). Conference report emphasizes the diversity of both nations represented by the participants and qualitative methodologies represented by the presentations. "What was shared across all these differences was the fundamental insight that human existence is best approached on its own terms—that is, with foundations and methods appropriate to it rather than borrowed uncritically from other preexisting sciences" (p. 126). Whereas "it often has been observed that groups frequently emerge advocating radical alternatives, only to die out without having had much impact" because they "remain isolated" and "each must 'reinvent the wheel'" (p. 126). Accordingly, the conference provided "a much-needed opportunity to communicate in depth ... and thereby overcome that isolation" (p. 126).

"Are qualitative methods always best for humanistic psychology research? A conversation on the epistemological divide between humanistic and positive psychology" (Franco, Friedman, & Arons, 2008). An e-mail exchange between the three authors on humanistic philosophy of science. Arons' contributions cover: (a) the distinction between explanation and understanding (pp. 172–173); (b) Ricoeurian hermeneutics as allegorical of Maslow's proposal for humanistic psychology's place in science as "not replacing the old models but completing them" (p. 175); (c) the distinction between humanistic psychology's focus on intersubjectivity as distinct from solipsistic subjectivity (p. 176); (d) clarification of Comte's role in science compared to that of his followers (p. 179); (e) the contradictions in "sense-based" natural science's failure to account for wisdom and intuition (pp. 181–183); (f) the problems of modern science claiming sole propriety of validation, knowledge, and explanation ("Don't you think that *homo-habilus* 'knew' he came up with something new or unique when he turned a rock into a useful tool? Or when one of our other ancestors drew a symbol that joined the sky and the earth, life and death?") (p. 184); (g) prediction and control, while making methodological sense, limited the scope of science to meeting utilitarian ends (p. 187); (h) the importance of scientific inquiry employing "appropriate method for appropriate questions" (p. 188); (i) clarification of the place of empirical science methodologies in humanistic psychology (p. 194); (j) his disagreement with Maslow's take on existentialism (p. 194); and (k) his personal experience with the "abuse to my humanness of empirical science in psychology" (p. 196). Franco reflects that Arons, first of all, provides "a philosophical perspective challenging the fundamental assumption of objectivity in the practice of science, noting that even the most systematic research efforts are replete with examples of unexplained insight, personal creativity, and intuition" (p. 199) and then "cautions against using intuition inappropriately to anchor weak assertions while simultaneously reminding us that traditional science has neglected to address areas of human behavior it cannot yet (or would prefer not to) measure" (p. 199).

Humanistic Ethics

In these papers, Arons addresses the ethical crises posed by the war in Vietnam (Arons, 1972b) and by the absence of emotions in Western rationalism (Arons, 1993b).

"A Humanistic Psychologist's View of Our Government's Action in Vietnam" (Arons, 1972b)

"Psychologically healthy, or fully functioning [humans are] obliged from the center of [their] being to resist … assaults on basic human values. … I, as a psychologist, a humanistic psychologist, but particularly as a human who refuses to lose touch with his humanness ... ask that the government recognize beyond its clever and effective neutralizing techniques, that all of humanity is having its psychological bones crushed, and that no preservation of personal or national pride, no military victory, can compensate for the spiritual destruction its actions in Viet Nam are wreaking" (p. 4).

"Philosophy, Psychology, and the Moral Crisis: Reflections on Compassion 'Between Tradition and Another Beginning'" (Arons, 1993b)
Arons dialogues with Werner Marx's writings on compassion, purposive rationality (that which "puts emotions *in the service* of ends, not the kind that opens, by insights ... to the expressions of the emotions," p. 315), and post-conventional morality to "inquire if reason and faith cannot be resurrected in intrinsic and holistic form" to facilitate the "transition between failed modern and ethically vulnerable postmodern paradigms" (p. 296).

Arons' Final Musings

Below are three papers that Arons composed during the last decade of his life, each of which set the stage for the subsequent one as he prepared his *Standing Up for Humanity* project (unfinished book but published in briefer form in Arons, 2007, Chapter 7 in this volume). First, Arons (1998a) explores the value of tolerance of ambiguity and openness to experience for optimal functioning. Second, he discusses how going out on a limb provides platforms for new outlooks of consciousness (Arons, 1999c). Third, Arons (2001) culminates the themes from throughout his career to apply the platform experience to the upright body posture.

"A Cook's Tour of the Edge" (Arons, 1998a)
Arons employs the resurrection of the human pyramid by the Flying Wallendas as a metaphor for the wisdom of insecurity, of living on the razor's edge, in the here and now. "For Socrates, human best—the

excellence of excellence itself, wisdom—is to constantly encounter the gods on all fronts. The greatest and most enduring advantage to the mortal soul is where it doesn't know the outcome of anything" (p. 8).

"The Platform Experience: Eidetic of Posture, Perspective, and Leveraging Our Way Home" (Arons, 1999c)

A precursor to Arons (2007). Arons reflects on how his experience of building a deck behind his wooded home—and the affordances it provided for "a new lookout which sparked a new outlook" (p. 9)—contributed to him developing "a different understanding ... on science ... and its changing status, consequent to newly seen relationships to the pre-sciences, its own ground in creativity and language, and the developing human sciences" (p. 2). Applying numerous metaphors from baseball to staircases to the Riddle of the Sphinx, he traces the circumstances by which modern science managed to outsource itself to outer space via the adoption of a linear, vertical view of progress in the same way that, by way of technology, humans have outsourced themselves to automation (Carr, 2014; F. Foer, 2017).

"Standing Up for Humanity: Reflections on the Heuristics of New–Old" (Arons, 2001)

An expansion of Arons (1999c). In addition to being a compendium of notes he prepared for a string of conference presentations, this 91-page document also was an early draft of his ultimately unfinished book on the connections between upright body posture and human freedom, creativity, reason, consciousness, language, and growth. Arons reviews and revisits threads, themes, and vignettes that constituted the crux of his writings throughout his career, situating them in the context of a dialectic between progressive (vertical, distal) rationalist science and what its proponents regard as its regressive (lateral, proximal) critics. He concludes by emphasizing (a) both the importance and the possibility of transcendence *and* inclusion (i.e., creative integration) of *both* worldviews ("[rejoining] consciousness with body ... without reducing one to the other," p. 88) in the emerging era and (b) the role of qualitative research for that reconciliation ("standing as go-between the natural attitude of science and the pre-reflective calls of experience, in the way Ricoeur stands between philosophy and the instincts and following the admonition of Merleau-Ponty to join fact and essential structure," p. 88). "Given our reflections on the upright body posture, are these really different formulations of the *human condition* and *human dilemma*—or two sides of the same coin? I'll *stand up* for the latter. But to check this out, a phenomenology of wisdom is awaited" (p. 91).

Mike announcing his retirement from (then) State University of West Georgia, 2000.
(Photographer unknown. Contributed by Sandrine Arons.)

References

Note: ^ = Included as a chapter in this book. * = Entries in the annotated bibliography (Appendix).

Aanstoos, C. (1989). The West Georgia story. *The Humanistic Psychologist, 17*, 77–85. doi:10.1080/08873267.1989.9976843

Aanstoos, C. (1991). The West Georgia College graduate psychology program. In C. Aanstoos, C. (Ed.). *Studies in humanistic psychology: West Georgia College studies in the social sciences, Vol. XXIX* (pp. 163–208). Carrollton, GA: West Georgia College.

Aanstoos, C. (2008). A tribute to Mike Arons. *The Humanistic Psychologist, 36*, 375–377. doi:10.1080/08873260802575214

Aanstoos, C. (2017, October). *Psychology at West Georgia over the years.* Presentation at the University of West Georgia Psychology 50th Anniversary Reunion and Conference, Carrollton, GA. Retrieved from https://www.youtube.com/watch?v=-gvXpwSvqG0

* Aanstoos, C., & Arons, M. (1985). Report on the 1984 Human Science Research Conference. *Journal of Humanistic Psychology, 25*, 125–127. doi:10.1177/0022167885252012

Aanstoos, C., Serlin, I., & Greening, T. (2000). *History of Division 32 (Humanistic Psychology) of the American Psychological Association.* Retrieved from http://www.apadivisions.org/division-32/about/history.pdf

Allender, J. A., & Richards, A. C. (1986). Association for Humanistic Education: Tenth anniversary conference. *The Humanistic Psychologist, 14*, 134–137. doi:10.1037/h0101363

Annas, J. (1993). *The morality of happiness.* New York, NY: Oxford University Press.

* Arons, M. (1965). *Le problème de la creativité: Discussion méthodologique, reactions dans la psychologie américaine* [The problem of creativity: Methodological discussion, reactions in American psychology] (Unpublished doctoral dissertation). Sorbonne, Paris, France.

Arons, M. (1967, December 7). [Letter to Abraham Maslow]. Abraham Maslow Papers (Box M4413, Folder 1). Drs. Nicholas and Dorothy Cummings Center for the History of Psychology, University of Akron, Akron, OH.

* Arons, M. (1969, May). *Humanistic psychology and the academic curriculum.* Paper presented at the meeting of the Georgia Psychological Association, Pine Mountain, GA. Copy in possession of author.

* Arons, M. (1970). Foreword. In H. Stewart & J. Thomas, *Introductory experiential psychology: A book of readings* (pp. viix). Dubuque, IA: Kendall Hunt.

* Arons, M. (1972a, August). *Creativity, humanistic psychology, and the emerging American consciousness*. Paper presented at the meeting of the Association for Humanistic Psychology, Oahu, HI. Retrieved from https://www.westga.edu/academics/coss/psychology/assets/docs/AronsCreativity.pdf

* Arons, M. (1972b). A humanistic psychologist's view of our government's action in Vietnam. *PsycEXTRA Database*. doi:10.1037/e512732011-003

* Arons, M. (1972?c). Humanistic psychology: West Georgia College. In Department of Psychology, West Georgia College, *The first annual disorientation handbook for the Psychology Department* (pp. 2–3). Department of Psychology Records (Box 2). Ingram Library Special Collections, University of West Georgia, Carrollton, GA.

* Arons, M. (1976a). The changing winds. *Newsletter: Division of Humanistic Psychology, 4*, 4–5. doi:10.1037/e586482009-010

^, * Arons, M. (1976b). Presidential address (1976): Transformations of science and religion through humanistic psychology. *Newsletter: Division of Humanistic Psychology, 4*, 6–7. Retrieved from https://www.westga.edu/academics/coss/psychology/assets/docs/AronsTransformation.pdf

* Arons, M. (1977a, April). *The future of humanistic education at the heart of crisis*. Paper presented at the Conference on Humanistic Education, Boston, MA. Retrieved from https://www.westga.edu/academics/coss/psychology/assets/docs/AronsTheFuture.pdf

* Arons, M. (1977b, September). *The group oral: An exam which is not inhuman*. Paper presented at the meeting of the Association for Humanistic Psychology, Berkeley, CA. Retrieved from https://www.westga.edu/academics/coss/psychology/assets/docs/AronsTheGroupOral.pdf

* Arons, M. (1977c, December). Humanistic psychology versus human potentials movement. *Association for Humanistic Psychology Newsletter*.

* Arons, M. (1977d). O. J. and teacher selection. *Journal of Humanistic Education, 1*, 57–66.

* Arons, M. (1978a). The humanistic orientation. In Department of Psychology, West Georgia College, *Self-study: The undergraduate program* (pp. 23–27). Department of Psychology Records (Box 3). Ingram Library Special Collections, University of West Georgia, Carrollton, GA. Retrieved from https://www.westga.edu/academics/coss/psychology/assets/docs/AronsTheHuman.pdf

^, * Arons, M. (1978b, March). *The value of the arts for special populations*. Paper presented at the Conference on Arts and Special Populations: A

Beginning Look, Atlanta, GA. Retrieved from
https://www.westga.edu/academics/coss/psychology/assets/docs/Aro
nsValueof.pdf

* Arons, M. (1982). *Hermeneutic of a complementarity between energy and meaning in Freud.* Paper presented at Southeastern Psychology Association Meeting, New Orleans, LA. Retrieved from https://www.westga.edu/academics/coss/psychology/assets/docs/Aro nsHermeneutic.pdf

* Arons, M. (1985a, March). *Humanistic zeitgeist, science, and religion: A meta-historical account.* Paper presented at the Quarter Century Conference on Humanistic Psychology, San Francisco, CA. Copy in possession of author.

* Arons, M. (1985b). A quarter century of humanistic psychologies. *The Humanistic Psychologist, 13,* 55–60. doi:10.1080/08873267.1985.9976733

* Arons, M. (1986, February). *Memory of things: Convergence toward a plausible psi context* (AKA *Plausible psi context: Convergence of Soviet, transpersonal, and psi approaches to memory*). Paper presented at the meeting of the Southeastern Regional Parapsychology Association, Charlottesville, VA. Copy in possession of author.

* Arons, M. (1987). Creativity and the methodological debate: A mytho-historical reflection. In F. J. van Zuuren, F. J. Wertz, & B. Mook (Eds.), *Advances in qualitative psychology: Themes and variations* (pp. 79–97). Lisse, Netherlands: Swets and Zeitlinger.

* Arons, M. (1988a, April). *The legacy of Maslow and Rogers* (AKA *Humanistic psychology and the humanities: Knowing ourselves as middle aged and ageless*). Paper presented at the conference of the Association for Humanistic Education, Paducah, KY. Retrieved from https://www.westga.edu/academics/coss/psychology/assets/docs/Aro nsTheLegacy.pdf

* Arons, M. (1988b). A proposal for credentialing humanistic practice. *The Humanistic Psychologist, 16,* 382-383. doi:10.1080/08873267.1988.9976834

^, * Arons, M. (1990a). The growing chasm between mission and job (1989 presidential address). *Journal of Humanistic Education, 14,* 124–127.

* Arons, M. (1990b, May). *Intuition and the intimacy of instinct and consciousness.* Paper presented at the Psi, Sexuality, and Intimacy Conference, Carrollton, GA. Retrieved from https://www.westga.edu/academics/coss/psychology/assets/docs/Aro nsIntuition.pdf

* Arons, M. (1990c, Fall). A new look at the enemies of parapsychology. *Theta: Contemporary Issues in Parapsychology,* 24–26.

* Arons, M. (1991a). Creativity and the methodological debate: A mytho-historical reflection. In C. Aanstoos (Ed.), *Studies in humanistic*

psychology: West Georgia College studies in the social sciences, Vol. XXIX (pp. 12–32). Carrollton, GA: West Georgia College.

^, * Arons, M. (1991b). The politics of education, a critical tribute: From the heart of Rogers to the heart of education. *Journal of Humanistic Education, 15*, 6–17.

^, * Arons, M. (1992a). Creativity, humanistic psychology, and the American zeitgeist. *The Humanistic Psychologist, 20*, 158–174. doi:10.1080/08873267.1992.9986788

* Arons, M. (1992b, January). Letters: An open mind. *APA monitor on psychology, 4.*

^, * Arons, M. (1992c). Two suns of my student years. *Journal of Humanistic Psychology, 32*, 46–50. doi:10.1177/0022167892321004

^, * Arons, M. (1993a). Instinct, intuition, and supraconscious: De-alienating reflections. *The Humanistic Psychologist, 21*, 158–179. doi:10.1080/08873267.1993.9976915

* Arons, M. (1993b). Philosophy, psychology, and the moral crisis: Reflections on compassion "between tradition and another beginning." *The Humanistic Psychologist, 21*, 296–324. doi:10.1080/08873267.1993.9976925

* Arons, M. (1994a). Creativity, humanistic psychology, and the American zeitgeist. In F. Wertz (Ed.), *The humanistic movement: Recovering the person in psychology* (pp. 45–61). Lake Worth, FL: Gardner.

^, * Arons, M. (1994b). Recognizable paths of humanistic psychology. *The Humanistic Psychologist, 22*, 371–378. doi:10.1080/08873267.1994.9976960

* Arons, M. (1996). Frank Barron and the creativity revolution. In A. Montouri (Ed.), *Unusual associates: A festschrift for Frank Barron* (pp. 57-68). Catskill, NJ: Hampton.

* Arons, M. (1997a). Jim Klee, 1916-1996. *Journal of Humanistic Psychology, 37*, 7–8. doi:10.1177/00221678970372003

* Arons, M. (1997b). Jim Klee 1916–1996. *The Humanistic Psychologist, 25*, 111–115. doi:10.1080/08873267.1997.9986874

* Arons, M. (1998a, June). *A Cook's tour of the edge.* Paper presented at the 17th Human Science Research Conference, Sitka, AK. Copy in possession of author.

* Arons, M. (1998b, August). Sacred and symbol: From Ricoeur's *Freud and philosophy.* In *Symbol and Sacred.* Symposium conducted at the meeting of the American Psychological Association, San Francisco, CA. Copy in possession of author.

* Arons, M. (1999a). Abraham Maslow: Yesterday, tomorrow, and yesteryear. In D. Moss (Ed.), *Humanistic and transpersonal psychology: A historical and biographical sourcebook* (pp. 334–346). Westport, CT: Greenwood.

* Arons, M. (1999?b). *New vocation for an age-old market.* Unpublished manuscript. Copy in possession of author.

* Arons, M. (1999c, August). *The platform experience: Eidetic of posture,*

perspective, and leveraging our way home. Paper presented at the International Qualitative Research Conference, Perugia, Italy. Copy in possession of author.

^, * Arons, M. (1999d). Self, multiple selves, and the illusion of separate selfhood. *The Humanistic Psychologist, 27,* 187–211. doi:10.1080/08873267.1999.9986904

^, * Arons, M. (2000a, July). *At the juncture: Creativity, humanistic, and transpersonal psychologies.* Paper presented at the Conference on Humanistic–Transpersonal Psychology, Wuhan, China. Copy in possession of author.

* Arons, M. (2000b). [Curriculum vita]. Copy in possession of author.

* Arons, M. (2001, August). *Standing up for humanity: Reflections on the heuristics of new–old.* Paper presented at the Human Science Research Conference, Tokyo, Japan. Copy in possession of author.

* Arons, M. (2003a). Dr. Earl Brown: Diplomat, personalist, visionary. *Division 32 Newsletter,* 9-10. Retrieved from http://www.apadivisions.org/division-32/publications/newsletters/humanistic/2003/04-issue.pdf

* Arons, M. (2003b). A tribute to Frank Barron: He helped bend a century. *Journal of Humanistic Psychology, 43,* 26–33. doi:10.1177/0022167802250105

^, * Arons, M. (2004). *My passage through Maslow.* Unpublished manuscript. Copy in possession of author.

^, * Arons, M. (2007). Standing up for humanity: Upright body, creative instability, and spiritual balance. In R. Richards (Ed.), *Everyday creativity and new views of human nature: Psychological, social, and spiritual perspectives* (pp. 175–193). Washington, DC: American Psychological Association.

* Arons, M., & Graham, S. (1976). President's column. *Newsletter: Division of Humanistic Psychology, 4*(2), 1–2. doi:10.1037/e586492009-002

* Arons, M., & Harari, C. (Eds.). (1992). Recollections and reflections: Snippets from an oral history of humanistic psychology. *The Humanistic Psychologist, 20,* 189–201. doi:10.1080/08873267.1992.9986790

* Arons, M., & Harari, C. (Eds.). (1994). Recollections and reflections: Snippets from an oral history of humanistic psychology. In F. Wertz (Ed.), *The humanistic movement: Recovering the person in psychology* (pp. 76–88). Lake Worth, FL: Gardner.

* Arons, M., Harari, C., & O'Donovan. (1972, Summer). What's it all about? *Association for Humanistic Psychology Newsletter, 8,* 1–3. Retrieved from https://www.ahpweb.org/images/stories/archive_pdfs/1972/ 08-72.pdf

* Arons, M., Harari, C., & O'Donovan. (1973). Humanistic psychology: An overview. In F. Richards & I. D. Welch (Eds.), *Sightings: Essays in humanistic psychology* (pp. 3–7). Boulder, CO: Shields.

* Arons, M., & London, H. (1969). Correcting for compensation in studies of

time estimation. *Psychonomic Science, 17,* 319–320.
doi:10.3758/bf03335258

* Arons, M., & Richards, R. (2015). Two noble insurgencies: Creativity and
humanistic psychology. In K. J. Schneider, J. F. Pierson, & J. F. T. Bugental
(Eds.), *Handbook of humanistic psychology* (2nd ed., pp. 161–175). Los
Angeles, CA: Sage.

Asch, S. E. (1952). *Social psychology.* Englewood Cliffs, NJ: Prentice Hall.

* Barrell, J. H., Aanstoos, A., Richards, A. C., & Arons, M. (1987). Human
science research methods. *Journal of Humanistic Psychology, 27,* 424–
457. doi:10.1177/0022167887274004

Barron, F. (1963). *Creativity and psychological health: Origins of personal
vitality and creative freedom.* New York, NY: van Nostrand.

Barron, F. X. (1968). *Creativity and personal freedom* (rev. ed.). Princeton, NJ:
Van Nostrand.

Barron, F. X. (1969). *Creative person and creative process.* New York, NY: Holt,
Rinehart & Winston.

Bergson, H. (1940). *L'evolution créatrice.* Paris, France: Presses Universitaires
de Paris.

Bergson. H. (1992). *The creative mind: An introduction to metaphysics.* New
York, NY: Carol.

Bland, A. (2002). *An excursion with Mike Arons: Standing up for humanity, the
backbone of creativity.* Retrieved from
https://www.westga.edu/academics/coss/psychology/assets/docs/Aro
nsStandingUp.pdf

Bland, A. (2003). *A brief history of the West Georgia psychology program.*
Retrieved from
https://www.westga.edu/academics/coss/psychology/assets/docs/Aro
ns-Brief_History.pdf

Bland, A. (2008, February). Obituary for Mike Arons. *AHP (Association for
Humanistic Psychology) Perspective,* 9.

Bland, A. M., & DeRobertis, E. M. (2019). The humanistic perspective. In V.
Zeigler-Hill & T. K. Shackelford (Eds.), *Encyclopedia of Personality and
Individual Differences.* Cham, Switzerland: Springer. Advance online
publication. doi:10.1007/978-3-319-28099-8_1484-2

Bloom, A. D. (1987). *The closing of the American mind.* New York, NY: Simon
and Schuster.

Bohm, D., & Peat, F. D. (1987). *Science, order, and creativity.* London, UK:
Routledge.

Bronowski, J. (1958). The creative process. *Scientific American, 199,* 63–64.
doi:10.1038/scientificamerican0958-58

Bühler, C. (1968). Fulfillment and the value of life. In F. Massarick (Ed.), *The
course of human life* (pp. 127–168). New York, NY: Springer.

Café philosophique. (n.d.). Retrieved from
https://en.wikipedia.org/wiki/Caf%C3%A9_philosophique

Camus, A. (1955). *The myth of Sisyphus and other essays* (J. O'Brien, Trans.).

New York, NY: Vintage.

Cardeña, E. (2018). The experimental evidence for parapsychological phenomena: A review. *American Psychologist, 73*, 663–677. doi:10.1037/amp0000236

Carr, N. (2014). *The glass cage: Automation and us.* New York, NY: Norton.

Chaudhuri, H. (1965). *Integral yoga: A concept of harmonious and creative living.* Wheaton, IL: Theological Publishing House.

Chaudhuri, H. (1977). *The evolution of internal consciousness.* Wheaton, IL: Theological Publishing House.

Chobe, M. (1993). *Differentiated consciousness.* Doctoral dissertation in process.

Cooper, D. (1997). *God is a verb: Kabbalah and the practice of mystical Judaism.* New York, NY: Riverhead.

Crutchfield, R. S. (1963). Conformity and creative thinking. In W. Henry (Ed.), *Contemporary approaches to creative thinking.* New York, NY: Atherton.

Csikszentmihalyi, M. (1996). *Creativity.* New York, NY: HarperCollins.

DeCarvalho, R. J. (1991). *The founders of humanistic psychology.* New York, NY: Praeger.

DeRobertis, E. M. (2017). *The phenomenology of learning and becoming: Enthusiasm, creativity, and self-development.* New York, NY: Palgrave-Macmillan.

Dreikurs, R. M. D. (1987). *Children: The challenge.* New York, NY: Hutton.

Dufrenne, M. (1966). *The notion of the a priori* (E. S. Casey, Trans.). Evanston, IL: Northwestern University Press.

Einstein, A. (1934). *Essays in science.* New York, NY: The Philosophical Library.

Eliade, M. (1969). *Yoga: Immortality and freedom* (2nd ed.). Princeton, NJ: Princeton University Press.

Elkins, D. N. (2000). Old Saybrook I and II: The visioning and revisioning of humanistic psychology. *Journal of Humanistic Psychology, 40*, 119–127. doi:10.1177/0022167800402002

Erikson, E. H. (1959). *Identity and life cycle.* New York, NY: International Universities Press.

Ferren, J. (1953). *The nature of creative thinking.* Industrial Relations Institute.

Flanagan, J. C. (1963). Definition and measurement of ingenuity. In C. W. Taylor & F. Barron (Eds.), *Scientific creativity: Its recognition and development* (pp. 89–98). New York, NY: Wiley.

Foer, F. (2017). *World without mind: The existential threat of big tech.* New York, NY: Penguin.

Foer, J., & Siffre, M. (2008, Summer). Caveman: An interview with Michel Siffre. *The Underground, 30.* Retrieved from http://www.cabinetmagazine.org/issues/30/foer.php

* Franco, Z., Friedman, H., & Arons, M. (2008). Are qualitative methods always best for humanistic psychology research? A conversation on the

epistemological divide between humanistic and positive psychology. *The Humanistic Psychologist, 36*, 159–203. doi:10.1080/08873260802111242

Frankl, V. (1950). *From death camp to existentialism*. New York, NY: Beacon.

Fromm, E. (1941). *Escape from freedom*. New York, NY: Holt, Rhinehart, & Winston.

Gallagher, S., & Zahavi, D. (2012). *The phenomenological mind* (2nd ed.). New York, NY: Routledge.

Gallegos, E. S. (1990). *The personal totem pole: Animal imagery, the chakras, and psychotherapy* (2nd ed.). Velarde, NM: Moon Bear.

Gergen, K. J. (1991). *The saturated self.* New York, NY: Basic.

Getzels, J. W., & Jackson, P.W. (1962). *Creativity and intelligence*. London, UK: Wiley.

Ghiselen, B. (1952). *The creative process*. Berkeley: University of California Press.

Ghiselen, B. (1963). Ultimate criteria for two levels of creativity. In C. W. Taylor & F. Barron (Eds.), *Scientific creativity: Its recognition and development* (pp. 30–43). New York, NY: Wiley.

Gilbert, R. (1977, July). Humanistic psychology and the human potential movement. *Association for Humanistic Psychology Newsletter*, 1–2.

Goldberg, P. (1983). *The intuitive edge*. Los Angeles, CA: Tarcher.

Goodall, J. (1986). *The chimpanzees of Gombe: Patterns of behavior*. Cambridge, MA: Harvard University Press.

Goodman, P. (1960). *Growing up absurd.* New York, NY: Random House.

Guilford, J. P. (1950). Creativity. *American Psychologist, 5*, 444–453. doi:10.1037/h0063487

Harman, W. & Rheingold, H. (1984). *Higher creativity: Liberating the unconscious for breakthrough insights.* Los Angeles, CA: Tarcher.

Harner, M. (1990). *The way of the shaman: A guide to power healing*. New York, NY: Harper & Row.

Heinze, R. I. (1991). *Shamans of the 20th century*. New York, NY: Irvington.

Hoffman, E. (1985). *The heavenly ladder: Kabbalistic techniques for inner growth*. New York, NY: Harper & Row.

Hoffman, L., Stewart, S., Warren, D. M., & Meek, L. (2015). Toward a sustainable myth of self: An existential response to the postmodern condition. In K. J. Schneider, J. F. Pierson, & J. F. T. Bugental (Eds.), *Handbook of humanistic psychology* (2nd ed., pp. 105–133). Los Angeles: Sage.

Houston, J. (1992). *The hero and the goddess*. New York, NY: Ballantine.

Howard, G. S. (2019). The present and future of methodology and statistics in psychology. *The Humanistic Psychologist, 47*, 26–51. doi:10.1037/hum0000111

Ito, J., & Howe, J. (2016). *Whiplash: How to survive our faster future*. New York, NY: Grand Central.

James, W. (1985). *The varieties of religious experience*. Cambridge, MA:

Harvard University Press. (Original work published 1902)

Keleman, S. (1981). *Your body speaks its mind*. Berkeley, CA: Center.

Klee, J. (1982). *Points of departure: Aspects of the Tao*. South Bend, IN: And Books.

Krippner, S. (1994). Humanistic psychology and chaos theory: The third revolution and the third force. *Journal of Humanistic Psychology, 34*, 48–61. doi:10.1177/00221678940343005

^, * Krippner, S., & Arons, M. (1973a). Creativity: Person, product, or process. *Gifted Child Quarterly, 17*, 116–123, 129. doi:10.1177/001698627301700207

* Krippner, S., & Arons, M. (1973b). Creativity east, creativity west. *Fields within fields within fields: Journal of the World Institute Council, 10*, 25–31.

Kris, E. (1952). *Psychoanalytic explorations in art*. New York, NY: International Universities Press.

Kris, E. (1953). Psychoanalysis and the study of the creative imagination. *Bulletin of the New York Academy of Medicine, 29*, 334–351.

Laing, R. D. (1965). *The divided self*. New York, NY: Penguin.

Lakoff, G. (1987). *Women, fire, and other dangerous things: What categories reveal about the mind*. Chicago, IL: University of Chicago Press.

Lange-Eichbaum, W. (1962). *The problem of genius* (E. Paul & C. Paul, Trans.). New York, NY: Wiley. (Original work published 1932)

Laski, M. (1962). *Ecstasy: A study of some secular and religious experiences*. Bloomington: Indiana University Press.

Leary, T. (1990). *Flashback: An autobiography*. Los Angeles, CA: Tarcher.

Lee, D. (1959). *Freedom and culture*. Englewood, NJ: Prentice-Hall.

Lee, J. (Director and Producer). (2009). *East and west* [documentary film]. Seoul, South Korea: Educational Broadcasting System. Retrieved from https://www.youtube.com/watch?time_continue=1&v=ZoDtoB9Abck

Leontiev, A. N. (1984). *Soviet psychology (Psikhologicheskiy Zhurnal)*. Moscow, Russia: Nauka.

Marx, W. (1992). *Toward a phenomenological ethics: Ethos and the life-world*. Albany: State University of New York Press.

Maslow, A. H. (1962). *Toward a psychology of being*. Princeton, NJ: Van Nostrand.

Maslow, A. H. (1964). *Religions, values, peak experiences*. Columbus: Ohio State University Press.

Maslow, A. H. (1965). *Eupsychian management: A journal*. Homewood, IL: Irwin-Dorsey.

Maslow, A. H. (1966). *Psychology of science: A reconnaissance*. New York, NY: Harper & Row.

Maslow, A. H. (1968). *Toward a psychology of being* (2nd ed.). New York, NY: van Nostrand.

Maslow, A. H. (1971). *The farther reaches of human nature*. New York, NY: Viking.

Matt, D. C. (1997). *The essential Kabbalah: The heart of Jewish mysticism.* Edison, NJ: Castle Books.

Maugham, S. (1944). *The razor's edge.* London, UK: Heinemann.

May, R. (1969). *Love and will.* New York, NY: Norton.

May, R. (1975). *The courage to create.* New York, NY: Norton.

McCarthy, K. (1991, November). Belief in paranormal isn't OK, it's harmful. *APA monitor on psychology.*

McGregor, D. (1960). *The human side of enterprise.* New York, NY: McGraw-Hill.

Merleau-Ponty, M. (1951). *Les sciences de l'homme et la phenomenologie.* Cours de la Sorbonne, Introduction and Premiere Partie.

Merleau-Ponty, M. (1962). *Phenomenology of perception.* (C. Smith, Trans.). London, UK: Routledge & Kegan.

Miller, W. R., & Thoresen, C. E. (1999). Spirituality and health. In W. R. Miller (Ed.), *Integrating spirituality into treatment: Resources for practitioners* (pp. 3–18). Washington, DC: American Psychological Association.

Moustakas, C. (Ed.). (1956). *The self: Explorations in personal growth.* New York, NY: Harper and Row.

Moustakas, C. (1990). *Heuristic research: Design, methodology, and applications.* Newberry Park, CA: Sage.

O'Hara, M. (2009, January). Boston hospitality suite: The society honors our beloved Mike (Myron) Arons. *Society for Humanistic Psychology Newsletter.* Retrieved from http://www.apadivisions.org/division-32/publications/newsletters/humanistic/2009/01/boston-hospitality-suite.aspx

Ornstein, R. (1991). *Evolution of consciousness: Darwin, Freud and cranial fire—The origins of the way we think.* New York, NY: Prentice Hall.

Pagels, E. (1943). *Gnostic gospels.* New York, NY: Random House.

Pinsker, J. (2016, September 12). Ask an economist: How can today's college students future-proof their careers? *The Atlantic.* Retrieved from https://www.theatlantic.com/business/archive/2016/09/ how-can-todays-college-students-futureproof-their-careers/499244/

Pirsig, R. (1991). *Lila: An inquiry into morals.* New York, NY: Bantam.

Polanyi, M. (1958). *On personal knowledge.* Chicago, IL: University of Chicago Press.

Polkinghorne, D. E. (2015). The self and humanistic psychology. In K. J. Schneider, J. F. Pierson, & J. F. T. Bugental (Eds.), *Handbook of humanistic psychology* (2nd ed., pp. 87–104). Los Angeles: Sage.

Questlove. (2018). *Creative quest.* New York, NY: HarperCollins.

Read, H. (1957). *Poetic consciousness and creative experience.* Zurich, Switzerland: Rhein-Verlag.

Read, H. E. (1967). *Art and alienation: The role of the artist in society.* New York, NY: Norton.

Richards, R. (2000). Millennium as opportunity: Chaos, creativity, and J. P. Guilford's Structure-of-Intellect Model. *Creativity Research Journal, 13,*

249–265. doi:10.1207/s15326934crj1334_03

Richards, R., Kinney, D., Benet, M., & Merzel, A. (1988). Assessing everyday creativity: Characteristics of the Lifetime Creativity Scales and validation with three large samples. *Journal of Personality and Social Psychology, 54*, 476–485. doi:10.1037//0022-3514.54.3.476

Richards, R., & Whitehouse, H. (2008). Subtle mind, open heart: Mike Arons remembered (1929-2008). *Psychology of Aesthetics, Creativity, and the Arts, 2*, 264–270. doi:10.1037/a0014189

Ricoeur, P. (1967). *Husserl: An analysis of his phenomenology.* Evanston, IL: Northwestern University Press.

Ricoeur, P. (1970). *Freud and philosophy: An essay on interpretation.* New Haven, CT: Yale University Press.

Ritkin, S. (1987). *Time wars.* New York, NY: Holt.

Roe, A. (1951). A psychological study of eminent biologists. *Psychological Monographs, 64*, 1–68. doi:10.1037/h0093639

Rogers, C. R. (1959). Toward a theory of creativity. In H. H. Anderson (Ed.), *Creativity and its cultivation* (pp. 69–82). New York, NY: Harper.

Rogers, C. R. (1969). *Freedom to learn. A view of what education might become.* Columbus, OH: Merrill.

Rose, T. (2015). *The end of average: How we succeed in a world that values sameness.* New York, NY: HarperCollins.

Rowan, J. (2001). *Ordinary ecstasy: The dialectics of humanistic psychology* (3rd ed.). Philadelphia, PA: Taylor & Francis.

Runco, M. A, & Pritzker, S. R. (1999). *Encyclopedia of creativity* (Vols. 1–2). San Diego, CA: Academic Press.

Runco, M. A., & Richards, R. (Eds.). (1998). *Eminent creativity, everyday creativity. and health.* Greenwich, CT: Ablex.

Sartre, J. P. (1947). *No exit.* New York, NY: Knopf.

Sartre, J. P. (1948). *Being and nothingness.* (H. E. Barnes, Trans.). New York, NY: Philosophical Library. (Original work published 1943)

Schneider, K. (2004). *Rediscovery of awe: Splendor, mystery, and the fluid center of life.* St. Paul, MN: Paragon House.

Schneider, K. J. (2013). *The polarized mind: Why it's killing us and what we can do about it.* Colorado Springs, CO: University Professors Press.

Schneider, K. J. (2019). *The spirituality of awe: Challenges to the robotic revolution* (rev. ed.). Colorado Springs, CO: University Professors Press.

* Schor, L., & Arons, M. (2007). Tribute to Duncan Blewitt. *Journal of Humanistic Psychology, 47*, 514–516. doi:10.1177/0022167807308013

Scorsese, M. (Director). (2005). *No direction home: Bob Dylan* [DVD]. Los Angeles, CA: Paramount.

* Serlin, I., & Arons, M. (2004). Carmi Harari (1920-2003). *American Psychologist, 59*, 642. doi:10.1037/0003-066x.59.7.642

Siffre, M. (1963). *Hors du temps.* Julliard.

Skolimowski, H. (1984). *The theatre of the mind: Evolution in the sensitive cosmos*. Wheaton, IL: Theosophical Publishing House.

Smith, H. (1972). *Requiem for a faith* [Film]. Cos Cob, CT: Hartley.

Smith, M. B., Moerman, C. L., & Wertz, F. J. (1986). Candidates for division elections. *The Humanistic Psychologist, 14*, 51–53. doi:10.1080/08873267.1986.9976753

Sophocles. (1982). *Oedipus Rex*. New York, NY: Cambridge University Press.

Spiegelberg, H. (1960). *The phenomenological movement: An historical introduction*. The Hague, Netherlands: Nijhoff.

Sprecher, T. B. (1964). Criteria of creativity. In Taylor & Calvin (Eds.), *Creativity: Progress and potential* (pp. 155–185). New York, NY: McGraw-Hill.

Stanford, G. (2001). *Significant others: The ape continuum and the quest for human nature*. New York, NY: Basic.

Steeves, H. P. (1999). *Animal others: On ethics, ontology and animal life*. New York, NY: State University of New York Press.

Sternberg, R. J. (1985). *Human abilities: An information processing approach*. New York, NY: Freeman.

Sternberg, R. J. (2013, December 11). *Robert Sternberg on culture, intelligence and education*. Retrieved from https://www.youtube.com/watch?v=5KKsf48_-A0

Sternberg, R. J. (2018). A triangular theory of creativity. *Psychology of Aesthetics, Creativity, and the Arts, 12*, 50–67. doi:10.1037/aca0000095

Straus, E. (1966). *Phenomenological psychology* (E. Eng, Trans.). New York, NY: Basic.

Taylor, E. (1991). William James and the humanistic tradition. *Journal of Humanistic Psychology, 31*, 56–74. doi:10.1177/0022167891311006

Terman, L. M., & Olden, M. H. (1947). *The gifted child grows up*. Stanford, CA: Stanford University Press.

Torrance, E. P. (1964). Education and creativity. In Taylor and Calvin (Eds.), *Creativity: progress and potential* (pp. 49–128). New York, NY: McGraw-Hill.

Vygotsky, L. S. (1978). *Mind in society: The development of higher psychological processes*. Cambridge, MA: Harvard University Press.

Walsh, R. (2015). What is wisdom? Cross-cultural and cross-disciplinary syntheses. *Review of General Psychology, 19*, 278–293. doi:10.1037/gpr0000045

Watts, A. W. (1951). *The wisdom of insecurity: A message for the age of anxiety*. London, UK: Vintage.

Wilber, K. (1983). *Up from Eden: A transpersonal view of human evolution*. Garden City, NY: Anchor/Doubleday.

Wilber, K. (2017). *Trump and the post-truth world*. Boulder, CO: Shambhala.

Wilson, C. (1966). *Introduction to the new existentialism*. Boston, MA: Houghton Mifflin.

Wilson, K. G., Bordieri, M., & Whiteman, K. (2012). The self and mindfulness. In L. McHugh & I. Stewart (Eds.), *The self and perspective taking:*

Contributions and applications from modern behavioral science (pp. 181–197). Oakland, CA: New Harbinger.

Zinker, J. (1977). *Creative process in gestalt therapy.* New York, NY: Vantage.

Index

Mike at his home in Carrollton, GA, 2004.
(Photo by Christiane Arons. Contributed by Andrew Bland.)

About the Editors

Andrew M. Bland is a member of the graduate clinical psychology faculty at Millersville University in Lancaster County, PA. He received a master's degree from the University of West Georgia's humanistic–existential–transpersonal psychology program (2003) and a Ph.D. in counseling psychology from Indiana State University (2013). He is a licensed psychologist, currently practicing at Samaritan Counseling Center in Lancaster, PA. He serves on the executive committees of the Society for Humanistic Psychology (Division 32 of the American Psychological Association, APA) and the Society for Qualitative Inquiry in Psychology (Section 3 of Division 5 of APA) and on the editorial boards of the *Journal of Humanistic Psychology* and the *Journal of Theoretical and Philosophical Criminology*. His scholarship provides both qualitative and quantitative support for the practical application of themes and principles from contemporary existential–humanistic psychology in the domains of love and intimate relationships, work and career development, the processes of therapy and education, creativity, and lifespan development.

Sandrine M. Arons lives in Marseille, France, where she works as a fine art photographer. She received an MA in psychology from University of West Georgia (1997), an MA in French language and literature from University of Pittsburgh (2010), and an MFA in photography from Savannah College of Art and Design (2015). Her studies in psychology and French literature have guided her photographic work, which centers on themes of self-

exploration, multiculturalism, and autobiography. She is represented by UPA Gallery in Tampa, FL and exhibits her work nationally and internationally. Beyond producing photographs, she also has enjoyed working in arts administration, where she has taken on roles of gallery assistant as well as exhibition chair. www.sandrinearons.com.